Autonomy without Collapse in a Better European Union

Autonomy without Collapse in a Better European Union

Editors

MARK DAWSON
MARKUS JACHTENFUCHS

OXFORD
UNIVERSITY PRESS

OXFORD
UNIVERSITY PRESS

Great Clarendon Street, Oxford, OX2 6DP,
United Kingdom

Oxford University Press is a department of the University of Oxford.
It furthers the University's objective of excellence in research, scholarship,
and education by publishing worldwide. Oxford is a registered trade mark of
Oxford University Press in the UK and in certain other countries

Impression: 1

Published in the United States of America by Oxford University Press
198 Madison Avenue, New York, NY 10016, United States of America

British Library Cataloguing in Publication Data
Data available

Library of Congress Control Number: 2022935973

ISBN 978–0–19–289754–1

DOI: 10.1093/oso/9780192897541.001.0001

Printed and bound by
CPI Group (UK) Ltd, Croydon, CR0 4YY

Contents

List of Contributors

Catherine Barnard, Professor of European & Employment Law, University of Cambridge

Ana Bobić, Référendaire, Court of Justice of the European Union

Sarah Fraser Butlin, Affiliated Lecturer, University of Cambridge

Damian Chalmers, Professor of Law, National University of Singapore

Gareth Davies, Professor of EU Law, VU Amsterdam

Mark Dawson, Professor of European Law & Governance, Hertie School, Berlin

Christian Freudlsperger, Postdoctoral Researcher, ETH Zürich

Markus Jachtenfuchs, Professor of European & Global Governance, Hertie School, Berlin

Frank Schimmelfennig, Professor of European Politics, ETH Zürich

Susanne K. Schmidt, Professor of Political Science, University of Bremen

Bruno de Witte, Professor of European Union Law, University of Maastricht

PART 1

THEORIZING AUTONOMY AND COLLAPSE

1

Autonomy without Collapse

Towards a Better European Union?

Mark Dawson and Markus Jachtenfuchs

1. Introduction

The EU's history, at least since the adoption of the Maastricht Treaty, demonstrates numerous episodes in which individual or groups of member states have sought to reinforce their national autonomy in the face of deepening integration. The latest instance of this is the most dramatic, the attempt by one state to leave the Union altogether. All of these attempts have one common ingredient; efforts to regain autonomy are often accompanied by fears that autonomy will lead to disintegration or will have wider destructive consequences. Maastricht's own opt-outs for three states from joining the common currency for example was accompanied by the demand that they join once certain convergence criteria were met. Its development of 'enhanced cooperation' was similarly coupled with the requirement that cooperation was a 'last instance' effort in which the ordinary methods of legislation via all member states had first failed (see Art. 20(2) TEU). Divergence from commonly agreed rules and procedures was seen both as inevitable/necessary and as limited/dangerous.

The Brexit example illustrates the quandary starkly. There can be no clearer call for autonomy than the attempt to exit the Union altogether. Faced, however, with a member state seeking to establish close trading and other ties post-exit, the Union's approach to Brexit has been influenced by the fear that it could lead to disintegrative effects, either breaking the 'indivisibility' of the internal market, or leading to states outside the Union enjoying the benefits of membership without its obligations. As a result, the UK has been given a rather stark choice: undisrupted trade (a choice eventually rejected by the Conservative government) was conditional upon accepting the full gamut of EU law, including the jurisdiction of the Court of Justice and a close, even permanent alignment of regulatory standards. Autonomy must be restricted, even for states seeking to leave the Union altogether.

Mark Dawson and Markus Jachtenfuchs, *Autonomy without Collapse*. In: *Autonomy without Collapse in a Better European Union*. Edited by Mark Dawson and Markus Jachtenfuchs, Oxford University Press.
 DOI: 10.1093/oso/9780192897541.003.0001

The EU thus faces a dilemma. As the next section will discuss, it faces an unprecedented degree of contestation emerging from the national level[1] and increasingly assertive calls for national autonomy. These calls cannot all be dismissed as mere populist rhetoric or national egoism but represent a consistent (and legitimate) questioning of the degree of uniformity that EU law and politics presently carry. At the same time, the fear that greater autonomy may carry disintegrative effects is also legitimate; uniformity is no mere accidental by-product of the EU's construction but intrinsically related to its policy goals of creating an area without internal borders for market transactions and people and often hailed by commentators as a key ingredient for overcoming collective action problems. Giving too much room for autonomy might create an opportunity structure leading to the loss of collective goods and deficits in problem-solving (and perhaps even to self-destruction). The EU requires autonomy, but in doing so, it must also avoid collapse. Can it achieve it, and if so, how?

2. The Problem: No Way Forward, or Back

Where does the dilemma come from? In its most general form, it is an intrinsic feature of all systems of multilevel governance, federal states as well as international institutions, as they involve the sharing of powers between different levels of governance over the same territory. These systems have an inherent tension between scaling up powers for furthering integration or scaling them down in order to increase the autonomy of constituent units, which leads to a constant struggle between the social forces behind either direction. Multilevel systems are constantly striving for a fragile and dynamic balance which is changing over time, and which needs to be renewed in light of changing circumstances, social forces, or normative evolution.[2] Such systems are not only preoccupied with the substance of policy—what is to be done?—but also and sometimes predominantly with the distribution of power between levels of government and institutional design: who does it and how?[3] These conflicts are often long-standing and very intense.

[1] De Vries, *Euroscepticism and the Future of European Integration* (Oxford University Press, 2018); Hobolt and Tilley, *Blaming Europe? Responsibility without Accountability in the European Union* (Oxford University Press, 2014).

[2] Benz, *Constitutional Policy in Multilevel Government: The Art of Keeping the Balance* (Oxford University Press, 2016).

[3] Pierson, 'Fragmented Welfare States: Federal Institutions and the Development of Social Policy', 8 *Governance* (1995), 449–478.

In the EU, the dilemma between autonomy and integration is particularly important as it is indeed a halfway house between a federal state and an international institution. Federal states usually have a settled constitution that assigns specific powers to institutions and levels of government but largely refrains from making highly specific regulatory policy prescriptions. These are left instead to the political process. The central government of a federal state enjoys a high degree of autonomy and considerable coercive, fiscal, and administrative capacity.[4] It thus has considerable leverage to ease claims for autonomy by either helping or coercing subnational governments into compliance with central rules. Exit of dissatisfied territorial units is often not foreseen but always carries major economic, legal, or political costs. The mandate of international institutions in turn is often rather narrow (although there are a number of general purpose organizations such as the United Nations),[5] and the autonomous coercive, fiscal, and administrative capacities of the centre are usually weak to non-existing. Exit of dissatisfied member states is comparatively easy.

The EU seems to combine the disadvantages of both forms. It has an evolving quasi-constitution with a huge number of detailed policy provisions which are difficult to change in a system with high consensus requirements and a high number of veto players. The EU deals with virtually every conceivable policy issue and produces far more legislative acts than any other international institution. This legislation is usually extremely precise and detailed, often highly intrusive into domestic politics and overseen by a highly active (and for some, activist) court. As Susanne Schmidt explains in her contribution to this volume, the 'over-constitutionalizing' tendencies of the EU's political system—and the shadow of judicial rulings of its highest Court—severely constrains its responsiveness to citizens and states. In comparison to established federal states, Christian Freudlsperger argues in his contribution, the reason for the EU's use of highly detailed and constraining regulation is its absence of fiscal capacities which those states use for reducing diversity. In other words, while federal states can afford to leave more room to subunits because they have a large budget, the EU has to resort to detailed regulation because it has no other means of dealing with diversity which might lead to collapse.

Yet, the EU's central institutions have no coercive power and comparatively little administrative and fiscal capacity to force, help, or convince member

[4] For the distinction between regulation and capacity as instruments of governance, see Genschel and Jachtenfuchs (eds.), *Beyond the Regulatory Polity? The European Integration of Core State Powers* (Oxford University Press, 2014).

[5] Hooghe et al., *A Theory of International Organization* (Oxford University Press, 2019).

states seeking more autonomy. And in the only case where the EU de facto possesses this capacity (with the ECB), its use is politically contested, legally challenged, and tightly circumscribed (leading most infamously to the 2020 ultra vires challenge from the German Constitutional Court). The EU is thus a case of an extremely ambitious programme of abolishing physical borders among its member states and increasing interdependence between highly heterogeneous member states with the aim of increasing collective welfare but without the capacities of a federal state. As Damian Chalmers explains in his contribution, the EU carries an 'ambition-authority' deficit; it has been given responsibility by its member states for a range of increasingly onerous tasks (precisely those tasks that states themselves—with all of their tools—cannot solve) while simultaneously lacking the necessary political and legal authority to deliver them.

The exit of a large member state, as well as the asymmetric shocks and the internal imbalances of two core areas of statehood—economic and monetary policy as well as migration—have thus exposed the precarious stage of integration. Part of this precariousness concerns capacity. In a number of crucial policy fields, from Economic and Monetary Union (EMU) to refugee and asylum policy, the EU has established a policy framework that few see as adequate. The challenges these policy fields involve—reducing economic divergences between Eurozone states, regulating the entry and stay of newcomers, or providing the vaccination capacity to overcome a pandemic—overwhelm the EU's historical regulatory model.

It is not clear, for example, that harmonizing asylum standards (a typical EU mechanism) can do much to facilitate the integration of refugees or ensure their fair distribution across European states.[6] Similarly, a common rule book for European banks may help manage market expectations but will not provide the fiscal and monetary instruments required to meet a future financial emergency (such as the need to resolve multiple financial institutions simultaneously).[7] Finally, as the vaccination campaign illustrated, while the EU's regulatory approach can bring benefits in avoiding interstate competition, its unwieldy decision-making structure is poor at acting decisively in moments of crisis. The lack of EU capacity in these fields (and others) has established a severe mismatch between the mechanisms available to the EU to meet its goals

[6] Costello and Guild, 'Fixing the refugee crisis: Holding the Commission accountable', Verfassungsblog, 2018. https://verfassungsblog.de/fixing-the-refugee-crisis-holding-the-commission-accountable/ (accessed 18 June 2021).

[7] Enderlein, 'The Euro as a Showcase for Exploratory Governance: Why There Are No Simple Answers', in Dawson et al. (eds.), *Governance Report 2015* (2015), 25–40; Grauwe and Ji, 'Governing a Sustainable Eurozone', 2 *Rivista Internazionale di Scienze Sociali* (2017), 173–194.

and the policies experts within these fields see as necessary for their long-term sustainability. The new fiscal capacities created during the pandemic are a highly specific reaction to a symmetrical crisis with few moral hazard concerns.[8]

The problem does not merely consist in a lack of coercive, fiscal, or administrative capacity of the member states or central EU institutions for dealing with external shocks. Rather, it is endogenously intensified and perhaps even created by the tight straitjacket of European regulation, and court rulings that substantially reduce the ability of member states to pursue their own policy preferences. Even in the field of tax policy, which is strictly limited in scope and subject to unanimity (Art. 113 TFEU), the ability of the member states to pursue their own tax policies is severely limited by a rich body of secondary legislation and a high number of court rulings. The EU does not have its own taxes and has a budget too small to have a significant macro-economic impact, but limits and constrains the taxing and increasingly the spending policies of its member states.

The EU's ability to break this impasse is hindered by another source of precariousness, political dissensus. Potentially, the capacity problem could be addressed either by furthering integration or loosening it. In the field of EMU, numerous proposals have been advanced on 'completing' EMU, principally by providing a fiscal counterpart to the EU's advanced monetary tools. Alternatively, proposals have been oriented towards dissolving EMU altogether, breaking it into constituent parts [9] or providing it with competition via 'parallel currencies'.[10] The field of asylum has faced similarly diverging calls to either entirely centralize EU policy around a common transnational border or return responsibility for the admission and integration of refugees fully to the EU's member states.

Even if, however, one or both of these alternatives would be preferable to the present halfway house, political forces mitigate against either path. Further capacity building runs against the obvious problem of severe and consistent national resistance to further integration; a resistance which is unevenly distributed between policy fields and between European states. As has been remarked, the EU's 'permissive consensus' has been replaced by a 'constraining

[8] Genschel and Jachtenfuchs, 'Postfunctionalism reversed: Solidarity and rebordering during the COVID-19 pandemic', 28 *Journal of European Public Policy* (2021), 350–369.

[9] Scharpf, 'There Is an Alternative: A Two-Tier European Currency Community', *MPIfG Discussion Paper* (2018), 18/7.

[10] Siekmann, 'Exit, Exclusion, and Parallel Currencies in the Euro Area', Institute for Monetary and Financial Stability, Goethe University Frankfurt, Working Paper Series No. 99. (2015).

dissensus' where all of the EU's activities take place under heightened domestic scrutiny.[11] Support for or resistance against supranational integration is slowly becoming part of political conflict in Europe.[12] Ambitious plans, even where backed by powerful members, such as the 'Macron plan' inspired by the 2017 Sorbonne speech of the French president, are likely to face severe obstacles, leaving them watered down to precisely the lowest common denominator of regulatory tightening without capacity building embodied by the 'halfway house'. Although the Eurozone crisis and the refugee crisis did not lead to disintegration but rather to more powers for EU institutions, their increasing influence was accompanied by an unprecedented rise in political contestation. Solving crises by strengthening the EU has at least become much more difficult.

Even if, however, integration might have gone too far,[13] political dissensus also impedes the path backwards. The EU's consensus-based decision-making structure (as David Cameron discovered in his 2015 attempt to renegotiate aspects of free movement) makes repatriating powers to the national level difficult. Consensus-based intergovernmental decision-making does not protect national sovereignty but the status quo, even if it is a highly institutionalized status quo.[14] In areas with close connections to general economic policy such as EMU,[15] or where member states carry high interdependencies (such as migration in a borderless area), a return to national solutions carries high costs and uncertain benefits. As Horst Seehofer, Sebastian Kurz, and Matteo Salvini discovered when trying to restrict the number of asylum seekers entering German, Austrian, or Italian territory and sending back those who had already entered (only to discover that their ability to do so depended on the goodwill of other states), there seem few alternatives to the EU when managing cross-border problems. In order to manage negative externalities from strong interdependence, cooperation is indispensable unless a member state is willing and able either to shape the rules for all or to shoulder the costs of externalities, inside the EU or outside. To put it crudely, there is no obvious way forward, but also no clear path 'back'.

[11] Hooghe and Marks, 'A postfunctionalist theory of European integration: From permissive consensus to constraining dissensus', 39 *British Journal of Political Science* (2009), 1–23.

[12] Kriesi, 'The politicization of European integration', 54 *Journal of Common Market Studies* (2016), 32–47.

[13] Majone, *Rethinking the Union of Europe Post-Crisis. Has European Integration Gone Too Far?* (Cambridge University Press, 2014).

[14] Tsebelis and Garrett, 'The institutional foundations of intergovernmentalism and supranationalism in the European Union', 55 *International Organization* (2001), 357–390.

[15] Lapavitsas, 'The redenomination risk of exiting the Eurozone: An estimation based on the Greek case', 24 *European Law Journal* (2018), 226–243.

The EU's constitutional structure adds a further ingredient to this challenge. On the one hand, the legal system is also an unsatisfactory halfway house. The difficulties of the EU in fully constitutionalizing its core legal values have been laid bare in the EU's confrontation with illiberal tendencies in its own member states.[16] There have thus been multiple calls to take a further leap in legal integration, for example, by abolishing the current restrictions on the use of the EU Charter of Fundamental Rights in domestic situations or establishing new frameworks to enforce rule of law values.[17] The EU's budget has recently been enlisted as a further tool in this fight, through making budgetary payments conditional on respect for rule of law values.

At the same time, the legal system faces continuous accusations that it is centralizing and unwieldy, 'emptying out' the essential constitutional functions of national courts, and failing to respect the limits on EU interference in national identity protected under Art. 4(2) of the Treaty.[18] The very tools developed by the Union to fight rule of law backsliding have themselves been accused of carrying dubious legality, with Treaty rules stretched to deal with the consistent resistance of the Polish and Hungarian governments to greater supranational supervision of their constitutional orders. At the same time, as explored by Catherine Barnard and Sarah Fraser Butlin in Chapter 9, the scope of the EU's free movement rules has been continuously expanded in spite of increasing political contestation of their content. The legal order seems to carry neither the tools to enforce its central 'fundamental' values nor the flexibility to accommodate 'legitimate diversity' between EU states.

More importantly, the legal structure also seems to hinder both the forward and backward paths. In effect, the Treaty (by writing certain substantive commitments into its text) commits the EU to a certain level of integration that restricts its ability either to further integrate in particular areas to meet pressing challenges or to 'disintegrate' in response to strong political calls for autonomy emerging from its member states.[19] This is not just a Treaty problem: the EU's

[16] Pech and Scheppele, 'Illiberalism within: Rule of law backsliding in the EU', 19 *Cambridge Yearbook of European Legal Studies* (2017), 3–47.

[17] Bogdandy et al., *A Constitutional Moment for the European Rule of Law—Upcoming Landmark Decisions Concerning the Polish Judiciary*, Max Planck Institute for Comparative Public Law & International Law (MPIL) Research Paper No. 2018-10 (Heidelberg, 2018).

[18] Claes and Reestman, 'The protection of national constitutional identity and the limits of European integration at the occasion of the Gauweiler Case', 16 *German Law Journal* (2015), 917–970; Polzin, 'Constitutional identity, unconstitutional amendments and the idea of constituent power: The development of the doctrine of constitutional identity in German constitutional law', 14 *International Journal of Constitutional Law* (2016), 411–438.

[19] Grimm, *The Constitution of European Democracy* (Oxford University Press, 2017); Schmidt, *The European Court of Justice and the Policy Process: The Shadow of Case Law* (Oxford University Press, 2018).

legal structure carries a number of strong centralizing constitutional principles, such as supremacy, direct effect, the duty of consistent interpretation, and others, all of which make national efforts to restrict the disruptive domestic impact of EU law difficult. In effect, the legal and Treaty structure limits the ability of the EU to be fully responsive to new political and functional demands, either for grand new projects or for decentralization.

At the same time, loosening Treaty rules also poses severe risks. In an EU marked by increasing contestation of the legal order and severe questioning of shared values, legal scholars might legitimately ask whether now is the right time to jettison principles such as supremacy and direct effect that seek to insulate EU law from cherry-picking and freeriding at the national level. Distinguishing between what Ana Bobić in Chapter 8 of this volume terms constructive versus destructive forms of national contestation of EU law seems a perilous task. Traditional solutions along the more/less integration axis seem to offer little promise at either the legal or the political levels.

3. Autonomy without Collapse? Towards a Better Union

If neither a radical leap forward nor a significant step back are wanted or likely, how can the Union maintain its effectiveness and legitimacy within the 'halfway house'? Answering this question depends on achieving a level of autonomy that does not risk collapse, or disintegration.[20] Let us deal with the 'autonomy preserving' element of the equation first. Efforts to recapture national autonomy would be oriented towards providing space for national political communities to diverge from common European standards in order to fulfil goals or recognize institutional or cultural norms that are unique to their national context.[21]

In this sense, the effort to recapture autonomy cannot be reduced to the classical EU subsidiarity test—of which level of governance regulates 'better'—because the subsidiarity principle is only meaningful in highly specific contexts.[22] Instead, it involves a recognition that national communities have particular forms of cultural and political reproduction that are unique, worthy

[20] For an early analysis, see Scharpf, 'Community and autonomy. Multi-level policy-making in the European Union', 1 *Journal of European Public Policy* (1994), 219–242.

[21] Scharpf, 'De-constitutionalisation and majority rule: A democratic vision for Europe', 23 *European Law Journal* (2017), 315–334; Schimmelfennig and Winzen, *Ever Looser Union?: Differentiated European Integration* (Oxford University Press, 2020).

[22] Jachtenfuchs and Krisch, 'Subsidiarity in global governance', 79 *Law and Contemporary Problems* (2016), 1–26.

of respect, and are damaged by efforts to harmonize rules and standards across the European area.[23] This speaks to a number of criticisms of the European lawmaking process, particularly the fear that integration increasingly follows a path of 'adversarial legalism' in which processes of informal cooperation are displaced by detailed legislative rules and the individualizing discourse of 'rights' and 'interests'.[24] It also speaks to the excessive formalism of EU law discussed in Damian Chalmers' contribution: namely that EU law carries legal priority in the European legal order *simply for being EU law*, regardless of its democratic quality. An autonomy-preserving approach is thus about providing space for diversity, and with it, *freedom from* the strictures of common European rules and standards.

In this sense, autonomy can be defended from both a normative and systems perspective. From a normative perspective, national autonomy seems to provide a mechanism to respect and give value to processes of political self-determination found at the national level.[25] It also provides a way of ensuring that EU law respects the significant diversity of cultural, economic, and social systems found within European states. Legally, this normative demand to respect differences finds its expression in the national identity clause of Art. 4(2) TEU.

From a systems perspective at the same time, autonomy is a mechanism to protect the European system as a whole by addressing national contestation and binding states and citizens to the EU by demonstrating that meeting collective goals and respecting national imperatives can go hand in hand. There are thus good reasons for the EU to embrace national autonomy *beyond* the functional weighing of 'who does what best' suggested by the subsidiarity principle. To appropriate the language used by Ana Bobić and Gareth Davies in this volume, the need to defer in particular circumstances to national orders is not a 'bug' that must be overcome in the name of European unity but rather a 'feature' necessary for the EU's functioning and preservation.

We must not forget, however, the second 'collapse avoiding' element. There are good reasons to think that efforts to build in autonomy may carry disintegrative efforts and thus to explore safeguards to avoid them. The very notion of 'opting out' of elements of EU law challenges first and foremost the very core of

[23] Bartolini, *Restructuring Europe: Centre Formation, System Building, and Political Structuring between the Nation State and the European Union* (Oxford University Press, 2005).

[24] Kelemen, *Eurolegalism: The Transformation of Law and Regulation in the European Union* (Harvard University Press, 2011).

[25] Dawson and Witte, 'Self-determination in the constitutional future of the EU', 21 *European Law Journal* (2015), 371–383.

a mainstream historical explanation for the successful development of the integration project. Namely, this is the notion that the key advantage of the EU over other regional and international organizations is the quality of its Treaty structure as a 'new species' of international law, the obligations of which cannot be divided or derogated from, and which carries strong centralized compliance mechanisms.[26]

In that sense, many of the institutional rules and mechanisms seen as the source of the EU's centralizing tendencies (e.g., the supremacy principle or the 'indivisible' internal market) were also built as safeguards against the disintegration of transnational order. This risk is clear; if states are given the capacity to 'opt-out', they risk opting into rights (and the areas of cooperation most closely fitting their domestic agendas) and out of responsibilities.[27] For the provision of collective goods and the avoidance of freeriding, a substantial amount of central enforcement and oversight over common rules is necessary. Equally at risk is the destabilization of projects (e.g., the creation of a common set of standards for the free circulation of goods) that require broad buy-in, and a level regulatory playing field, in order to be successful. The end of this process could be a gradual erosion of mutual trust, both in the willingness of other governments to abide by common rules, and the ability of central institutions to enforce them.

The challenge is how to throw the bathwater out but hold onto the baby: how can autonomy be built without triggering processes of destabilization that risk the unity of the European project as a whole? How can member states have greater autonomy in EU law and policy without forgoing the collective gains that motivated cooperation in the first place: economies of scale and the management of externalities? Such gains should empirically exist rather than being assumed, and even if there are collective gains, losses for individual states or groups of individuals need to be taken into account.[28] At issue is thus not a return to sovereignty or intergovernmentalism but rather a rebalancing of a multilevel legal and political order. The essays in this volume all seek to use academic research to offer pathways towards such a rebalancing.

[26] Weiler, 'The transformation of Europe', 100 *Yale Law Journal* (1991), 2403–2483.

[27] Andersen and Sitter, 'Differentiated integration: What is it and how much can the EU accommodate?', 28 *Journal of European Integration* (2006), 313–330; Avbelj, 'Differentiated integration. Farewell to the EU-27?', 14 *German Politics* (2013), 191–211.

[28] Chalmers et al. (eds.), *The End of the Eurocrats' Dream: Adjusting to European Diversity* (Cambridge University Press, 2016); Colgan and Keohane, 'The Liberal Order Is Rigged', *Foreign Affairs* (Issue 9, May 2018).

4. Two Paths to Autonomy

In this volume, we principally explore two paths to achieving this balance: differentiated integration and the use of constitutional or legal principles to establish greater autonomy. While some research has explored the interrelation of these two paths),[29] they are largely complementary in nature, i.e., the use of one does not preclude the use of the other.

To begin with the first path, in a few years only, differentiated integration has evolved from an obscure niche topic to a booming research agenda. At first sight, differentiated integration seems to be an elegant and readily available solution for achieving autonomy without collapse in an increasingly heterogeneous union: member states which do not wish to participate in a certain policy area (such as Denmark in defence) or are not able to do so (such as some Eastern European member states in EMU) are temporarily or permanently exempted from participating while those who are willing and able can strengthen cooperation in the respective area. Differentiated integration thus reintroduces a certain dose of international relations into the EU: states only cooperate in specific areas and not in others, and there is no need to choose between uniform rules for all or no rules at all. In the past, differentiated integration has mostly been introduced in the area of core state powers where the heterogeneity of member states as well as the sensitivity of governments is strong.[30]

Differentiated integration is a nuanced way of varying both exit from collective policies and voice in collective decision-making.[31] It breaks the binary choice between either being part of the EU and subject to all of its laws or being outside of it and subject to none of its laws, and thus makes borders softer and more flexible. In this respect, differentiated integration, particularly if it extends to non-member states, is really an indication that the EU is a postmodern polity which differs from the classical territorial state, with its claim to uphold a clear inside/outside distinction, at least in principle. It is somehow in the middle between a federal state which allows for differentiation within a given territory and 'functional, overlapping and competing

[29] Miglio, 'Differentiated integration and the principle of loyalty', 14 *European Constitutional Law Review* (2018), 475–498.

[30] Schimmelfennig and Winzen, *supra* note 21.

[31] Jachtenfuchs and Kasack, 'Balancing sub-unit autonomy and collective problem solving by varying exit and voice. An analytical framework', 27 *Journal of European Public Policy* (2017), 598–614.

jurisdictions',[32] which almost abandon the idea of a centre of authority in a given polity altogether. Thus, differentiated integration has the potential to cope with the EU's increasing heterogeneity by providing for autonomy though selective exit while maintaining the EU as a distinct polity without the risk of collapsing into a series of overlapping functional regimes.

However, differentiated integration is not the solution for all claims to greater autonomy, and may have adverse consequences. As in classical federalism, differentiated integration practised in the EU assumes that heterogeneity is territorially organized, and that this territory ideally is identical to member states. It thus privileges claims to greater autonomy from member states and is less sensitive to claims from other territorial units or functionally defined groups.

Differentiated integration is also easier to practice *ex ante* than *ex post*.[33] When states decide by unanimity or by quasi-unanimity, it allows a small number of dissenting states to retain the status quo while the others deepen integration. Even here, however, sticking to the status quo is not necessarily cost free. While the UK has constantly maintained that it does not want to become a member of the Schengen area, most other member states felt excluded from the gains of borderless movement. And while the UK, Denmark, and Sweden do not wish to join the Eurozone (although Denmark pegs the crown tightly to the euro), other member states saw membership in the Eurozone as a benefit even during the crisis. Even *ex ante*, therefore, autonomy may come with a cost that not all member states want to accept.

Ex post, however, the costs of autonomy may be much higher, as the distributive implications are often more salient and interdependence is high. As Frank Schimmelfennig demonstrates in his contribution, the relationship between the demand and the supply of differentiated integration changes fundamentally in the case of differentiated disintegration. Whereas *ex ante* differentiated integration was a useful means to ease the accession of new member states and cooperation in highly controversial fields, differentiated disintegration risks to produce unsustainable group sizes and create massive harmful externalities. It is also made more difficult because it takes up in a highly institutionalized and legalized environment (see also Bruno de Witte's contribution). Expelling a member state from the Eurozone (leaving aside the legal difficulties) risks imposing dramatic costs of the country leaving but also a heavy backslash on those remaining inside. The reinstitution of border controls during the

[32] Frey and Eichenberger, *The New Democratic Federalism for Europe: Functional, Overlapping, and Competing Jurisdictions* (Edward Elgar, 1999); see also Leuffen et al., *Differentiated Integration: Explaining Variation in the European Union* (Palgrave Macmillan, 2013), p. 11.

[33] Genschel and Jachtenfuchs, 'From market integration to core state powers: The Eurozone crisis, the refugee crisis and integration theory', 56 *Journal of Common Market Studies* (2018), 178–196.

refugee crisis had a modest effect on refugee flows but threatened to be highly disruptive of economic exchanges. The Brexit debate also highlights that differentiated integration is perceived by some as freeriding and undermining collective goods. As a result, differentiated disintegration was not helpful during the polycrisis to accommodate claims for autonomy.

The second path concerns exploring the constitutional foundations of the EU order and the necessity and use of principles of EU law that are precisely designed to guard against the risk of 'disintegration' already discussed above. This begins with the EU Treaties themselves. They carry both an autonomy-preserving and a collapse-avoiding element. In the first case, the Treaties define the boundaries of the EU's action, anchoring the EU's activities in the principle of conferral and thereby limiting EU intervention in certain sensitive areas of national policy. In the second case, the Treaties bind the member states to common political and economic goals, and integrate them within a centralized system for the implementation of policies and the resolution of disputes.

More recent scholarship has pointed to the difficulties of reconciling the Treaties with rapid advances in the functional goals the EU is expected to meet, resulting in an 'imbalanced' or 'mutated' constitutional structure.[34] This raises the question of whether the EU's Treaty structure should be revisited. A 'deconstitutionalization' of certain Treaty rules, i.e., a shift from anchoring certain policies directly in the Treaties to making them a part of 'ordinary' EU legislation, would provide one route to providing the member states with greater freedom to depart from Treaty rules.[35] They could do so, however, only within the constraints of the EU's institutional system (where the full gamut of co-decision, judicial review, and other procedural safeguards would apply).

The purpose of such reform, as explored in the contribution of Susanne K. Schmidt, would be to provide a form of autonomy from central *substantive* aspects of EU law, without making radical changes to the Union's wider institutional framework. It would also not necessarily give individual member states more autonomy but rather allow decision-making by the member states collectively in a manner less constrained by substantial constitutional provisions. In her contribution, Schmidt focuses on the effect of constitutionalization on the relationship between the Court of Justice and the EU legislature, providing a typology for how legal rulings affect policymaking. As Schmidt argues, the EU's legal framework can disrupt policymaking in different ways, with the case law of court either foreclosing legislative action, establishing gaps that the legislature may engage with, creating a parallel regime to legislative provisions,

[34] Dawson and Witte, 'Constitutional balance in the EU after the Euro-Crisis', 76 *The Modern Law Review* (2013), 817–844; Witte, 'Euro crisis responses and the EU legal order: Increased institutional variation or constitutional mutation?', 11 *European Constitutional Law Review* (2015), 434–457.

[35] Grimm, *supra* note 19.

or leaving an unclear relation between legislative provisions and applicable Treaty law. In each case, the unique features of the EU's legal order create considerable flux and uncertainty. As she writes:

> With accumulating case law, much is already decided at the level of the EU's constitution, also implying a judicial closure of zones of agreement for legislative political compromises in a very heterogeneous EU. Under conditions of preference heterogeneity in a widened EU, over-constitutionalization may protect the 'deepened' integration, but Brexit shows how much it may also be a destabilizing force.[36]

The EU Treaties cannot, however, be seen in isolation. In the history of integration, the Treaties have been accompanied by the gradual development of a set of constitutional principles designed to strengthen the EU's legal and political order.[37] The reason the Treaties have such significant centralizing effects pertains not to their substantive rules as such but rather to the effect of accompanying principles of EU law which make departure from these rules difficult. The principle of supremacy for example, pre-empts the ability of the member states to legislate in areas where the Union has already done so; the principle of consistent interpretation demands that national courts, where possible, interpret national provisions in a manner consistent with EU law; the principle of direct effect allows individuals to directly apply provisions of EU law where their governments have failed to do so, and so on.

These principles have the 'avoidance of collapse' as their essence. Their goal is to ensure that, when EU obligations are agreed, either via the Treaties or via the legislative process, appropriate legal remedies are in place to enforce them. These principles thus significantly reduce the scope available to member states to depart from common EU standards. In doing so, however, these principles obviously significantly constrain national autonomy. In those areas where EU law applies, constitutional principles limit the ability of national institutions to modify or reinterpret EU law in order to meet the diverse demands that legitimate national interests require. The question that this element of this project seeks to address is therefore how general constitutional principles could be provided with an 'autonomy-preserving' role to temper their autonomy-constraining effects.

[36] Schmidt, Chapter 6, this volume.

[37] Lenaerts and Gutiérrez-Fons, 'The constitutional allocation of powers and general principles of EU law', 47 *Common Market Law Review* (2010), 1629–1669.

To take supremacy as a first example, what kind of supremacy principle is needed to retain EU law's authority and under what circumstances does EU law simply no longer deserve recognition as a 'superior' category of law?[38] Although the rationalist literature on international institutions insists on the need for centralized enforcement of rules in order to avoid freeriding, the functional need for supremacy can simply not be taken for granted—as a non-EU member, Norway is one state not bound by the principle but which carries an exemplary record in faithfully executing EU law obligations.[39] Even if not all member states can be expected to follow the Norwegian example, there may yet be circumstances where supremacy should be suspended or tempered (a boundary tentatively explored by a number of constitutional courts).[40] More academic work is needed to explore both the role of constitutional principles of EU law and how they might be limited or redesigned to answer demands for greater autonomy emerging from national law and politics.

Much of this work is started in the contributions to this volume by Ana Bobić and Gareth Davies. As Bobić argues, allowing a degree of national contestation of EU constitutional principles is a key means of preserving the EU system by allowing EU norms that damage important tenets of the national constitutional order to be identified and even reinterpreted. Constitutional conflict is therefore not a damaging bug in most instances—a signal of systems erosion or collapse—but rather a feature which promotes systems integration. At the same time, a constructive (as opposed to destructive) shared constitutional space can be built only where certain overarching principles—namely the values contained in Art. 2 TEU—are adhered to in good faith. As she explains:

> Constructive conflict is therefore characterized by the differing interpretation of shared values across member states. Still, so long as the national level interprets the 'constitutional', expressed through the values in Article 2 TEU, coherently within the limits of mutual respect and sincere cooperation, as well as by an independent judiciary, we can speak of constructive conflict, conducive to the dynamic development of the EU's constitutional sphere.[41]

[38] Joerges, *Rethinking European Law's Supremacy with Comments by Damian Chalmers, Rainer Nickel, Florian Rödl, Robert Wai*, EUI Working Paper LAW 2005/12 (Firenze, 2005).

[39] Burke et al., 'Life on the edge: EFTA and the EEA as a Future for the UK in Europe', 22 *European Public Law* (2016), 69–96.

[40] Albi, 'Erosion of constitutional rights in EU law: A call for substantive co-operative constitutionalism', 9 *Vienna Journal on International Constitutional Law / ICL Journal* (2015), 151–185.

[41] Bobić, Chapter 8, this volume.

Bobić's demand for a shared constitutional space resonates with Gareth Davies' contribution, which similarly argues that the EU benefits from acting as a contested constitutional polity in which there is no single locus of authority. The EU's existing preliminary reference procedure, however, sits uneasily with this notion of shared authority by casting the EU level as a unitary and binding interpreter of EU law, whose judgments national courts must apply and obey. Davies' answer to this problem is to maintain the role of the procedure as a feedback loop between the national and EU levels but to convert it from a binding to a non-binding procedure. For Davies, therefore, an autonomy-preserving preliminary reference procedure would start from the premises of interpretive pluralism, namely an approach that 'sees judicial disagreements in terms of different views of shared body of law rather than in terms of two bodies of law each put forward as a candidate for primacy'.[42] The key to autonomy without collapse in interpretative terms is thus about interpreting the body of EU law as a shared space of constitutional interpretation where courts may legitimately disagree but which can also find a reading of the law that does justice to the normative demands of both sides.

The drive to reimagine EU constitutional principles in this fashion need not be merely procedural in character but can also concern substantive rules, such as the four 'fundamental' market freedoms (explored in the contribution by Catherine Barnard and Sarah Fraser Butlin) or the idea, in citizenship law, of the need for EU citizens to enjoy the 'substance' of their rights. These substantive principles once again significantly limit the scope for national departure from EU rules to meet pressing policy objectives (with their boundaries drawn by the courts themselves and not merely via the legislative process).[43] These substantive principles once again significantly limit the scope for national departure from EU rules to meet pressing policy objectives (with their boundaries drawn by the courts themselves and not merely via the legislative process).

The contestation of principles like free movement via the Brexit process thus raises the obvious question of whether substantive principles of EU law also require revisitation and whether a more flexible, variegated, or limited conception of these principles ought to be developed.[44] Such a conception, as Barnard and Fraser Butlin explore, was proposed in the context of the UK's renegotiation of its relationship with the EU, but dropped following Brexit, in

[42] Davies, Chapter 7, this volume.

[43] *KA and Others v Belgium*, judgment of 8 May 2018, *CJEU*.

[44] Barnard and Fraser Butlin, 'Free movement vs. fair movement. Brexit and managed migration', 55 *Common Market Law Review* (2018), 203–226.

spite of indications that political contestation of free movement extends well beyond the UK case. Could this be, once again, a means of providing autonomy without risking a broader disintegration of the substantive projects underlying these principles (i.e., the building of a common market and shared 'European' form of citizenship, respectively)? Exploring the constitutional principles and foundations of EU law thus provides one promising route to explore how the EU's current political impasse can be breached.

5. Conclusion

Allowing member states more autonomy while preventing collapse is a difficult balancing act, as it involves contradictory goals: binding member states and giving them more autonomy; providing common rules, and allowing divergence from them. Differentiated integration and constitutional-legal principles are two means to achieve a temporary balance between those conflicting goals. However, we still need to know more about the precise conditions under which these two strategies can apply and about their effects.

With respect to differentiated integration, we still need to know more about its applicability for different types of goods, policy areas, or conflict types in order to understand under which conditions differentiated integration may help to realize autonomy without leading to negative side effects. While much of differentiated integration has been applied *ex ante*, Brexit, the Eurozone crisis, and the refugee crisis also highlight the importance of knowing more about its applicability *ex post* in order to accommodate demands for autonomy in the interest of the stability of the entire system without contributing to the demise of this very system. Finally, the legal feasibility and the consequences for accountability of differentiated integration (DI) also need to be better understood.

With respect to constitutional-legal principles, understanding the conditions under which constitutional principles might be *disapplied* requires a better understanding of the constraints these principles de facto impose in the first place. To what extent are internal market principles, the supremacy of EU law, the 'constitutionalizing effects' of the Treaty, or the duty of consistent interpretation significant constraints on national autonomy and how does this vary between national contexts and substantive areas of EU law? To what extent, and if so, how, are these principles being contested at the national level? And finally, if certain constitutional principles could be reformed, discarded, or tempered, what alternative principles are needed, and what normative criteria can be used to orient this exercise?

We seek through this project to find routes for autonomy without collapse, but we do so in the knowledge that the balance between these two poles is perilous and requires a deep engagement with more specialized debates in EU law and political science. It also requires engagement *between disciplines* (for example, coupling legal research on constitutional feasibility with research in political science on institutional and policy adaptation in the EU system). This volume is precisely devoted to this task.

2
The European Union as a Community of Super Wicked Problems and Its Ambition–Authority Deficit

Damian Chalmers

1. Introduction

The idea that member states should be granted more autonomy but not enough to risk Union collapse begs the question as to how we arrived here. It prompts curiosity about the relationship between those impulses that sustain Union restrictions on domestic autonomy and those that find these restrictions so challenging. And if answers to this are complex and multiple, none address a central puzzle. The European Union repeatedly fails to realize the goals set for it: be these those of the Lisbon Strategy, Banking Union, protecting the values in Article 2 TEU, or Europe 2020. But the rewards for such failure are to continue to be granted eyewatering responsibilities on matters as diverse as climate change, the finance system, or the Covid-19 pandemic.

The answer to this puzzle is that the central mission for the Union are problems that are insurmountable for member states. These problems are at best extremely difficult to resolve and, at worst, intractable. This is not all, however. The Union's mission also requires member states to address these in a manner which grants authority to certain other foreigners, Union citizens. Their interests and voice must be valued. The challenges of this mission create, it will be argued, an ambition–authority deficit. Limits on the Union's authority restrict how it realizes its mission and affect appraisal of its performance. If shrill and persistent demands for autonomy are a manifestation of this deficit, this deficit has also resulted in four strategies becoming Union leitmotivs. These strategies seek to manage this deficit by alleviating the demands made in the Union's name whilst enabling it to realize this mission.

A good part of this essay assesses how well these strategies—legislative pacts, administrative coordination, resourced co-option, and discounting of future

Damian Chalmers, *The European Union as a Community of Super Wicked Problems and Its Ambition–Authority Deficit.* In: *Autonomy without Collapse in a Better European Union.* Edited by Mark Dawson and Markus Jachtenfuchs, Oxford University Press. © Oxford University Press (2022). DOI: 10.1093/oso/9780192897541.003.0002

interests—have managed this deficit. It will be argued that only one, legislative compacts, has done this at all plausibly. Realization of the Union's mission is dependent, therefore, on generalization of this strategy. However, it will be argued that this strategy is hampered by two weaknesses: legal formalism and collective action problems. These have to be addressed in a way that retains the strategy's operational effectiveness and allows member states more autonomy. The final section proposes three reforms to do this: endowing the Union with a general legislative competence; allowing domestic parliaments to derogate from individual EU laws subject to certain constraints; and allowing groups of nine member states to develop, amend, or repeal EU laws provided that this does not unnecessarily affect the interests of other member states nor arbitrarily discriminate.

2. The Mission of the European Union: Super Wicked Problems and the Authority of Foreigners

As a public policy system, in almost all fields of competence, the scale of the challenge is what warrants Union action. It can only act if the objectives of the proposed action cannot be sufficiently achieved through domestic action.[1] In other words, it exists to do difficult things. And it must do these things well. It must aspire to policies that are at least the technical and moral match of national ones. Union policies must take into account a whole series of public goods.[2] In a whole range of policies, Union measures must secure a 'high level' of protection.[3] They must be consistent with one another and not exceed what is necessary to achieve Treaty objectives.[4] Impact assessments must identify the most efficient policy that best protects the environment and best manages the social consequences. There must be then ongoing analysis of this during the measure's life cycle.[5]

If these problems warrant Union action, they also impose extensive demands on it. Many are beset by what public policy literature identifies as 'super wicked' qualities.[6] They are difficult to complementalize satisfactorily

[1] Article 5(2) TEU.

[2] E.g., Articles 9–13 TFEU.

[3] Articles 9, 67(3), 114(3), 147, 168(1), 169(1), and 191(2) TFEU; Protocol on Services of General Interest, Article 1.

[4] Articles 7 TFEU and 5(4) TEU.

[5] European Commission, *Life Cycle Assessment for the Impact Assessment of Policies* (European Union, 2016).

[6] On these see Levin, Cashore, Bernstein, and Auld, 'Overcoming the tragedy of super wicked problems: constraining our future selves to ameliorate global climate change', 45 *Policy Science* (2012), 123–152; Crowley and Head, 'The enduring challenge of "wicked problems": revisiting Rittel and Webber', 50 *Policy Science* (2017), 539–547; Daviter, 'Coping, taming or solving: alternative approaches to

because they interact in complex ways with other problems (e.g., climate change, Covid-19, migration, the euro, and Brexit). Mission creep, domestic ringfencing, incomplete policy solutions, and unstable policy fields have, thus, become endemic features of Union activity. Super wicked problems also generate imperatives for action but have few discrete solutions. The Union persists, in part, therefore, because there is no resolution of issues such as migration, the weaknesses of the euro financial system, climate change, competitiveness of Union industry. However, it is perennially destined to fail because there is no resolution to these. Knowledge about these problems—be they climate change financial markets, Covid-19, or biotechnology—may be imperfect and contested. The consequence of actions or inaction are therefore uncertain, and there is more scope for post-truth politics.[7] And, finally, the Union is beset by conflicts of interests for, with issues such as the financial crisis or climate change, the parties responsible for resolving the problem are also those most responsible for creating it.

The political contestation associated with these problems becomes, furthermore, more difficult to manage over time, since the distributive issues become more salient. When the Union establishes a new policy, this policy usually establishes a new good (e.g., the single market, the euro, security information systems) that creates benefits for all member states. This incentivizes them to seek win–win solutions and takes the heat out of political contestation. Once the policy is established, by contrast, these benefits are factored in and attention turns to managing its externalities. The incentives for parties now are to maximize their share of the returns and reduce their share of the costs. The benefits from cheating are more evident, as they can freeride on the policy. There is no reason to downplay political contestation, as it can be deployed to secure leverage in distributive debates.[8] The central Union policies have all perennially struggled, therefore, to deal with distributive issues that have resulted from their operation: be this labour movements, fiscal competition, or climate change in the case of the single market; transfers to rescue stricken banks or deteriorating public finances in the case of the euro; or the reception of those seeking international protection in the case of the area of freedom, security, and justice.

the governance of wicked problems', 37 *Policy Studies* (2017), 571–588; Peters and Tarpey, 'Are wicked problems really so wicked? Perceptions of policy problems', 38 *Policy & Society* (2019), 218–236.

[7] Daviter, 'Policy analysis in the face of complexity: What kind of knowledge to tackle wicked problems?' 34 *Public Policy and Administration* (2019), 62.

[8] These incentives were first set out in Scharpf and Mohr, 'Efficient Self-Coordination in Policy Networks—A Simulation Study', in Scharpf (ed.), *Games Real Actors Play: Actor-Centered Institutionalism in Policy Research* (Westview, 1997).

However, the European Union is not just a public policy system. It is also a political community. This community's most distinctive feature is the authority granted to foreigners. The Union, thus, promotes values, interests or identities which counter the negative associations identified with the foreign: threat, rivalry, destabilization, or the absence of commitment.[9] Many EU laws require domestic decision makers to take the interests of other Union citizens into account.[10] Most significantly, the Union involves foreigners governing its national citizens. All member states constitute a minority within the European Union. The EU lawmakers adopting laws are, therefore, for all Union citizens laws overwhelmingly foreign, and the collective interest justifying their adoption, the Union interest, will be one in which the national interest is a minority voice.

This quality is what many (including this author) find most attractive about the Union. However, it complicates its problem-solving. For foreigners enjoy only an ambivalent authority within the Union. This ambivalence in the centrality of decision makers representing national positions within Union decision-making. The function of these decision makers is to mobilize disparate parties around a position which can be represented against foreign positions.[11] This reinforces strong cleavages. At its weakest, this position involves no duty of concern for other interests, providing no reason to reach out to these or even to accommodate them. At its strongest, it sets out these others' interests as inimical to the national community. Thus, even in a world where national actors deliberate with one another, and these cleavages are softened as possible, one still finds agreement harder to reach in the Council or intergovernmental bodies than supranational institutions, such as the Commission or European Parliament.

This ambivalence complicates matters, furthermore, in two particular ways within the Union.

First, it leads to institutional dissipation. If foreign actors dominate the lawmaking or policy formulation process, in most fields, domestic actors are exclusively responsible for implementation. A corollary is weak system

[9] Foret and Calligaro, 'Analysing European Values: An Introduction', in Foret and Calligaro (eds.), *European Values: Challenges and Opportunities for EU Governance* (Routledge, 2018).

[10] Jorges, 'Unity in Diversity as Europe's Vocation and Conflicts Law as Europe's Constitutional Form', in Nickel and Greppi (eds.), *The Changing Role of Law in the Age of Supranational and Transnational* Governance (Nomos, 2014), pp. 125–176.

[11] Naurin, 'Liberal intergovernmentalism in the Councils of the EU: A baseline theory?' 56 *JCMS* (2018), 1526–1543; Wratil, 'Modes of government responsiveness in the European Union: Evidence from the Council negotiation positions', 19 *EUP* (2018), 52–74.

formation.[12] Complex institutional settlements and supermajorities put checks on the law and policymaking processes to counter this foreign predominance.[13] Supranational actors acquire significant powers to police and mitigate the significant coordination and enforcement issues that arise from the domestic monopoly over implementation.[14]

Secondly, it distorts the distributive lens through which problems are addressed. The central point of comparison is the allocation of costs and benefits between states. This backgrounds intra-state distributive conflicts and leads to a perverse political economy. There are incentives for the interests represented in national positions to externalize the costs of any deal onto unrepresented interests as they both reduce their own costs and foist additional costs onto their competitors.

3. The EU Strategies for Managing the Ambition–Authority Deficit

These pressures create an ambition–authority deficit: a situation where the Union's commitments exceed its capacity to act authoritatively. As the Union spends so much more of its time proportionately addressing super wicked problems than other polities, the political contestation associated with these bedevils it. This contestation tears at the Union mission. It obstructs policymaking, weakens mutual commitments, and generates demands for political exit. The ambivalent authority granted to foreigners exacerbates this. It limits what the Union can do to manage these problems. It tarnishes the authority of its solutions, polarizes debate, and restricts Union mobilization of support. This deficit is significant and persistent. It generates demands for member state autonomy, which at their most intense threaten the Union with collapse.

Strategies for managing this deficit have, thus, been a central leitmotiv of the Union, with four central ones emerging over time: legislative compacts, administrative coordination, resourced co-option, and discounting.

[12] Bartolini, *Restructuring Europe—Centre Formation, System Building, and Political Structuring between the Nation State and the European Union* (Oxford University Press, 2005)

[13] Bellamy, *A Republican Europe of Sovereign States: Cosmopolitan Statism, Republican Intergovernmentalism and the Demoicratic Reconnection of the EU* (Cambridge University Press, 2018).

[14] Zhelyazkova, Kaya, and Schrama, 'Decoupling practical and legal compliance: Analysis of member states' implementation of EU policy', 55 *EJPR* (2016), 827–846; Dörrenbächer, 'Frontline uses of European Union (EU) law: A parallel legal order? How structural discretion conditions uses of EU law in Dutch and German migration offices', 38 *Journal of Public Policy* (2018), 455–479; Trein, Thomann, and Maggetti, 'Integration, functional differentiation and problem-solving in multilevel governance', 97 *Public Administration* (2019), 339–354.

The effectiveness of these strategies can be gauged, first, by their political authority. This goes to whether they become *the* place where conflicts arising from this deficit are managed. If parties use other processes, there is a decline in Union authority and a risk the deficit becomes unmanageable, as these other processes may not be interested in managing it but simply giving expression to voices which oppose Union policies. If a strategy fails to induce engagement, therefore, there is as much a collapse in Union policymaking as when a policy becomes operationally ineffective.

They can be gauged, second, by their realization of the Union's missions. The Union collapses if it does not pursue these, as it becomes a different beast. The formal organizational structures might remain, but the justifications for its existence, the quality of its actions, and its identity change. Such failures can take a number of forms. The Union response may be so weak to be implausible as a response. It may be operationally ineffective. As super wicked problems rarely have definitive solutions, a failure to adapt its policies is also an abandonment of its mission, since the Union replaces addressing the problem with preserving the policy for its own sake. Alongside this, the Union can fail to grant authority to foreigners. This is done most directly by failing to represent the interests of Union citizens from different member states. However, the commitment extends beyond that because it is an emancipatory commitment. Considering only the interests of rich or male Union citizens would, therefore, not be honouring it. For the commitment is a pluralist one which requires heed to be paid to the diversity of the Union citizenry.

3.1 Legislative Compacts

Associated with the Community method, this is the longest established strategy. The problem is identified and framed by Action Plans or Programmes, which are usually drafted by the Commission and signed off by the Council or European Council. These settle expectations by providing a timetable of measures to address the problem, identifying each measure's contribution and relating it to other measures, and allocating institutional and domestic responsibilities. Political contestation is managed at a number of points throughout the process. These plans are, thus, only mid-level commitments which do not specify the content of legislation or commit member states to it. Binding EU laws are often very specialized, regulating a particular sector or industry and thereby limiting the number of competing interests at stake. Administrative actors dominate the lawmaking process, with the one non-administrative actor, the European Parliament, adopting a similar managerial style to secure influence.[15] Adaptiveness is secured by extensive provision for the Commission to adopt implementing and delegated measures to specify what was agreed initially. If credibility is secured by the Commission pursuing infringement proceedings against states that do not transpose these EU laws into their laws, contestation is restricted by its focusing its resources on policing this transposition rather than wider questions of application of and compliance with these laws.[16]

Notwithstanding this, a number of issues have bedevilled this strategy in terms of problem management.

It has encountered significant collective action challenges with responses to these challenges, weakening the Union's problem management. There have been many instances of a 'Christmas tree' effect where additional national demands are lain on top of the original proposal, making the Union measure overly complex and incoherent. The 2004 enlargement led, for example, to the length of EU laws increasing by approximately 15 per cent.[17] There has been hogwiring of national diffentiation into EU law, with one study showing one in six pieces of EU legislation marked by this special pleading.[18] EU legislation is also often kept vague, with detailed content subsequently determined by the Commission or EU agencies. In 2018 and 2019 combined, the EU legislative procedures adopted 269 Regulations and Directives, whilst the Commission adopted 2142 delegated or implementing acts.[19] The focus has led to concerns of a broader compliance deficit. Over time, therefore, the Commission has increasingly set out enforcement standard for national authorities,[20] and EU institutions and agencies has been granted direct enforcement powers over commercial actors.[21]

Its reliance on binding laws also leaves this strategy vulnerable to legal formalism. Treaty strictures prevent a number of policy responses,[22] and EU legal

[15] Brandsma, 'Transparency of EU informal trilogues through public feedback in the European Parliament: promise unfulfilled', 26 *JEPP* (2019), 1464–1483; Novak, Rozenberg, and Bendjaballah, 'Enduring consensus: why the EU legislative process stays the same', (2021) 43, *Journal of European Integration* 475.

[16] European Commission, *EU law: Better results through better application*, OJ 2017, C 18/10 at 14–15.

[17] Best and Settembri, 'Legislative Output after Enlargement: Similar Number, Shifting Nature', in Best, Christiansen, and Settembri (eds.), *The Institutions of the Enlarged European Union: Change and Continuity* (Edward Elgar, 2008), pp. 183–203 at 187.

[18] Duttle, Holzinger, Malang, Schäubli, Schimmelfenning, and Winzen, 'Opting out from European Union legislation: the differentiation of secondary law', 24 *JEPP* (2017), 406–428.

[19] https://eur-lex.europa.eu/statistics/legislative-acts-statistics.html

[20] Bastings, Mastenbroek, and Versluis, 'The other face of Eurolegalism: The multifaceted convergence of national enforcement styles', 11 *Regulation and Governance* (2017), 299–314.

[21] Scholten, 'Mind the trend! Enforcement of EU law has been moving to "Brussels"', 24 *JEPP* (2017), 1348–1366.

[22] Herdegen, 'Price stability and budgetary restraints in the economic and monetary union: The law as guardian of economic wisdom', 35 *CMLRev* (1998), 9–32.

objectives frequently frame problems in confining ways.[23] The primacy of EU law over national law limits domestic responsiveness to subsequent issues. There are also limited prospects that EU law will deal with these expeditiously. A 2014 study found the average EU law was amended once every seven years.[24] The focus on compliance with EU law limits policymakers' adaptiveness to the changing demands of the problem at hand and the circumstances surrounding it.[25]

Over time, these limitations to the strategy have shaped the quality of political community engaged with it. The specialized nature of many EU measures has generated a political economy of a stable group of interests resistant to change[26] but little wider mobilization.[27] This lack of pluralism and mobilization has also made a European Union political space a fragile one. The managerialization of the legislative process has weakened the range and vibrancy of debate, with influence more easily secured by purveyors of expertise than representatives of different societal interests,[28] and industrial actors looking to other fora where EU legislative processes do not suit them.[29]

3.2 Administrative Coordination

Policy coordination was first formalized in EU law by the Single European Act in relation to economic and monetary policy and foreign policy,[30] and has since spread Union activity across almost all walks of governmental engagement.[31] Its modes vary. In some instances, healthcare systems are an example; policy coordination takes the form of developing tools and methodologies to assess performance, share experiences, and collective assessment of national

[23] Sangiovanni, 'Debating the EU's raison d'être: On the relation between legitimacy and justice', 57 *JCMS* (2019), 13–27.

[24] Borghetto and Mäder, 'EU law revisions and legislative drift', 15 *EUP* (2014), 171–191.

[25] Thomann and Zhelyazkova, 'Moving beyond (non-)compliance: the customization of European Union policies in 27 countries', 24 *JEPP* (2017), 1269–1288.

[26] Eising, Rasch, Rozbicka, Fink-Hafner, Hafner-Fink, and Novak, 'Who says what to whom? Alignments and arguments in EU policymaking', 40 *WEP* (2017), 957–980.

[27] Rauh and de Wilde, 'The opposition deficit in EU accountability: Evidence from over 20 years of plenary debate in four member states', 57 *European Journal of Political Research* (2018), 194–216; Winzen, de Ruiter, and Rocabert, 'Is parliamentary attention to the EU strongest when it is needed the most? National parliaments and the selective debate of EU policies', 19 *EUP* (2018), 481–501.

[28] Gornitzka and Krick, 'The expertisation of stakeholder involvement in EU policymaking', in Góra, Holst, and Warat (eds.), *Expertisation and Democracy in Europe* (Routledge, 2017), pp. 51–70; Krick and Gorntizka, 'Tracing scientisation in the EU Commission's expert group system' *Innovation* (2020), early view.

[29] Chalmers and Chaves, 'EU law-making and the state of European democratic agency', in Hobolt and Cramme (eds.) *Democratic Politics in a European Union under Stress* (Oxford University Press, 2014), pp. 155–179.

[30] Articles 20 and 30 SEA.

[31] Jachtenfuchs and Genschel, 'More integration, less federation: the European integration of core state powers', 23 *JEPP* (2016), 42–59.

performance. Alongside this, platforms are provided for interest groups and stakeholders to input into the process and share their own best practices. In others, the role of the EU institutions is more central and the process more directed. In the European Semester, the European Council adopts Country-Specific Recommendations which are to inform individual national budgetary policies. The Commission drafts these Recommendations with input from national stakeholders and in the light of EU institution assessment of prior national performance and the collective priorities set by the EU institutions. These Recommendations are underpinned by the possibility of the instigation of the sanction procedures provided for by the six pack if they are disregarded.

Coodination's problem-solving promise lies in its enlargement of the knowledge base through its bringing together public, private, foreign, and domestic expertise. It stimulates reflection and scrutiny of this knowledge through the subsequent deliberation that takes place and national and Union responses being adapted on an ongoing basis in the light of the experiences of each other.[32] The authority of foreigners is secured by the Union framing the ambitions and values of the process; governments justifying themselves to other governments and Union institutions; and the possibility for private parties to input directly into this transnational process rather than through the intermediary of their national governments.[33]

The central limitation of this approach is insufficient appreciation of the super wicked qualities of many EU problems: their intractability, deep distributive conflicts, and conflicts of interest. The central national administrative actors and the Commission predominate,[34] and policies reflect prevailing thinking with little evidence of significant policy innovation.[35] Little is done to challenge existing geographies of power with correspondingly low levels of implementation. The most extensive study suggested there is only between 29 and 40 per cent implementation rates,[36] with particular challenges where distributive issues are salient.[37] The European Union has, thus, not come close

[32] Sabel and Zeitlin, 'Experimentalism in the EU: Common Ground and Persistent Differences', 6 *Regulation and Governance* (2012), 410–426.

[33] de Búrca, 'Human Rights Experimentalism', 111 *AJIL* (2017), 277–316.

[34] On this see Dawson, 'New governance and the displacement of Social Europe: the case of the European Semester', 14 *EuConst* (2018), 191–209.

[35] Haas, D'Erman, Schulz, and Verdun, 'Economic and fiscal policy coordination after the crisis: is the European Semester promoting more or less state intervention?', 42 *Journal of European Integration* (2020), 327–344; Crespy, 'The EU's socioeconomic governance 10 years after the crisis: Muddling through and the revolt against austerity', 58(1) *JCMS* (2020), 133–146.

[36] Darvas and Leandro, *The Limitations of Policy Coordination in the Euro Area Under the European Semester* (Bruegel, 2015), p. 6. There is a chance actual rates are lower as this study looked at the European Semester, which is underpinned by binding laws.

[37] Eberlein, 'Experimentalist Governance in the Energy Sector', in Sabel and Zeitlin (eds.), *Experimentalist Governance in the European Union: Towards a New Architecture* (Oxford University Press, 2010), pp. 61–78; Börzel, 'Experimentalist governance in the EU: The emperor's new clothes?' 6 *Regulation & Governance* (2012), 378–384, but cf. Rangoni and Zeitlin, 'Is experimentalist governance

to realizing the targets set by it in all the major fields where this strategy is predominant (e.g., the Stability and Growth Pact, Lisbon Agenda, Europe 2020). This strategy has also struggled to mobilize a sufficiently diverse array of voices, in large part, because it has been treated as a policy process rather than a political one. Parliaments have been marginalized and the influence of civil society interests on the process is questionable.[38] This has allowed no significant voice for traditional intermediaries of public opinion, such as political parties, with a consequent failure to engage public opinion.

3.3 Resourced Co-option

The increased polarization surrounding European integration in the last decade has led to increased mistrust about States implementing EU laws or coordinating their actions with others. A third strategy has emerged to mark this: resourced co-option. Resources are granted to a member state to participate in a policy with effective participation a condition for continued grant of resources. Examples include the European Stability Mechanism;[39] the grant of budgetary payments in proportion to the scale of member state asylum and migration responsibilities;[40] linking budgetary payments to compliance with the rule of law;[41] and the proposed precautionary financial assistance to euro area states which will link access to their continually meeting the criteria set out in the six pack.[42]

The logic is a hard-nosed one in which individual states are provided financial resources in return for implementing policies that would otherwise be

self-limiting or self-reinforcing? Strategic uncertainty and recursive rulemaking in European Union electricity regulation', 15 *Regulation and Governance* (2020), 822.

[38] Crum, 'Parliamentary accountability in multilevel governance: what role for parliaments in post-crisis EU economic governance', 25 *JEPP* (2018), 268–286; Barrett, 'European economic governance: deficient in democratic legitimacy?', 40 *Journal of European Integration* (2018), 249–264.

[39] Article 12(1) of the Treaty Establishing the European Stability Mechanism (2012). https://www.esm.europa.eu/sites/default/files/20150203_-_esm_treaty_-_en.pdf (accessed May 2021).

[40] Article 7 of Regulation (EU) No 515/2014 Establishing, as part of the Internal Security Fund, the instrument for financial support for external borders and visa OJ 2014 L 150/143; Articles 15–18 of Regulation (EU) No 516/2014 establishing the European Asylum, Migration and Integration Fund, OJ 2014 L 150/68.

[41] Article 4(1) of Regulation (EU) No 2020/2092 on a general regime of conditionality for the protection of the Union budget, OJ 2020 L433l/1. Measures can only be taken if the breaches of the rule of law affect the sound financial management of the Union or its financial interests in a sufficiently direct way.

[42] Article 14(1) of the Agreement Amending the Treaty Establishing the European Stability Mechanism (2020). https://www.esm.europa.eu/sites/default/files/esm-treaty-amending-agreement-21_en.pdf (accessed April 2021).

politically unacceptable. States are, in effect, bought off. This logic is ill-suited to super wicked problems. The issues must be simplified and bounded to allow it to be clear what the state must do to access the financial resources. This does little justice to the complexity, scope, or intractability of the Union's super wicked problems. The issues surrounding constitutional democracy in Central and Eastern Europe cannot be reduced compliance with the rule of law,[43] and neither can the performance of the South European political economies be reduced, as the European Stability Mechanism (ESM) did, to public finances, regulatory reform, and public administration.[44]

The surrounding politics is, moreover, too fissile to allow any bargain to be stable. As a consequence, the focus of the arrangement can turn all too easily from problem-solving to monitoring non-compliance. The policing of financial support offered to euro area states, thus, transformed the euro area into a debt community where a central preoccupation is minimizing threats to the recovery of financial support to the detriment of wider consideration of the area's performance.[45]

The quality of authority shown to foreigners is also highly questionable. The provision of resources is alternately characterized as solidarity,[46] recognition of that state's solidarity with others,[47] or as realizing the constitutional democratic values set out in Article 2 TEU.[48] The deeply transactional nature of the arrangement belies all this, however. Its hallmarks are often polarization and institutional sniping. The Commission and European Central Bank (ECB) aggressively patrolled implementation of programmes entered into under the ESM just as constitutional courts frequently pushed back at these.[49] In like vein, the Commission has used infringement proceedings to undermine the populist government in Hungary, on occasion at some human cost,[50] whilst the latter called a referendum and enlisted the constitutional court to limit the application of EU fundamental rights norms.[51]

[43] Krastev and Holmes, *The Light That Failed: A Reckoning* (Penguin Random House, 2019), pp. 27–75.

[44] Hall, 'Varieties of capitalism in light of the euro crisis', 25 JEPP (2018), 7–30.

[45] Losada, 'A Europe of creditors and debtors: Three orders of debt relations in European integration', 58 JCMS (2020), 787–802.

[46] Treaty establishing the European Stability Mechanism, *supra* note 39, Preamble, para 5.

[47] Regulation 516/2004, *supra* note 40, Articles 1(2)(d) and 18.

[48] Regulation 2020/2092, *supra* note 41, Preamble paras 1 and 2.

[49] Beukers, de Witte, and Kilpatrick (eds.), *Constitutional Change through Euro-Crisis Law* (Oxford University Press, 2017).

[50] Case C-179/14 *Commission v Hungary*, EU:C:2016:108.

[51] *Decision 22/2016 Interpretation of Article E(2) of the Fundamental Law*, Judgment of 30 November 2016.

3.4 Discounting

The distributive conflicts that mark and debilitate the third strategy can be tempered if the costs of the Union are offloaded onto unrepresented parties, be it non-EU citizens or future generations. This has emerged as a significant strategy as a consequence of the Recovery and Resilience Facility (Council of the EU 2020). The Union will borrow on the capital markets against its own resources and provide grants of 384.4 billion euros and loans of 360 billion euros to member states.[52] These are to realize 'national recovery and resilience plans' which must meet objectives set out in the European Semester, enable recovery from the Covid-19 crisis, support EU climate change objectives, and contribute to moving to the digital economy.[53] The size of the facility mean that it will be a central part of what the Union is about in these fields. It dissolves many of the distributive conflicts associated with these by generating benefits (i.e., access to cheap capital and grants) that most member states would otherwise not be able to obtain and defraying the costs for these.

This is extremely attractive in the midst of a pandemic, but there are concerns. The frontloading of resources means that decision-making can be rushed and problems poorly identified. The Czech prime minister, for example, put forward the Czech plan without its even having been even discussed by the Czech government.[54] Future interests are historically poorly represented within decision-making, leading to their often being undervalued both in the terms of the scale of repayment and the wider human cost. Organizational literature suggests, therefore, their interests are best protected when decision makers are required to identify a significant concrete legacy that will be left to these interests.[55]

There is also little about this approach which requires national institutions to value foreigners. Their relationship with foreigners is a debtor–creditor one. The conditions of the loan come to epitomize the relationship, with instalments only paid on national authorities meeting certain milestones.[56]

[52] Article 2 of Regulation (EU) No 2020/2094 establishing a European Union Recovery Instrument to support the recovery in the aftermath of the COVID-19 crisis, OJ 2020 L 433l/23.

[53] Articles 4 and 7 of Regulation (EU) No 2021/241 establishing the Recovery and Resilience Facility, OJ 2021 L 57/17.

[54] 'EU countries warm up recovery fund engine', *euractiv*, 16 October 2020. www.euractiv.com/section/politics/news/eu-countries-warm-up-recovery-fund-engine/ (accessed May 2021).

[55] Fox, Tost, and Wade-Benzoni, 'The legacy motive: a catalyst for sustainable decision making in organizations', 20 *Business Ethics Quarterly* (2010), 153–185; Hurlstone, Price, Wang, Leviston, and Walker, 'Activating the legacy motive mitigates intergenerational discounting in the climate game', 60 *Global Environmental Change* (2020), 102008.

[56] Regulation 2021/241, *supra* note 53, Articles 4(2), 14(7), and 20(5)(d).

Moreover, the arrangements consolidate the power of national administrations by providing them with a powerful source of patronage. There is notably no requirement for them to engage with national parliaments or civil society in the development or implementation of their plans. The quality of domestic governance alone is, thus, likely to be central to how well these funds are spent and whether they exacerbate existing geographies of power.[57]

4. Towards a European Community of Super Wicked Problems

Two things emerge when assessing whether each strategy has been sufficiently successful at overcoming the Union's ambition–authority deficit to allow it to manage super wicked problems in a way that grants authority to foreigners. The first is that earlier strategies do not die. They just atrophy. This persistence might be evidence that their possibilities and achievements are too easily disregarded. It might also be evidence of institutional inertia. Presence without significance. This raises the second point. Anxieties about Union collapse mask the fact that much of it has collapsed. Julia Gray has, thus, observed that when regional organizations collapse, they rarely disappear. Instead, they become moribund (about 20 per cent of all organizations in her view) or acquire a zombie existence with little autonomy or significance (about 50 per cent in her view).[58] In this regard, the imperative of super wicked problems form the context for assessing whether a Union strategy has collapsed. If that strategy cannot mobilize action with a measure of authority when confronted with these imperatives, one is talking about a de facto collapse. It is fiddling whilst the Union burns. It condemns itself either to irrelevance, with other for a taking on the mantle, or policy failure.

On this basis, it is difficult to argue that the second and third strategies, administrative coordination and resourced co-option, have not collapsed.

Administrative coordination has failed to generate sufficient action to meaningfully address the demands of super wicked problems. Most notably, economic policy coordination generated only inconsequential reforms in the period prior to 2008, leaving many states woefully exposed at the onset of the sovereign debt crisis. The inconsequentiality of administrative coordination is

[57] Hagemann, 'How politics matters for EU funds' absorption problems—a fuzzy-set analysis', 26 *JEPP* (2019), 188–206; Incaltarau, Pascariu, and Surubaru, 'Evaluating the determinants of EU funds absorption across old and new member states—the role of administrative capacity and political governance', 58 *JCMS* (2020), 941–961.

[58] Gray, 'Life, death, or zombie? The vitality of international organizations', 62 *International Studies Quarterly* (2018), 1–13.

illustrated by its use in areas as salient as poverty, healthcare, and education. However, it is impossible to talk of significant European politics of poverty, healthcare, or education that has emerged from this coordination. As noted earlier, even its most vaunted example, the European Semester is more often ignored than followed, and it is particularly telling that there is little significant difference in implementation rates between euro area states, who have a bigger stake in its making the euro work, and non-euro area states.[59]

Equally, resourced co-option has oscillated between two situations, which both deprive it of any effectiveness beyond the short term. One is where significant resources have been used to leverage action from member states which generated high social costs and had little local support. The most dramatic example is the Memoranda of Understanding agreed under the ESM and similar programmes. The brutality of these makes it unlikely they will be repeated. Their bullying of weaker states, undermining of democratic institutions, and dramatic social consequences so corrodes Union authority that it cannot regularly deploy them. The other is where resources are used to buy unpopular policies. However, the resources do not shift the political dynamics underlying the opposition. Significant payments to member states since 2014 to police migration more effectively and take more asylum seekers have, thus, been tangential to European migration politics. Similarly, conditioning EU accession on the quality of a states' constitutional democracy has not prevented regression with sanctions having little effect against established regimes.[60]

It is too early to know whether the fourth strategy, discounting, will be successful. The Union's history is, however, replete with examples of the first strategy's (legislative compacts) successes: competition, equal opportunities, consumer protection, data protection, chemicals, motor vehicles, and many environmental standards. A policy was established which mobilized subsequent wider support within the Union and was often copied by many jurisdictions around the world. These successes point to the advantages enjoyed by the Union in relation to super wicked problems. It can pool resources and expertise in unrivalled ways. It is less likely to be deterred by the risks to a politician's reputation or to their re-election. Its diversity of arenas provides opportunities for policy entrepreneurs—be these supranational institutions, national administrative rent-seekers, epistemic communities, or repeat litigators—to forum shop and incubate ambitious and innovative policies. Its scale grants it a regulatory autonomy enjoyed by few jurisdictions around the world. Finally, the

[59] Darvas and Leandro, *supra* note 36, at 2.

[60] Sedelmeier, 'Political safeguards against democratic backsliding in the EU: the limits of material sanctions and the scope of social pressure', 24 *JEPP* (2017), 337–351.

authority granted to foreigners is not simply appealing on its own terms but opens the Union up to considering a plurality of interests that are historically poorly represented by political institutions.

That being so, the central antidote is a more general use of this strategy in a way that addresses the problems that bedevil it, those of legal formalism and collective action. Legal formalism, it will be remembered, can unduly frame and confine how the problem is initially addressed, and can also unnecessarily limit domestic democracy and unduly restrict domestic responsiveness. Collective action problems generate a series of pathologies to overcome them: Christmas tree effects, overdifferentiation, and vagueness. The challenge of autonomy without collapse is a straightforward one: to address these in a way that protects the Union's operational effectiveness. Three reforms would help.

4.1 Reform One: The Union should be granted a general legislative competence.

The central feature confining problem-solving is the programmatic nature of the Treaties. They set up a number of projects to be realized, methods for realizing them, and restrictions that must be observed. This framing and programming is not so extensive in other settlements with comparable powers (i.e., many federal governments). It looks all the more anachronistic as Union activities now pervade almost all fields of policymaking. The question has long ceased to be about the remit of European integration but rather about its quality.

Granting the Union a general legislative competence would have a number of advantages.[61] Union action would no longer be just tied to realizing particular policies with their particular teleologies and path dependencies. Success would not be measured by the chimera of the effective operation of these policies. Instead, there would be a more open-ended engagement with the challenges of the age, with more possibility for the Union both to be more creative and to move away from past measures where these are no longer optimal. It might also allow a more diverse political mobilization. All policy entrepreneurs would see the Union as a potential vehicle for their ambition where other arenas were not available. The wider range of policies consequently put forward before Union arenas would draw domestic political

[61] For an earlier argument to this effect see Garben, 'Confronting the competence conundrum: democratizing the European Union through an expansion of its legislative powers', 35 *OJLS* (2015), 55–89.

parties more actively into Union politics as they both saw possibilities for advancing their preferences and threats to their positions.

The concern with this reform is that it overextends the Union. It can do things that are not currently possible and restrict domestic action that is now free from the possibility of constraint. As already mentioned, the Union already has this possibility of action through administrative coordination, which has few limits on its scope. The real question is, therefore, whether member states retain their veto over such action. They would if Article 352 TFEU, the flexibility provision, were reformed. This Article, it will be remembered, allows the Union to adopt legislation to attain one of the objectives set out in the Treaties. These objectives are, however, so vague as to include almost any general interest.[62] The Article is, therefore, sufficiently broad to be a general power. Member states also have a veto, and national parliaments' attention must be drawn to any use of it.[63] The current constraints needing reform are an opaque requirement that it be used within the framework of policies defined in the Treaties;[64] and that it neither be used for harmonization in fields where this is not provided[65] or common foreign and security policy.[66] These requirements would all have to be deleted.

There remains the question of whether such a reform would unduly restrict domestic action. The second proposed reform addresses this.

4.2 Reform Two: Parliamentary statutes can deviate from EU law. Such deviation should be referred to the Conference of Parliamentary Committees for Union Affairs of Parliaments of the European Union (COSAC) to verify it does not unduly affect other EU interests. In such instances, COSAC may refer the matter to the European Council, which can sanction the state if a satisfactory solution is not found.

Allowing domestic parliaments to derogate from EU law would enable greater responsiveness to local circumstances. It would increase incentives for Union institutions to be more generally responsive as such derogations would provide pressures to rethink that law. It would also address the issue that EU

[62] One objective, therefore, is promoting economic and social progress. Preamble to the TEU, para 9.

[63] Article 352(2) TFEU.

[64] Article 352(1) TFEU.

[65] Article 352(3) TFEU.

[66] Article 352(4) TFEU.

decision-making processes do not enjoy the democratic authority held by domestic legislatures. There is less political mobilization and debate, and the centre of gravity of political identities within the Union is domestic then European.

In that context, the arguments for a priori EU legal primacy over domestic law are weak. Any concern that, otherwise, EU law's unity and effectiveness is compromised is belied by the high level of differentiation already present within EU law. Stronger concerns are that member states might game the system by seeing EU law as something for others to observe or engage tit-for-tat reprisals by retaliating against derogations. It is for those making those claims to substantiate them, however, and the evidence suggests the opposite. There is already high non-compliance with EU law without any of this being present. This non-compliance is evidenced in the Commission's policing of EU law. It only takes up cases where it find a prima facie breach of EU law, taking forward just over 10 per cent of cases notified to it.[67] It settles the overwhelming majority of cases either before[68] or after formally launching proceedings,[69] and wins 89.5 per cent of the few cases that reach the Court.[70] High settlement rates securing compliance with EU law would only be plausible if the Commission lost more cases before the Court, as this would evidence doubt about the law in a high proportion of cases settled. The only plausible alternate explanation is that the Commission settles a large number of cases where the breach of EU law persists and it does not regard that breach as serious. A more structured settlement of non-compliance would be more honest, more democratic, and more transparent. It would not threaten the operational effectiveness of EU law.

There are, thus, reasons to police but not ban derogations from EU law. Domestic controls would be necessary. Only statutes enacted by domestic parliaments would enjoy the democratic authority to derogate from EU law. To prevent abuse, these statutes could not be omnibus statutes but must address individual EU laws. Furthermore, to prevent this derogation being

[67] Between 2014 and 2018, the Commission registered 18,010 complaints, but only took 1889 cases further. European Commission, *Monitoring the Application of Union Law: 2018 Annual Report, Part I Statistical Overview* (European Commission, 2019), p. 14.

[68] In the five years up to 2018, between 73 and 77 percent of all cases were resolved within EU Pilot, the online process that allows for resolution of the matter before formal initiation of proceedings. Ibid. European Commission (2019).

[69] In the five years up to 2018, the Commission formally initiated 2952 proceedings, Ibid. European Commission (2019), p. 18; In that period, there were 159 judgments. See Court of Justice, *Annual Report 2018: Judicial Activity* (Official Publications of the European Union, 2019), p. 132.

[70] The Commission won 128/143 of the cases that reached Court in the 2015–19 period. See Court of Justice, *Annual Report 2019: Judicial Activity* (Official Publications of the European Union, 2020), p. 170.

leveraged as a negotiating strategy in EU lawmaking, derogation should not be possible until at least two years after the law has come into effect. Alongside this, the duty to grant authority to foreigners would require an impact assessment and hearings to consider how the derogation would affect the interests of EU citizens and EU enterprises from other states, and to limit the adverse consequences on these to those necessary for the statute to serve its purpose.

There would also be Union controls. The best policing mechanism would be that COSAC assess the proposed statute. If national parliaments have incentives to provide each other with some freedom from EU law as they may wish to exploit this freedom, they are also likely to be responsive to the views of constituents potentially adversely affected by the proposed law. COSAC would look at whether the impact assessment and hearings had been effectively carried out, and whether the measure unnecessarily affects other parties' interests. If over half of the COSAC representatives found any of this to be so, the Commission would refer the proposed statute to the European Council under Article 7(2) TEU on the grounds of a serious and persistent breach of the values in Article 2 TEU. If a satisfactory solution could not be found with the member state, the Council could impose sanctions under Article 7(3) TEU on the grounds that the member state was proposing a serious and persistent breach of the values in Article 2 TEU.

4.3 Reform Three: Nine member states should be able to adopt, amend, or repeal EU legislation between themselves subject to Commission verification that it does not unnecessarily affect the interests of other EU states or arbitrarily discriminate.

The most direct way to address collective action problems is to reduce the threshold for action. Lowering the threshold would not only make action easier. It would also alter the Union legislative dynamics. Parties would be willing to make more ambitious proposals as these now stood a greater chance of being adopted. Veto players would also be warier. The choice is no longer between the status quo or leveraging their veto to secure something better, as others now may be able to make legislative changes with some costs to them.

The Treaties set the number of states able to take action at nine.[71] Two further things would secure better responsiveness.

[71] Article 20(2) TEU.

First, the Commission should lose its monopoly over proposing legislation. This monopoly allows Union responsiveness to be determined by the preferences and institutional imagination of a single administrative actor with a stake in system building. This is not fit for purpose for a Union which tackles super wicked problems and embraces diversity. The green card proposal should be adopted, which would require the Commission to adopt any proposal put forward by a quarter of national parliaments.[72] This grants more direct voice in agenda-setting to political parties as these are represented most directly in national parliaments. These not only often represent different interests from those staked in Brussels but have incentives to mobilize a wider array of constituencies to support the legislation as their electoral appeal depends on it.

Secondly, the provisions on Enhanced Cooperation should be amended to allow EU laws to be adopted, amended, or repealed by nine member states or more where this neither unnecessarily affect the interests of other member states nor arbitrarily discriminates. These reforms are necessary because the current regime on Enhanced Cooperation imposes so many restrictions on action that it is rarely used.[73] More specifically, the current requirement that such action 'reinforce the integration process' is outdated in a world where most Union activity is managing existing policies rather than creating new ones.[74] It is particularly inappropriate where the intention is to make the Union a more responsive arena which allows more space for institutional imagination and political competition in addressing problems.

To be sure, other member states must be protected from abuse of this process or significant externalities generated by its use. In that regard, national measures derogating from EU single market legislation must currently simply neither unnecessarily restrict trade nor arbitrarily discriminate.[75] A similar standard should apply to EU laws for a collective group of member states. These should not unnecessarily affect the interests of other member states nor arbitrarily discriminate. These laws are, after all, less vulnerable to abuse, as they are harder to adopt than individual national laws and less likely to be focused around a narrow national self-interest. They should, therefore, be subject to the same procedure as these national laws, namely they can be enacted once the Commission has verified that they do neither of these things.

[72] COSAC, *Twenty-fifth Bi-annual Report: Developments in European Union Procedures and Practices Relevant to Parliamentary Scrutiny* (COSAC, 2016), pp. 12–13.

[73] See the paper by de Witte, Chapter 4, this volume.

[74] These are set out in Articles 20 TEU and 326–334 TFEU.

[75] Article 114(4) TFEU.

5. Conclusion

Arguments for institutional reform risk overstating the capacity of institutions, particularly as many of the Union's super wicked problems are intractable. However, there can be no escaping the fact the Union's ambition–authority deficit needs to be managed. Addressing the challenges of the Union's mission directly is likely to be more effective at this than treating the limits of problem-solving capacity and the ambivalent authority it accords foreigners as guilty secrets. And that is what happened with the two strategies, administrative coordination and resourced co-option, that followed legislative compacts. They were responses to the limitations of that strategy rather than plausible attempts to manage the deficit. Addressing the limitations of legislative compacts mean addressing its formalism and collective action problems in a way that retains its operational effectiveness. This involves granting member states more autonomy. However, it does not threaten collapse but rather rescues the Union from it.

PART 2

DIFFERENTIATED INTEGRATION

3

Overcoming Crisis in the European Union

The Limits of Differentiated Integration

Frank Schimmelfennig

1. Introduction

Since the mid-1980s, differentiated integration has become a core feature of European integration. Of their own accord or forced by negative referendums, individual governments have refused to sign up to new policy regimes such as Economic and Monetary Union (EMU), Schengen, and defence. Alternatively, the EU has refused states access to the Eurozone or Schengen area. As a result, the EU has developed from a system of (largely) uniform integration, in which integrated policies applied to all members (and members only) to a system of differentiated integration, in which the territorial validity of integrated policy regimes is not congruent with formal membership.[1]

Differentiation has proved to be an important and often indispensable facilitator of integration. Major institutional and policy changes in the EU continue to require intergovernmental unanimity, the consent of the European Parliament, and domestic ratification in each member state, thus creating numerous veto points. At the same time, the heterogeneity of member state preferences and capacities and the domestic contestation of EU policies have grown and increased the probability that veto players use their powers. Under these conditions, agreement on the uniform introduction or reform of EU policies has become ever more difficult to achieve. Differentiated integration accommodates international heterogeneity, removes veto points, and thus reduces the probability that member states block agreement. It offers member states the possibility to opt out of EU policies they reject. In addition, it allows for exempting or excluding member states from demanding policies that exceed their capacity.

[1] Schimmelfennig, Leuffen, and Rittberger, 'The European Union as a system of differentiated integration: interdependence, politicization, and differentiation', 22 *Journal of European Public Policy* (2015), 764–782.

Frank Schimmelfennig, *Overcoming Crisis in the European Union.* In: *Autonomy without Collapse in a Better European Union.* Edited by Mark Dawson and Markus Jachtenfuchs, Oxford University Press. © Oxford University Press (2022).
DOI: 10.1093/oso/9780192897541.003.0003

Differentiated integration thus appears to be a clever solution to the autonomy–collapse dilemma.[2] It protects the autonomy of member states, especially in domains of core state powers that some regard as the basis of national sovereignty and self-determination. At the same time, differentiation allows willing and able member states to deepen their integration without being blocked by veto or uniformity rules. Far from putting the European Union on a slippery slope towards collapse or disintegration, differentiated integration has been an indispensable instrument in the dynamic integration progress of the 1990s and 2000s. Counterfactually speaking, without differentiation, the EU would not have a common currency, a free-travel zone, or integrated justice and home affairs policies.

The challenges to European integration have fundamentally changed in the 'polycrisis' of the 2010s however. Rather than struggling to muster support for integrating new member states and policies, the EU has had to deal with old member states threatening to leave (Brexit) or crash out (Grexit) and with already highly integrated policies threatening to disintegrate (such as monetary union and asylum policy).

To cope with these crises, academics and policymakers have again brought differentiated integration into play, most prominently in the European Commission's 'White paper on the future of Europe' which proposed 'Those who want more do more' as one of five scenarios for reforming the EU.[3] Given that the crises of the EU have exposed and reinforced the heterogeneity of integration preferences and capacities between member states, while at the same time demonstrating the need for far-reaching reform to prevent integrated policies from collapsing, differentiated integration may indeed appear to be the perfect solution.

However, I argue that differentiated integration is generally less helpful to facilitate reform in already highly integrated policy areas threatened with disintegration than it has been in the integration of new policies and new member states, especially if these integrated policies are constitutional or redistributive. Whereas international heterogeneity generates demand for differentiation in both contexts, supply conditions differ considerably. The differentiation of existing policies might generate subcritically small groups of member states. Splitting up highly integrated policy areas is also likely to lead to detrimental positive and negative externalities between the groups. Moreover, EU

[2] Dawson and Jachtenfuchs, 'Autonomy without Collapse: Towards a Better Union?', Chapter 1, this volume.

[3] COM(2017) 2025, 'White paper on the future of Europe. Reflections and scenarios for the EU27 by 2025'.

decision-making rules, supranational actors, informal integration norms, high path dependencies, and constitutional as well as redistributive policy purposes reduce the efficiency, legitimacy, and feasibility of differentiation in highly integrated domains. In sum, for all its benefits in boosting the integration of new members and policies, differentiated integration is not the EU's silver bullet for coping with crises of advanced integration.

The chapter starts with a review of the demand and supply factors of differentiated integration.[4] It then applies these factors to the reform needs and prospects in major EU policy domains that have faced or are facing crisis: the Eurozone crisis, the migration crisis, Brexit, and the rule of law. In each case, I show that in spite of high demand and several proposals for differentiated integration, unfavourable supply conditions have thwarted attempts to overcome these crises through differentiation. The chapter concludes with general considerations on the limits of differentiated integration as a solution to the autonomy–collapse dilemma.

2. Demand and Supply of Differentiated Integration

Demand factors create an interest in differentiated integration; supply factors facilitate or inhibit the realization of this demand. The literature shares the assumption that demand for differentiated integration results from international heterogeneity in a context of consensual decision-making.[5] In a homogeneous union, uniform integration is feasible; in a majoritarian system, heterogeneity can be overcome by voting. In the EU, however, where major decisions on integration require the consensus of an increasingly heterogeneous membership, differentiated integration helps to avoid negotiation deadlock.

Differentiated integration addresses two major types of heterogeneity: heterogeneity of state preferences and capacities. Heterogeneity of preferences refers to the desired level and scope of integration. Member states have always been differentially inclined to delegate and pool sovereignty in the Union, especially in the domain of core state powers such as defence, fiscal, and monetary policy. Differentiated integration has allowed member states concerned about national self-determination—such as Denmark and the UK—to opt out

[4] Schimmelfennig and Winzen, *Ever Looser Union? Differentiated European Integration* (Oxford University Press, 2020).

[5] Holzinger and Schimmelfennig, 'Differentiated integration in the European Union. Many concepts, sparse theory, few data, 19 *Journal of European Public Policy* (2012), 292–305.

of supranational integration while allowing integrationist member states to move ahead.

Even if sovereignty concerns are not an issue, the heterogeneity of capacities may stand in the way of uniform agreement. On the one hand, affluent member states with high state capacity may have reservations about integration. When it comes to regulatory compliance in the internal market, budget discipline in monetary union, or effective border protection in Schengen, they may be concerned about the financial resources and bureaucratic quality of lower capacity states. For these reasons, they may make their participation dependent on the conditional entry or exclusion of such countries. Accession conditionality for new member states and the convergence criteria of the monetary union produce such capacity-based differentiation. On the other hand, low-capacity member states sometimes fear the costs of adaptation and participation in integrated EU policies and ask for temporary exemptions from the application of demanding regulations.

Heterogeneity of integration preferences and capacities thus creates demand for differentiation. This demand cannot always be realized, however. Whether differentiated integration is feasible, and acceptable to all relevant states, depends on several 'supply conditions'.

First, the size of the integrationist group needs to be large enough to deal efficiently with the policy problem at hand. A small group of willing and able member states may not generate the economies of scale and the pooling of resources that would make the effort worthwhile. Moreover, a large integrationist group that spans different (regional or economic) groups of member states increases the legitimacy of differentiation against accusations of exclusion and discrimination.

Second, the feasibility and stability of differentiated integration depends on the externalities it produces between insiders and outsiders.[6] If differentiated integration creates positive externalities, outsiders can freeride on the integration efforts of insiders. For instance, the differentiated integration of ambitious climate policies would be costly for insiders but would benefit non-participants too. Substantial positive externalities thus reduce the likelihood that states agree on differentiation or create centrifugal tendencies later on. Why contribute to deeper integration if you can enjoy the benefits outside? By contrast, differentiated integration that imposes negative externalities on outsiders turns happy bystanders into dissatisfied integration losers. For

[6] Kölliker, 'Bringing together or driving apart the Union? Towards a theory of differentiated integration', 24 *West European Politics* (2001), 125–151; Kölliker, *Flexibility and European Unification: The Logic of Differentiated Integration* (Rowman and Littlefield, 2006).

instance, states that refuse to join, or are excluded from access to an integrated market, may find themselves disadvantaged in attracting foreign investment. Substantial negative externalities thus create centripetal tendencies: outsiders prefer to join in anticipation or after realizing the costs of exclusion. Either way, substantial intergroup externalities cause differentiation to be unlikely or short-lived.

Third, the suitability of differentiation depends on the policy type. In particular, differentiated integration is inappropriate to overcome international heterogeneity regarding constitutional and redistributive issues. Constitutional issues concern the fundamental values and norms as well as the basic organizational set-up and institutional rules of a polity. The differential validity of fundamental values and norms—such as human rights or the rule of law in the member states—is generally considered illegitimate even if it were technically feasible and did not create externalities. Moreover, EU-level institutional rules need to be uniform for all member states for reasons of political equality and the proper functioning of the institutions. Therefore, differentiated integration in institutional provisions is extremely rare and limited.

In redistributive policies, differentiated integration tends to be self-defeating. For instance, risk-sharing arrangements are most efficient if they consist of a large number of participants with a high diversity of risk profiles. If they bundle very low risks only, they are unnecessary. If they bundle only a few participants with extremely high risks, they are unsustainable. Likewise, burden-sharing arrangements need to join low-capacity and high-burden members with those that have high capacity or a lower burden so that redistribution produces manageable burdens for all participants. Voluntary arrangements that allow member states to opt out inevitably lead to the exit of the countries with the lowest risks and the lightest burdens, or to a significant reduction of their contribution.

Finally, the institutional context of negotiations on differentiated integration matters. Here I distinguish four typical contexts: no, low, uniform, and differentiated integration. These contexts differ with regard to bargaining power of the status quo countries, the normative legitimacy of differentiation, and the effect of path dependencies.

In a situation of no prior integration, institutional norms, rules, and path dependencies do not exist. The heterogeneity of preferences and material bargaining power is all that counts. Integrationist states can move ahead without the formal agreement of states that refuse or are refused to join. A context of no prior policy integration thus facilitates differentiation, *ceteris paribus*.

Once integration is established, it generates formal decision-making rules, informal norms, and common institutions. Supranational actors enter the stage, and path dependencies are likely to develop. Specifically, the decision-making rule of unanimity weakens the institutional bargaining power of states interested in changing the status quo. If integrationist countries seek more integration, status quo states can threaten to use their veto. In addition, the EU has a normative bias in favour of 'ever closer union' and uniform integration. Unlike other constitutional principles such as proportionality, subsidiarity, and conferral (Art. 5 TEU), the Treaties do not mention, let alone approve, differentiation explicitly. Supranational actors such as the European Commission, Parliament, and Court favour uniform integration in principle, too. Finally, path dependencies of integration build up over time as integration creates sunk costs, triggers endogenous interdependencies, and raises exit costs.[7] To what extent these factors constrain differentiation depends on the level and type of prior integration.

As long as integration remains at a low level, supranational actors and path dependencies are absent or weak. Outsiders are less likely to object to differentiation in policy areas, in which they are only weakly invested. And even though uniform integration would be normatively preferable, differentiated integration is legitimate if it promises major progress in integration, especially if differentiation is limited in time and integration remains open to later joiners. For these reasons the institutional constraints on the differentiated integration of hitherto weakly integrated policies or states are minor.

By contrast, in deeply integrated policies, major institutional constraints on differentiation are in place. Supranational actors favouring uniformity are powerful. Path dependence locks in the existing membership and creates incentives for further uniform integration. The EU's normative bias works in the same direction. In general, states have more incentives to block differentiation if they are part of a deeply integrated group and are heavily invested in the existing level of integration.

The institutional constraints are particularly high where states demand 'differentiated disintegration', i.e., seek to move to a lower level of integration.[8] In this situation, the integrationist states become defenders of the status quo and benefit from the unanimity requirement. Each integrationist government

[7] Pierson, 'The path to European integration. A historical-institutionalist analysis', 29 *Comparative Political Studies* (1996), 123–163.

[8] Schimmelfennig, 'Brexit: differentiated disintegration in the European Union', 25 *Journal of European Public Policy* (2018), 1154–1173.

becomes a veto player, and the member state that is most averse to disintegration defines the limits of change. Veto threats do not preclude disintegration because states always have the option to exit the EU (under Article 50). Yet full exit may impose prohibitive costs on governments that only want to renegotiate the conditions of their membership and reduce their level of integration slightly. Moreover, demands for (differentiated) disintegration face opposition from supranational actors, trigger concerns about 'cherry picking', and are least legitimate in the perspective of 'ever closer union'.

Finally, a context of pre-existing differentiated integration mitigates the institutional constraints on further differentiation. For one, differentiation enjoys higher legitimacy in domains in which it is already an established practice. In addition, if the insiders decide to move ahead with integration, they can do so more easily, because the most sceptical member states do not take part in the decision.[9] Moreover, supranational actors may be 'differentiated' too (as in the case of the European Central Bank). Furthermore, path dependence tends to lock in differentiated integration. It puts states on two divergent trajectories of integration and increases the costs of changing paths over time.

In sum, the supply conditions of differentiated integration are most favourable in a context of no or shallow prior integration of regulatory or distributive policies, in which a large group of states agree on further integration and externalities between them and the outsiders are low. By contrast, demand for differentiation is most difficult to realize when constitutional and redistributive issues are at stake in deeply and uniformly integrated policies and differentiation threatens to shrink the size of the insider group and create significant externalities between them and the outsiders.

3. Differentiated Integration in Crisis-Induced Reforms?

The supply conditions discussed in the previous section limit the general prospects of future differentiated integration in the EU. Few 'low-hanging fruit' are left to pick. The EU already covers all policy domains. In most policies, it has advanced beyond the initial stage of shallow integration, which facilitate differentiated integration progress. Defence policy is one of the few policy areas in which the current level of integration is still low. Correspondingly, Permanent Structured Cooperation (PESCO) is the only example in which the member states have successfully introduced new differentiations

[9] Jensen and Slapin, 'Institutional hokey-pokey: the politics of multispeed integration in the European Union', 19 *Journal of European Public Policy* (2012), 779–795.

in recent years. Moreover, EU enlargement, a major source of differentiated integration in the past, has all but stopped since Croatia joined in 2013. One important reason is the stagnation or even backsliding in democratization in Eastern Europe: a constitutional issue that does not lend itself to differentiated integration.

Here, however, I focus on the integration crises that have defined the current period of European integration since the start of the Eurozone crisis in early 2010. I define an integration crisis as a situation in which an integrated EU policy is threatened with at least partial disintegration: the renationalization of policymaking competences, the disempowerment of supranational actors, or the loss of a member state. For instance, monetary union was manifestly threatened at least with the exit of Greece (if not the end of the euro). In the migration crisis of 2015, the breakdown of the 'Dublin' asylum regime and potentially the Schengen regime of free cross-border movement was at stake. The Brexit vote of 2016 threatened the EU with the loss of a member state. In the ongoing rule of law crisis, several member state governments undermine a fundamental value and institutional backbone of the EU. To qualify, it is sufficient if the crisis threatens the integration of a single policy; it does not have to put in question the survival of the EU as an organization. Indeed, none of the recent crises has gone that far.

In integration crises, the dilemma of autonomy and collapse comes to a head. On the one hand, integration crises are either caused or reinforced by the pursuit of national autonomy. The desire to 'take back control' from Brussels and from independent supranational and national judiciaries has been at the origin of the Brexit and rule of law crises. In the Eurozone and migration crises, governments pursued national policies to cope with rising balance of payment deficits and rising numbers of asylum seekers. On the other hand, these autonomous policies intentionally threatened integrated policy regimes with collapse, or risked their breakdown as a side effect.

Differentiated integration could potentially solve the dilemma by providing individual member states with more autonomy without leading to the collapse of the integrated policy. The EU's integration crises revealed and reinforced international heterogeneity of preferences and capacities among the member states. Regarding preferences, they have aggravated ideological conflicts on issues of macroeconomic policy, migration, sovereignty, and liberal democracy. Regarding capacities, the Eurozone and migration crises in particular have exposed and widened gaps in economic and administrative burdens and capabilities. For these reasons the integration crises have led to increased demand for differentiated integration to reform the integrated policies in crisis.

At the same time, this demand has run into major supply-side obstacles. For one, differentiated reform would have reduced the membership size of the integrated policy and produced significant positive and negative externalities. In addition, the crises have focused on constitutional and redistributive issues. Finally, supranationally and uniformly integrated policies generate important institutional constraints for reforms based on differentiation. Decision-making rules, integration norms, supranational actors, and path dependencies have worked in favour of maintaining uniform integration. To illustrate the dilemmas of differentiation in crisis-induced reform I briefly discuss the Eurozone crisis, the migration crisis, Brexit, and the rule of law crisis. In none of these cases have we seen differentiated integration in spite of pronounced international heterogeneity and academic as well as political forays in favour of differentiation.

3.1 Eurozone Crisis

Economic and Monetary Union (EMU) has been a differentially integrated policy area from the start. The British and Danish opt-outs from monetary union were codified in the Treaty of Maastricht, years before the Euro was introduced. These opt-outs resulted from heterogeneity of preferences. In addition, the Eurozone can exclude EU member states (which have a legal obligation adopt the euro) if they do not meet the economic and fiscal convergence criteria. On this basis, EMU initially excluded Greece (until 2000) and all new member states since 2004 based on heterogeneity of capacity.

In the Eurozone crisis the differentiation between euro-area and non-euro-area member states has remained stable. Yet the crisis has put in question uniform integration among the members of the Eurozone. Economists have asserted early on that the Eurozone was far from an 'optimum currency area', lacking in both labour mobility and fiscal integration.[10] Political economists have further pointed out that monetary union brings together countries pursuing opposite growth strategies: a supply-side or export-led growth strategy based on wage restraint, productivity, and competitiveness in the 'north' of the Eurozone, and a demand-led growth strategy based on fiscal expansion and wage inflation in the 'south'.[11] The Great Recession exacerbated

[10] Krugman, 'Revenge of the Optimum Currency Area', *New York Times*, 24 June 2012. https://krugman.blogs.nytimes.com/2012/06/24/revenge-of-the-optimum-currency-area/ (accessed 8 April 2021).

[11] Hall, 'The economics and politics of the Euro-crisis', 21 *German Politics* (2012), 355–371, at 358–359.

this heterogeneity by turning export-led Eurozone countries into surplus and creditor states and demand-led countries into deficit and debtor states with divergent preferences on crisis management. Whereas the northern countries sought to minimize their liabilities and financial assistance and called for austerity in the south, southern countries favoured the Europeanization or forgiveness of debt and financial transfers from the north. At the height of the crisis, the Eurozone member states were able to agree on the establishment of a rescue fund (the European Stability Mechanism), a fiscal compact, and a banking union. Yet north–south heterogeneity has blocked or whittled down further reaching reforms towards a fiscal union (before the Covid-19 pandemic).

The heterogeneity of state preferences and capacities in the Eurozone's non-optimal currency area has inspired numerous recommendations for differentiated disintegration, i.e., for reforming the Eurozone through the exit or exclusion of a group of its member states. For instance, Roger Bootle won the Wolfson Economics prize by proposing a northern monetary union led by Germany.[12] Fritz Scharpf favoured a two-tier 'European Currency Community' composed of (predominantly northern) EMU members and other (predominantly southern) member states, with national currencies pegged to the euro according to the EU's Exchange Rate Mechanism (ERM II).[13] Finally, Joseph Stiglitz regarded uniform reform of the Eurozone as the best way forward, but advocated 'amicable divorce' in its absence, preferably by the exit of Germany and other northern members from the Eurozone.[14]

Yet the differentiated disintegration of a highly integrated policy area such as EMU would be confronted with the most adverse supply-side conditions. First, the resulting currency union(s) would be much smaller than the current EMU. The EMU might well cease to be the political core of the EU and produce too few returns to scale. Second, the negative externalities of the split would be massive. In the Eurozone crisis, in spite of their conflicting fiscal interests, north and south agreed that a break-up had to be avoided for the prohibitive economic and political risks that it would entail. Even a post-crisis 'amicable solution' would require massive transfers and debt forgiveness to stabilize former Eurozone countries.[15] It would also cause the currencies of

[12] Bootle, *The Trouble with Markets. Saving Capitalism from Itself* (2nd ed., Nicholas Brealy Publishing, 2011).

[13] Scharpf, 'Forced Structural Convergence in the Eurozone—Or a Differentiated European Monetary Community' (2016) MPIfG Discussion Paper 16/15, 1–47. http://pubman.mpdl.mpg.de/pubman/item/escidoc:2385226:5/component/escidoc:2479325/mpifg_dp16_15.pdf (accessed 8 April 2021).

[14] Stiglitz, *The Euro and Its Threat to the Future of Europe* (Penguin Books, 2016), p. 292.

[15] Ibid., pp. 290–292.

the northern countries leaving the Eurozone to appreciate massively, with the likely effect of an export slump; and it would undermine the belief in the durability of the monetary union and invite speculative attacks by financial markets testing member states' commitment to the single currency.

Finally, the institutional context makes differentiated disintegration difficult. The Eurozone is designed to be permanent and has no exit procedures. It features the European Central Bank (ECB), a highly independent and powerful supranational agency with a vital interest in preserving the Eurozone, which has played a decisive role in preventing a break-up during the Eurozone crisis. A split of the Eurozone would also go against the prevailing integration norms and raise major legitimacy concerns, especially in case of a non-consensual break-up or forced exit (see the adverse political reactions to German Finance Minister Schäuble's proposal for a Greek 'time out' from the Eurozone in July 2015). In line with these considerations, the Eurozone crisis has not resulted in the differentiated disintegration of the Eurozone, in spite of the strong demand-based case.

Instead of differentiated disintegration, the Eurozone could have considered differentiated integration, i.e., a reform in which a group of member states moves ahead with fiscal integration without changing the monetary integration of the rest. Such a 'Eurozone Plus', including, for instance, a common bank deposit insurance, a back-up unemployment insurance, or Eurobonds could be sponsored either by the northern or southern group of Eurozone countries, each of which would have sufficiently homogeneous preferences and capacities to achieve agreement.

A Eurozone Plus would certainly be more acceptable than the 'Eurozone Minus' proposed by Bootle, Scharpf, or Stiglitz. It would not reduce the size, disrupt the institutions and interdependencies of EMU, or create significant externalities. A scheme for advancing integration differentially would also be more legitimate than one that reduces integration and expels member states.

Yet differentiated integration along the cleavage between north and south would defeat the basic purpose of fiscal union or risk-sharing. Whereas a Eurozone Plus of southern countries would not be sufficient to stabilize its members in a future economic crisis, a Eurozone Plus of fiscally healthy northern countries would not be necessary to stabilize its members and would not be helpful for stabilizing the south. Obviously, a fiscal union or risk-sharing community requires high- and low-capacity countries in a uniform regime to develop its potential. As with redistributive policies in general, differentiated integration is no recipe for overcoming lack of international solidarity. It is therefore small wonder that proposals for differentiated fiscal integration in

EMU have remained absent from the policy debate. Rather, EMU reform has largely stalled after the Eurozone crisis had abated in 2015. It took the shock of the Covid-19 pandemic for the member states to agree on a recovery fund involving substantial international fiscal transfers. Yet this major (if temporary) advance towards fiscal union was designed as uniform integration across not only the Eurozone, but including non-euro area member states as well.

3.2 Migration Crisis

Like the Eurozone crisis, the 2015–16 migration crisis has exposed serious problems and heterogeneities within the EU. The so-called 'Dublin rules' of EU asylum policy normally allocate responsibility to the country where the asylum seeker first applies for asylum, i.e., in most cases the country of first arrival. Consequently, the migration flows from Northern Africa and the Middle East affected the Mediterranean member states almost exclusively. The front-line states were neither capable of blocking unauthorized migration at the external Schengen border nor did they possess the infrastructure to handle such a high number of asylum seekers. Yet the Schengen area lacks a system of burden-sharing among member states or supranational organizations that could effectively support the border countries.

The policy failure in the migration crisis prompted the European Commission to propose a major reform of the Common European Asylum System including the establishment of an EU asylum agency, a common asylum procedure, further harmonization of the qualification and protection standards, reception conditions, and a permanent resettlement framework. The most contested centrepiece of the reform, however, was a change to the Dublin rules that would allow for a permanent quota system for the allocation of asylum seekers across the member states and thus provide for a fairer sharing of the asylum burdens. However, the member states have not been able to reach agreement since 2015.

The intergovernmental preference heterogeneity mirrors variation in affectedness. Because of their geography, front-line states like Greece and Italy are affected most immediately by the migrant flows. In addition, destination states like Germany and Sweden, prosperous countries with a comparatively liberal asylum regime, are strongly affected by secondary migrant movements. Both groups of member states have supported the corrective allocation system to alleviate their burden. By contrast, transit countries that lay on the migration routes from the front line to the destination states and bystander countries that were located off-route and therefore not directly affected oppose the quota system.[16] The most vocal and uncompromising opposition came from Central and Eastern European member states, not only because they were either bystander or transit countries but also because they were most ideologically and culturally opposed to extra-European migration.

Would differentiated integration offer a way out of non-agreement and confrontation over the reform of the Schengen area's asylum policy? Both the Viségrad countries and French President Macron have made suggestions that would amount to differentiation in the Schengen area. The Central and Eastern European opponents of corrective reallocation proposed 'flexible solidarity' as an alternative in 2016. Like its successor concept 'effective conditionality', however, it does not entail a formal differentiation of the Schengen area with two groups governed by different asylum rules. It rather means that each member state ought to decide individually 'on specific forms of contribution taking into account their experience and potential. Furthermore any distribution mechanism should be voluntary.'[17] In practice, 'flexible solidarity' would allow willing member states to engage in burden-sharing while unwilling countries opt out.

In March 2019, President Macron addressed the 'citizens of Europe' ahead of the European elections and proposed to 'rethink the Schengen area: all those who want to be part of it should comply with obligations of responsibility (stringent border controls) and solidarity (one asylum policy with the same acceptance and refusal rules)'.[18] The proposal leaves open how the differentiation would be implemented. Would it lead to a 'Schengen Plus', in which those wanting to participate would agree to a deepening of asylum and border control integration, or to a 'Schengen Minus', from which those refusing 'obligations of responsibility ... and solidarity' would be excluded?

In September 2020 the European Commission published its compromise proposal for a migration and asylum pact. On the one hand, the proposal keeps the Dublin rules of responsibility for asylum request in place and abandons mandatory reallocation. On the other hand, it introduces a quota-based mechanism to support overburdened member states that gives other member states

[16] Biermann, Guérin, Jagdhuber, Rittberger, and Weiss, 'Political (non-)reform in the refugee crisis: a liberal-intergovernmentalist explanation', 26 *Journal of European Public Policy* (2019), 246–266.

[17] Visegrad Group, 'Joint Statement of the Heads of Governments of the V4 countries', 16 September 2016. http://www.visegradgroup.eu/calendar/2016/joint-statement-of-the-160919 (accessed 8 April 2021).

[18] Macron, 'For European Renewal', Élysée, 4 March 2019. https://www.elysee.fr/emmanuel-macron/2019/03/04/for-european-renewal.en (accessed 8 April 2021).

a choice between relocation and 'return sponsorships'. Where this choice introduces flexibility in implementation, it is not differentiated integration because the same rules apply to all member states. Yet several Central European governments immediately opposed any quota-based obligations, whereas a group of Mediterranean countries insisted on firmer relocation commitments.[19]

In general, like EMU, a differentiation of EU asylum policy faces adverse supply conditions. Both are highly integrated policy areas, but because asylum policy is less centralized and interdependent than monetary policy, and covers a larger membership, some of the conditions are more favourable towards differentiation. In particular, asylum policy lacks powerful supranational actors like the ECB in EMU. Moreover, a split in the Schengen area would be less disruptive than a break-up of the Eurozone. Even according to the most pessimistic scenario, the annual 'cost of non-Schengen' would not have amounted to more than 0.2 per cent of GDP annually,[20] a hundred times less than even the most optimistic models forecast for a Eurozone breakdown.[21] Yet, as in the case of the Eurozone, the core conflict is about redistribution, and differentiation would defeat the purpose of reform: a burden-sharing and harmonization scheme that would stabilize the EU asylum regime. Schengen Plus would most likely bring together only those front line and destination countries that would benefit from relocation. Whereas Schengen Plus might provide for a fairer and more orderly distribution of migrants across the most affected countries, it would not lower their collective burden if transit and bystander countries remained outside.

Additionally, Schengen Plus would generate positive externalities. An improved asylum regime might make it even more attractive for migrants to seek asylum in one of the Schengen Plus countries. Unless the origin of the major migration flows shifted from the south to the east, the Eastern member states would fare best by remaining outside of Schengen Plus while benefiting from the current regime. A differentiated arrangement would thus not only institutionalize the freeriding behaviour of the non-affected countries, it might also create incentives for the insiders to defect.

[19] Zalan, 'Visegrad countries immediately push back on new migration pact', *EUobserver*, 25 September 2020. https://euobserver.com/justice/149537 (accessed 8 April 2021); Nielsen, 'EU "front-line" states want clearer migration rules', *EUobserver*, 26 November 2020. https://euobserver.com/migration/150196 (accessed 8 April 2021).

[20] PE 581.383, 'The Cost of Non-Schengen. Impact of border controls within Schengen on the Single Market', April 2016. http://www.europarl.europa.eu/RegData/etudes/STUD/2016/581383/EPRS_STU(2016)581383_EN.pdf (accessed 8 April 2021).

[21] Schimmelfennig, 'European integration (theory) in times of crisis. A comparison of the Euro and Schengen crises', 25 *Journal of European Public Policy*, 969–989.

In order to change the incentives of the opponents of asylum policy reform, the integrationists would therefore have to be able to threaten them credibly with expulsion from the Schengen free-travel area—amounting to 'Schengen Minus'—in the hope that they value free movement more highly than migration control. If Schengen/Dublin was still regulated by an intergovernmental agreement, as it was until the mid-2000s, such a threat might work. Because it is an integral part of the EU Treaties, however, refounding the Schengen regime would require a renegotiation of the Treaties. The threat to exclude unwilling Schengen countries thus lacks credibility.

3.3 Brexit Crisis

In his January 2013 Bloomberg speech, UK Prime Minister David Cameron promised to negotiate a new settlement for the UK, to be followed by an in–out referendum, in order to appease the EU opponents in the Conservative Party and to deflect the challenge posed by the UK Independence Party (UKIP). Initially, the referendum pledge bought Cameron time, but he had to make good on his promise after leading the Conservatives to victory in the 2015 general elections. In his November 2015 letter to Donald Tusk, President of the European Council, Cameron sought a legally binding opt-out from the Treaty obligation to 'ever closer union' and limits to the free movement of citizens within the internal market.[22]

For many years Cameron had sought in vain to renegotiate the freedom of movement principle with the EU in order to take back national control over immigration. He knew that most member states considered a general opt-out from the freedom of movement non-negotiable[23] and did not want to be in a position in which he would have to recommend British voters to leave the EU because too far-reaching demands were rebuffed. Cameron therefore put forward measures that would limit the free movement for citizens of *future* new member states only, fight the abuse of free movement, restrict in-work benefits to EU citizens for a period of four years, and end the sending of child benefit payments overseas. Even with these limitations, the demands would have amounted to differentiated disintegration, which would have exempted Britain from existing Treaty obligations and discriminated against current and

[22] Cameron, 'A New Settlement for the United Kingdom in a Reformed European Union', 10 Downing Street, 10 November 2015. https://www.gov.uk/government/uploads/system/uploads/attachment_data/file/475679/Donald_Tusk_letter.pdf (accessed 8 April 2021).

[23] Weiss and Blockmans, 'The EU deal to avoid Brexit: take it or leave', CEPS Special Report 131, 2016.

future member states. In contrast to the euro and migration cases, this is a case of heterogeneity of preferences only, and one in which heterogeneity pitted one country against the rest of the EU.

Even though the UK was a major recipient country of intra-EU migrants, these temporal, indirect, or future measures would probably not have led to major reductions or distortions in the free movement of persons across the EU. The size condition therefore did not stand in the way of agreement. Yet the British demands meant disintegration in a highly and uniformly integrated core policy area of the EU: the single market. The UK therefore faced highly adverse institutional conditions.

First, the UK suffered from weak institutional bargaining power when asking for disintegration. Whereas the UK has typically been the least integrationist member state, and therefore in a strong position to bargain for red lines and opt-outs in negotiations on integration progress, it now found itself in the position of requiring the consent of the other member states in the favourable bargaining position of status quo defenders. Unsurprisingly, the strongest opposition came from the new member states whose citizens benefited most from the freedom of movement to the UK.

Second, the UK attacked the integrity of the internal market. Not only is the internal market the single most important policy area of the EU; it is also the classic example of supranational and uniform integration. Even though the member states have regularly agreed to exempt or exclude new member states from provisions of the internal market, and the freedom of movement of labour in particular, these differentiations have generally been temporary and short-lived. Moreover, the integrity of the internal market, i.e., the adherence to all four market freedoms, is a cherished principle, firmly anchored in the Treaties and the jurisdiction of the Court. Whereas demands for differentiated disintegration are always likely to provoke resistance, it was bound to be particularly strong in this case.

Finally, concerns about cherry-picking ranked high. The UK was not the only country in which immigrants from other EU member states and their entitlement to social benefits were contested. In addition, the member states tend to benefit unequally from the different market freedoms. If the EU were to grant an opt-out from the freedom of movement of persons to one country, other countries would likely demand the same. And if the EU were to grant opt-outs from the freedom of movement of persons, other countries might ask for opt-outs from other market freedoms.

In line with these considerations, the EU decided to accommodate British concerns without agreeing to differentiation. The agreed measures, an 'emergency brake' for in-work benefits and the indexing of child benefits, affected secondary legislation but not the Treaties. They also applied to all member states and not just the UK; and they were exceptional and conditional measures to be authorized collectively (rather than decided by the UK alone).

In sum, the British renegotiation demonstrates the particular difficulties of agreeing on demands for differentiated *dis*integration. Even though the policy in question was neither constitutional nor redistributive, the British demand affected a highly and uniformly integrated domain, raised concerns about positive externalities, violated informal norms about acceptable differentiation, and was constrained by weak UK institutional bargaining power.

3.4 Rule of Law Crisis

According to Article 2 of the TEU, 'The Union is founded on the values of respect for human dignity, freedom, democracy, equality, the rule of law and respect for human rights.' Adherence to these liberal democratic values is a key prerequisite for countries to be eligible for membership (Art. 49 TEU) and serious and persistent breaches justify the suspension of member states' rights (Art. 7).

Such breaches have occurred in two Central European member states, in Hungary under the Fidesz government headed by Prime Minister Viktor Orbán since 2010, and in Poland under the PiS government since 2015. In both countries these populist radical right governments have launched massive attacks on the independence of the judiciary, a cornerstone of the rule of law. Together with curbing the rights of parliaments, the opposition, and minorities; expanding governmental control of the media; and changing electoral laws, these attacks served to ensure the dominance of the executive in the political systems and to safeguard the power of the incumbents.

The EU was slow to react to this democratic backsliding, especially in the Hungarian case, and when EU institutions finally decided to take action to protect their fundamental values, the available instruments turned out to be ineffective. Article 7 envisages tough sanctions against a rule-violating member but requires a consensus of all the other member states to impose them. Because Article 7 proceedings were launched against both Hungary and Poland, this consensus is out of reach.

In reaction to the failure of Article 7, EU institutions have proposed to reform the protection of fundamental EU values and the rule of law in particular. In 2014, the European Commission launched a new Rule of Law Framework as a preventive mechanism based on dialogue with the member state in question and on assessments and recommendations of the Commission. The only time it was used—in relation to Poland in 2016 and 2017—it did not, however, produce any tangible results. The annual Rule of Law Report, published in 2020 for the first time, was again a preventive tool and put public pressure on the rule-violating member states at best. To increase the bite of the EU's measure, the Commission proposed a rule of law mechanism in 2018 that would allow the EU to withhold payments from its budget in order to sanction rule of law breaches. The regulation codifying this mechanism was approved by qualified majority voting (QMV) in the Council and by the European Parliament in November 2020. In return, however, the Hungarian and Polish government threatened to veto the EU's budget and the own resources decision to establish the Covid-19 recovery fund. In the end, the member states reached a consensus that delays the application of rule of law conditionality until the European Court of Justice decides on Hungary's and Poland's action for annulment.[24]

Again, differentiated integration would hardly have been a suitable way to get out of the negotiation deadlock and to agree on a stronger text. For one, it could have followed the 'Eurozone' and 'Schengen Plus' options by bringing together a group of countries willing to subscribe to an effective rule of law mechanism. It is clear, however, that exactly those governments that cause the rule of law concerns, or that fear they might incur sanctions in the future, would opt out of such a mechanism. Differentiated integration of the rule of law would thus be as self-defeating as the other 'Plus' options, even though it does not raise concerns of size and externalities. The ability of a member state to respect the rule of law is not directly affected by how well the independence of the judiciary is guaranteed in other member states or by how many other member states respect it.

Rather, the rule of law is a constitutional policy that relates to the fundamental values and collective identity of the EU and its overall functioning as a political system. It concerns a core component of what it means to be member state of the EU, and it represents the 'integration through law' that is a hallmark of European integration. The differentiation of such a policy would not

[24] EUCO 22/20, 'European Council meeting (10 and 11 December 2020)—Conclusions', December 2020. https://www.consilium.europa.eu/media/47296/1011-12-20-euco-conclusions-en.pdf (accessed 20 April 2021).

only be normatively inappropriate but also disrupt the enforcement of EU law against national governments and administrations by national courts.

Alternatively, differentiated rule of law integration could exclude all member states that are unwilling to subject themselves to exacting monitoring and sanctioning mechanisms. Yet because the rule of law is a constitutional issue, it does not simply affect a single policy, from which a member state could be excluded. Rather, 'Rule of Law Minus' would be equivalent to exit from the EU. In other words, neither the Plus nor the Minus options have the potential to solve the EU's rule of law crisis.

4. Conclusions

Differentiated integration provides the EU with a powerful tool to facilitate and lubricate integration under conditions of increasing international heterogeneity among its member states. As European integration has expanded to countries with increasingly diverse integration preferences and capacities, and to the controversial integration of core state powers, differentiated integration has allowed the EU to overcome national vetoes by exempting or excluding member states from participating in individual EU policies. In the past, differentiated integration has struck a balance between preserving the autonomy of member states and facilitating the deepening and widening of the EU.

Differentiated integration is, however, unable to play a similarly constructive role in the present and near future. For one, differentiated integration is losing its traditional role of kick-starting the integration of new members and new policies. It is unclear if and when the EU will admit new member states whose accession could be facilitated by transitional arrangements for differentiation. In addition, there a few policies left, in which the EU does not already have some competence, and there is little appetite among the member states for Treaty revisions that might require differentiated integration to achieve consensus.

Rather, it has been the priority of EU policymakers to avoid the collapse of common policies in the EU's polycrisis. As I have argued in this chapter, however, differentiated integration is ill-suited for this purpose. A differentiated policy response to crisis in highly integrated policies risks pushing group size to unsustainable levels and producing major externalities between the differentially integrated groups. Crisis-induced reforms tend to take place in an institutional environment—decision-making rules favouring the status quo, sceptical supranational actors, and informal norms of uniform integration—that inhibits differentiated integration. Finally, the EU's crises have raised problems of risk-sharing, burden-sharing, and constitutional values, for which differentiated integration is counterproductive.

Correspondingly, the EU crises have generally not resulted in reforms based on differentiation, beyond already existing divides such as between euro area and non-euro area member states. There has either been uniform agreement or no agreement at all. Member states have concluded that differentiation would not produce a better outcome, or might even be worse, than non-agreement.

In the Eurozone, initial reforms at the height of crisis (such as the European Stability Mechanism (ESM) and banking union) apply uniformly to all Eurozone countries. Far-reaching reforms aiming at a form of fiscal union have not produced any substantive agreement before the Covid-19 pandemic paved the way for the—uniform—'Next Generation' fund. The reform of the common asylum policy has foundered altogether in spite of a series of proposals for 'flexible solidarity'. Ahead of Brexit, the EU refused the UK's demand for differentiated integration into the internal market: a decision that has arguably contributed to, or at least done nothing to prevent, the British vote to leave the EU altogether. Proposals for strengthening the EU's rule of law mechanisms have all been based on the uniform validity of the rule of law and have either failed or produced minimalist compromises.

Differentiated integration helped overcoming the dilemma between autonomy and integration when the EU faced the problem of reaching consensus on 'more integration'. The challenges of preventing 'less integration', however, demonstrate the limits of differentiated integration in working around the dilemma between autonomy and collapse.

4

The Law as Tool and Constraint of Differentiated Integration

Bruno de Witte

1. Introduction

This chapter deals with the legal rules that govern the use of differentiated integration. The law provides the *tools* for differentiated integration but also imposes *constraints* on the member states and the EU institutions when engaging in differentiated integration projects. Differentiated integration is often (and rightly) portrayed as a way to protect the diversity of capacities and preferences of the member states of the EU, but the way this works depends on the type of mechanism that is used. Section 2 of this chapter emphasizes the role of the law as having provided *tools* for differentiated integration that are either regulated by the EU Treaties (first subsection) or that leave wide room for discretionary action to the national governments involved (second subsection). Section 3 examines the role of the law as imposing *constraints* on policy decisions to use differentiated integration; again, a first subsection will discuss the constraints on the use of the regulated forms of cooperation, whereas the second one discusses the constraints on the discretionary forms of à la carte cooperation.

2. The Legal Toolbox of Differentiated Integration: Strictly Regulated or À la Carte

In a lecture given in Florence in 1979, Ralf Dahrendorf (who had previously been a member of the European Commission) stated the following: '*Europe à la carte*, that is, common policies where there are common interests without any constraint on those who cannot, at a given point of time, join them, must

Bruno de Witte, *The Law as Tool and Constraint of Differentiated Integration*. In: *Autonomy without Collapse in a Better European Union*. Edited by Mark Dawson and Markus Jachtenfuchs, Oxford University Press. © Oxford University Press (2022). DOI: 10.1093/oso/9780192897541.003.0004

become the rule rather than the exception, if European union is not to get stuck.'[1]

A remote echo of this view can be found in a special report by *The Economist* on the future of the European Union, published in March 2017 on the sixtieth anniversary of the Treaties of Rome. The report was significantly entitled 'The case for flexibility'. It argued that 'the EU must embrace greater differentiation or face potential disintegration', and that 'a more differentiated Europe, based around the idea of variable geometry, a range of speeds or concentric circles, would be a good way to ease the tensions and problems that afflict the present, overly rigid EU.'[2]

Around that same time, the European Commission published its White Paper on the Future of Europe.[3] Among the five possible scenarios for the EU's future, one was identified by the Commission as: 'Those who want more do more': this scenario envisages the creation of several 'coalitions of the willing' that would carry forward new cooperation projects in areas such as defence, security and justice, taxation, and social policy; and the other member states would be able to join those projects at a later stage, as soon as they would be ready or willing to do so. The Commission did not add further detail, for example, on the legal form that those cooperation projects would take. Indeed, the White Paper states that the scenarios 'deliberately make no mention of legal or institutional processes—the form will follow the function'.

These approaches to differentiated integration (from Dahrendorf in 1979 to the Commission in 2017), whilst not identical, all sound very favourable to the idea that the discretion of the member states should be preserved as much as possible when deciding how, and in which areas, the European integration project should be developed. More particularly, the à la carte approach protects both the autonomy of those countries who want to deepen cooperation, and that of the countries who prefer not to engage in such deeper cooperation.

The actual legal regime of differentiated integration came into life rather late in the life of the European Union, namely with the Treaty of Maastricht, and was further developed by later Treaties. These Treaty changes made differentiated integration into a structural element of the EU legal order, but not

[1] Dahrendorf, *A Third Europe?* Third Jean Monnet lecture, Florence, European University Institute, 1979. I owe the reference to Schimmelfennig, 'Is differentiation the future of European integration?', in Fägersten and von Sydow (eds.), *Perspectives on the Future of the EU* (Swedish Institute for European Policy Studies (SIEPS), 2019), p. 99, at 100.

[2] John Peet, Special report on the future of the European Union: 'The case for flexibility', *The Economist* (March 2017), p. 15, http://www.economist.com/news/special-report/21719188-it-marks-its-60th-birthday-european-union-poor-shape-it-needs-more

[3] European Commission, *White Paper on the Future of Europe—Reflections and scenarios for the EU27 by 2025*, COM(2017) 2025 of 1 March 2017.

in the way advocated by Dahrendorf or by *The Economist*. The member state governments and the EU institutions shunned the *à la carte approach*, and instead a restrictive regime of differentiation was put in place. The combination of a number of opt-out regimes organized in detail in Protocols attached to the Treaties, and regimes of enhanced cooperation that are carefully regulated in the Treaty text, defines the current EU legal regime of differentiated integration. Added to this are the transitional arrangements for newly acceding member states, which create temporary modes of differentiated integration. This complex regime is far removed from the à la carte model and instead can be better described as a regulated and legally constrained regime of flexible integration. However, some à la carte elements are nevertheless present both inside, and alongside, that regulated framework, and act as a possible alternative to the regulated framework. We will, in the following pages, briefly describe the contours of the regulated and à la carte parts of the EU's current regime of differentiated integration.

2.1 Treaty-Regulated Forms of Differentiated Integration

The most prominent mechanisms of differentiated integration that we know today were enacted through revisions of the original EU Treaties. The negotiations of the Maastricht Treaty resulted in 'forced differentiation', as opt-outs for the UK (from monetary union and social policy) and Denmark (from monetary union) had been a condition for getting unanimous agreement on the Treaty as a whole. These opt-outs were thus not enacted with the deliberate aim of protecting the autonomy of the participating states, but rather as a necessary price to be paid for allowing the overall integration project to move forward. The dominant view inspiring those Treaty opt-outs was a 'multi-speed' one: sooner or later, it was thought, the opting-out countries would join the rest. This actually happened for social policy, when the Labour government scrapped the British opt-out on the occasion of the Amsterdam Treaty revision, but it did not really happen for EMU.

The same pattern was replicated in later Treaty revisions. The UK, in particular, was able to insist on new opt-out mechanisms as a condition for agreeing the overall Treaty revision packages at the Amsterdam, Nice, and Lisbon conferences. Again, the opt-outs were not based on a positive recognition of the need to preserve the autonomy of all member states in certain sensitive policy domains. They rather emerged from the political context of Treaty revision: most of the EU countries wanted to deepen the integration process into those new domains and they had to allow for opt-outs in order to be able to move forward.

Soon after the adoption of the Maastricht Treaty, the prospect of enlargement with a large number of new states promoted a broader debate on differentiated or 'multi-speed' integration. During the 1996 intergovernmental conference, there emerged a consensus among the member state governments that some mechanism of institutional flexibility (or of, as it was eventually called, 'closer cooperation') should be put in place, but that it should be encapsulated within the existing EU framework and be made subject to rather strict conditions. This particular form of differentiated integration was thus conceived as a 'safety valve' that would allow valuable integration projects to be carried out *within the EU legal order* even when opposed by a minority of members. By allowing for such intra-EU closer cooperation, it was hoped that Schengen-type cooperation *outside* the EU legal order would no longer be needed, or at least less often. Thus, the main aim of this mechanism was not the protection of the autonomy of the single member states, but the protection of the effective operation of the EU's institutional system.

The conditions for closer cooperation imposed by the Amsterdam Treaty were so rigid that both the Treaty of Nice and the Treaty of Lisbon loosened them up. Enhanced cooperation initiatives can now start on request of at least nine member states, and a qualified majority vote of the Council must authorize them. They can cover all areas of non-exclusive EU competence.[4]

It is probably fair to say that, leaving aside the temporary function of allowing for a 'smooth' incorporation of new member states, the main integrative function of differentiated integration has been to neutralize the rigidity caused by the unanimity rule in EU politics. That rigidity is most obvious when it comes to revisions of the Treaties, but it also impacts on many domains of EU policymaking, as was shown again in 2020 by the difficult negotiations of the Multiannual Financial Framework and the 'Next Generation EU' recovery plan, which took place 'in the shadow of the veto'.[5]

As was recalled above, the Treaty-based opt-outs for EMU, Justice & Home Affairs, and Schengen (as well as the short-lived one for Social Policy) did not

[4] Art. 20 TEU. The conditions and procedures are spelled out in considerable detail in Articles 326 to 334 TFEU.

[5] When Hungary and Poland threatened to veto the adoption of the Multiannual Financial Framework and the Next Generation EU programme, some other states and EU actors advocated a recourse to differentiated integration in order to overcome that blockage; see Merler and Nicoli, 'Beyond the veto of the EU Recovery Fund', *Verfassungsblog*, 27 November 2020; Graf von Luckner, 'A novel "reinforced cooperation" in the EU: The viable option of a NextGenEU without Poland and Hungary', *Verfassungsblog*, 9 December 2020.

come about as positive recognition of the value of member state autonomy in those domains, but as negative 'progression costs' incurred when carrying forward the European integration project. It is clear that 'given the existing constraint of consensual intergovernmental agreement on and ratification of European treaties, the deepening of European integration would have stopped at a much earlier stage',[6] if it had not been for those opt-out solutions.

Similarly, the enhanced cooperation mechanism was, so far, used only in cases where an EU-wide legislative instrument faced the veto of one or more member states.[7] A first and rather uncontroversial application happened for the regulation of transnational divorces.[8] A second, much more controversial application related to the creation of a new EU patent system; two countries (Italy and Spain) had refused to participate in an EU-wide solution, because they were unhappy with the language regime for patent applications that the other states supported. They challenged the recourse to enhanced cooperation before the Court of Justice, arguing among other things that enhanced cooperation had been used to bypass the veto power that the Treaty text gave to them in this area. In its judgment, the Court confirmed that the function of enhanced cooperation is indeed to advance European cooperation even where (or rather, *especially* where) the unanimity requirement makes 'normal' decision-making too difficult.[9]

Since then, a third piece of enhanced cooperation law was adopted, namely the twin Regulations on judicial cooperation in matters of matrimonial property and registered partnership property. A fourth Council authorization for enhanced cooperation was given for the creation of a financial transaction tax, but the directive itself was not adopted, or at least not yet. This failure was not due to legal impediments but to the lack of political commitment by the governments that had initially launched the project. Finally, the European Public Prosecutors Office was set up as an enhanced cooperation project between

[6] Schimmelfennig, *supra* note 1, at 107.

[7] See the overview by Kroll and Leuffen, 'Enhanced cooperation in practice. An analysis of differentiated integration in EU secondary law', 22 *Journal of European Public Policy* (2015), 353; and the study by Wessels and Gerards for the European Parliament, *The implementation of enhanced cooperation in the European Union*, Study requested by the AFCO committee of the EP, PE 604.987, October 2018.

[8] Council Regulation 1259/2010 of 20 December 2010 implementing enhanced cooperation in the area of the law applicable to divorce and legal separation, OJ 2010, L 343/10. The authorization had been given by Council Decision 2010/405 of 12 July 2010, OJ 2010, L 189/12. See Peers, 'Divorce European style: The first authorization of enhanced cooperation', 6 *European Constitutional Law Review* (2010), 339.

[9] Joined Cases C-274/11 and C-295/11 *Spain and Italy v Council*, EU:C:2013:240. The Council had authorized enhanced cooperation in this area by a Decision adopted (despite negative votes of Italy and Spain) on 10 March 2011, OJ 2011, L 76/53. See the comment by Pistoia, 'Enhanced cooperation as a tool to ... enhance integration? *Spain and Italy v Council*', 51 *Common Market Law Review* (2014), 247.

twenty-two member states, under slightly different procedural rules applying only to this policy domain (according to Article 86 (1) TFEU). In all five cases, recourse to enhanced cooperation was made in order to bypass the requirement of a unanimous Council decision—which is still the decision-making rule in a number of EU policy domains. This limited practice (situated entirely in the post-Lisbon period) shows that enhanced cooperation is a feasible option.

In addition to the general enhanced cooperation mechanism, the Lisbon Treaty created a specific regime of enhanced cooperation in the field of economic governance, which was grafted on the existing distinction between euro area and non-euro area countries. The legal basis allowing for the adoption of euro area–specific legislation on economic governance (Article 136(1) TFEU) was used, very soon after the entry into force of the Lisbon Treaty, for important parts of the 'six-pack' and 'two-pack' economic governance reforms. This special regime is distinct from the general mechanism of enhanced cooperation, in that there is no requirement for a prior authorization by the Council in its full composition. Rather, the Council in a reduced euro area composition can directly adopt the necessary measures (naturally, as always, after having received a proposal by the Commission). However, this form of enhanced cooperation is strictly constrained in two other ways. First, because it limits the format of cooperation to the euro areas states, that is, all of them and no others. Second, by the fact that Article 136(1) TFEU limits the domain in which such euro area–specific EU legislation is allowed to: (a) strengthening the coordination and surveillance of eurozone countries' budgetary discipline, and (b) setting out specific economic policy guidelines for them.

More generally, both opt-outs and enhanced cooperation are forms of differentiated integration that are heavily regulated by EU law. The legal constraints weighing on opt-outs stem from the fact that the scope of these opt-outs is 'set in stone' in the Treaty text so that a formal Treaty revision is required to change their mode of operation. The legal constraints of enhanced cooperation are less evident, since this is a tool of differentiation that is entirely open-ended as to its content and fields of application. The constraints weighing on enhanced cooperation are, however, very real and will be discussed in more detail in the second section of this chapter.

2.2 À la Carte Forms of Differentiated Integration

Europe à la carte was not a utopian construct at the time of Dahrendorf's speech, which was mentioned in the introduction of this chapter, but rather the living legal reality of the 'other Europe' that had existed alongside the European Community since the 1950s, namely the Council of Europe. The Strasbourg-based organization offered (and still offers) precisely what Ralf Dahrendorf recommended for the European Community, namely the possibility for states to cooperate only where they find a common interest, without being compelled to do so in other instances. That regime of perfectly variable geometry consists in the adoption of lawmaking Treaties (called conventions) within the organizational framework of the Council of Europe, followed by their separate signature and ratification by those Council of Europe states that choose to do so.[10] Moreover, states retain the option of making reservations to specific provisions of the conventions that they ratify. More than 200 conventions and additional protocols were adopted since the origins of the Council of Europe, and they show a widely varying pattern of participating states. Each country has created its 'unique national portfolio'[11] of Treaty commitments. There is only one Council of Europe convention whose ratification is now compulsory for every member state of the organization, namely the European Convention for the Protection of Human Rights (ECHR) of 1950. The flexibility offered by this regime favours the production of legal norms: as none of the member states of the Council of Europe is forced to accept a given convention, there is not much of an incentive to impede the others from going ahead with a lawmaking initiative that they care about.

The legal regime of the European Community was, from its early years, developed in marked (and deliberate) contrast with the à la carte model of the Council of Europe. There was an insistence on the uniform application of the Treaty and of the increasing bulk of secondary legislation to all the member states of the organization. This collection of legal norms constituted a 'Community legal order' marked by a sense of unity and uniform application across the territory of the member states. The Court of Justice insisted on the fact that EU legal rules were 'fully applicable at the same time and with identical effects over the whole territory of the Community'.[12] There is then no room for autonomous choices of the member states whether to participate in EU policies, and whether (or not) to apply EU legal norms. However, some à la carte elements have continued to exist on the 'outskirts' of the EU system. The most obvious one is that the member states have retained their capacity to conclude

[10] For a complete list of the conventions and protocols see https://www.coe.int/en/web/conventions/full-list. The convention-making system of the Council of Europe is analysed by Benoit-Rohmer and Klebes, *Le droit du Conseil de l'Europe. Vers un espace juridique européen* (Editions du Conseil de l'Europe, 2005), pp. 97–122.

[11] MacMullen, 'Intergovernmental functionalism? The Council of Europe in European integration', 26 *European Integration* (2004), 405, at 424.

[12] ECJ, Case 48/71 *Commission v Italy*, EU:C:1972:65, para 8.

international agreements not only with third countries (as in the context of the Council of Europe) but also among themselves and in close connection with the functioning of the EU. Less obviously, some intra-EU legal forms of differentiated integration display strong à la carte characteristics, in particular the enhanced cooperation in the field of defence. We will discuss these two forms of à la carte cooperation in turn.

The principal form of à la carte cooperation is formally situated outside the EU legal order. It consists of *agreements under international law* concluded between the 'willing and/or able' member states in matters connected with the EU project. This form of cooperation transposes the Council of Europe model, mentioned above, to the context of the European Union. It results from the simple fact that the member states of the EU are still states, that is, subjects of international law that have retained the capacity to conclude international treaties with other states, including with their fellow member states of the EU.

The model for this form of cooperation used to be the Schengen Convention and is nowadays the European Stability Mechanism (ESM), but, in a sense, one could say that this form of flexibility has always existed, since the early days of the European integration process. In those early days, the European Community was 'one of many'[13]: a number of other organizations had sprung up in Western Europe to deal with economic cooperation and other policy domains, most prominently the Council of Europe established in 1949. In addition, the EU member states have continued, throughout the history of the EU and until today, to conclude hundreds of bilateral and multilateral international treaties between themselves in areas such as tax law, environmental protection, defence, culture, and education. In some cases, the scope of that cooperation is quite broad and institutionally structured, as for example with the Nordic Council, the Benelux Union or the Franco-German partnership.[14]

Such cooperation by means of international law typically occurs in areas in which the European Union has no lawmaking competence at all. It also occurs in areas in which the EU possesses shared lawmaking competence but where a set of member states prefer to use their 'share' in order to conclude an agreement among themselves rather than acting in the framework of the European Union. For example, protecting the environmental quality of the Meuse river basin is a question of environmental policy which falls squarely within the

[13] The expression is used by Patel, *Project Europe—A History* (Cambridge University Press, 2020), p. 14. The first chapter of that book deals with the place of the early European Communities among the many other international organizations operating in Europe at the time.

[14] The latter partnership is now based, legally speaking, on the Treaty on Franco-German Cooperation and Integration (also known as Treaty of Aachen), signed on 22 January 2019. See Stark, 'Le traité d'Aix-la-Chapelle: Promesse de convergence pour couple divisé', 84(4) *Politique Etrangère* (2019), 73.

scope of the EU's shared competences, but since the concrete problem affects only some member states (namely France, Belgium, and the Netherlands), it was decided that concluding a separate international treaty was the better option.[15]

Many of those '*inter se* agreements'[16] are legally and politically irrelevant for the functioning of the European Union. However, some of them can be considered as instruments of differentiated integration, namely when they serve the purpose of allowing a group of member states to move European integration forward in the face of the opposition of other member states. In this respect, the Schengen experience is still referred to, in current discussions, as a positive model; it offers an example of both the potential of such agreements to overcome a blockage within the Union's decision-making system, and the possibility for their later reintegration within the EU legal system.

In the post-Lisbon years, the EU member states have reiterated the practice of concluding international treaties among themselves, even when the subject matter of their agreement is close to European Union policies. This happened, in particular, in the domain of Economic and Monetary Union. As part of the collective response to the sovereign debt crisis, a number of such international agreements were concluded between large groups of EU member states: the Decision of the Representatives of the euro area countries of 10 May 2010 to set up the European Financial Stability Facility (EFSF), the Treaty establishing the European Stability Mechanism (ESM Treaty), and the Treaty on Stability, Coordination and Governance in the Economic and Monetary Union (commonly known as 'Fiscal Compact').[17] They were followed, in May 2014, by the signature of yet another international agreement in the sphere of Economic and Monetary Union (EMU) law, namely the Agreement on the Single Resolution Fund, which is the intergovernmental part of the banking union package.[18] A further multilateral agreement closely connected with the functioning of the EU, but in a very different domain, was signed on 19 February 2013 between twenty-five member states (all except Croatia, Poland, and Spain), namely the

[15] Agreement on the Protection of the Meuse, signed at Charleville-Mézières on 26 April 1994.

[16] This is an expression from international law. It refers to the case where some, but not all, parties to a first international treaty (in this case, the EU Treaties) conclude a second international treaty among themselves that complements the first one.

[17] On the mix of reasons explaining recourse to international law in these EMU-related matters, see De Witte, 'Using international law in the Euro crisis—Causes and consequences', *ARENA Working Paper* 04/2013.

[18] In this case, the choice for an international agreement came about for a combination of legal and political reasons, see Asimakopoulos, 'International law as a negotiation tool in Banking Union: The case of the Single Resolution Fund', 21 *Journal of Economic Policy Reform* (2018), 118.

Agreement on a Unified Patent Court. That Court's main task is to adjudicate an EU law instrument, the Regulation on the creation of unitary patent protection, which is itself the outcome of an enhanced cooperation initiative.[19]

In the light of this recent and not so recent practice, we can see the advantages and disadvantages of recourse to international side agreements as compared to the more regulated forms of differentiated integration. The main advantage is the protection of the autonomy of the participating states. The participants to the cooperation project can freely choose their partners to the agreement: a self-proclaimed core group can indeed decide to act together without having to offer (as is the case with enhanced cooperation) a standing invitation to the other EU states to join at any time. Conversely, the states that do not share the wish to cooperate can stay away from the project (even though their autonomy may be constrained when non-participation would cause negative externalities for them). Seen from the perspective of national sovereignty, the negotiation of an international agreement leaves the member state governments fully in control, since they cannot formally be outvoted by the others (unlike what routinely happens for the adoption of EU legislation). However, those governments face the extra transaction costs of setting up a little diplomatic conference instead of being able to discuss within the tried and tested institutional framework offered by the EU system. Altogether, this method of differentiated integration, despite its great flexibility, has major shortcomings not only from the perspective of constitutional integrity (its intergovernmental nature excludes the institutional balance that is characteristic of EU decision-making), but also from a purely national interest perspective.

Given these shortcomings, the initiators of the earlier international agreements insisted on their temporary nature. The Schengen Agreement did not include an expiry clause setting a time limit for its existence, but, in a separate declaration, the Schengen states announced that the content of the agreement they had concluded would serve as a basis for the negotiation of equivalent measures to be adopted within the EU framework.[20] The Schengen regime was, indeed, eventually integrated within the EU legal order, as the Treaty of Amsterdam brought the Schengen Agreement and its implementing measures within the boundaries of EU law, by means of an additional Protocol

[19] Here, recourse to international law happened, essentially, in order to establish a Patent Court composed of specialized judges, and to remove adjudication of patent disputes from the 'generalist' Court of Justice of the EU; see De Witte and Martinelli, 'Treaties between EU Member States as Quasi-Instruments of EU Law', in Cremona and Kilpatrick (eds.), *EU Legal Acts—Challenges and Transformations* (Oxford University Press, 2018), p. 157, at 181–187.

[20] This declaration is cited and discussed by Schutte, 'Schengen: Its meaning for the free movement of persons in Europe', 28 *Common Market Law Review* (1991), 549, at 567–568.

to the Treaty.[21] As for the more recent satellite agreements, there are no signs yet that the participating states are willing to reintegrate them within the EU legal order. The European Commission made proposals, in December 2017, to transform part of the Fiscal Compact into an EU directive,[22] and to transform the intergovernmental ESM into an EU body called European Monetary Fund,[23] but neither of these proposals met with approval from the side of the national governments, and they are not going to be adopted any time soon. On the contrary, the state parties to the ESM (i.e., the euro area countries) started negotiations to entrust additional tasks to the ESM and to amend the ESM Treaty for that purpose. A political agreement was reached on a revised text of the ESM Treaty at the Eurogroup meeting of December 2019, but it took another year to iron out all the remaining wrinkles. The Amended ESM Treaty was finally signed by the Parties in January 2021,[24] after which the national ratification procedures started.[25] Among the new tasks given to the ESM, we find the creation of a backstop facility to support the operations of the Single Resolution Board (SRB), should the SRB run out of funds to undertake banking resolution operations. This new task ties in the ESM even more closely with the operation of the European Union than before, since it entails close cooperation between the ESM and an EU agency (the SRB) in implementing banking resolution operations.

Next to the recourse to international 'side agreements', à la carte cooperation has also been accommodated *within* the bounds of the EU legal order, namely in the field of *defence*. The specific enhanced cooperation regime for *defence*, created by the Lisbon Treaty, was implemented in December 2017 through the launch of a permanent structured cooperation scheme (PESCO).[26] This form

[21] Protocol No 19 on the Schengen *acquis* integrated into the framework of the European Union, OJ 2012 C 326/290.

[22] Commission proposal for a Council Directive laying down provisions for strengthening fiscal responsibility and the medium-term orientation in the Member States, COM(2017) 824 of 6 December 2017.

[23] Commission proposal for a Council Regulation on the establishment of the European Monetary Fund, COM(2017) 827, 6 December 2017.

[24] The text of the amendments is available at https://www.consilium.europa.eu/media/47294/sn04244-en19.pdf

[25] See, on the content of the ESM reform: Aerts and Bizarro, 'The reform of the European Stability Mechanism', 15 *Capital Markets Law Journal* (2020), 159; and Zaccaroni, 'The Future of the ESM within a Hybrid EMU Law', BRIDGE Working Paper 6 (September 2020).

[26] Council Decision (CFSP) 2017/2315 of 11 December 2017 establishing permanent structured cooperation (PESCO) and determining the list of participating Member States, OJ 2017, L 331/57; and the implementing measure Council Decision (CFSP) 2018/340 of 6 March 2018 establishing the list of projects to be developed under PESCO, OJ 2018, L 65/24. The suddenness of this development is illustrated by the fact that the European Commission's Reflection Paper, published only a few months earlier, does not even mention PESCO (European Commission, *Reflection Paper on the Future of European Defence*, COM(2017) 315 of 7 June 2017).

of cooperation is defined by Article 42(7) TEU. It provides that those member states whose military capabilities fulfil higher criteria and who agree to make binding commitments with a view to the most demanding missions shall establish permanent structured cooperation within the Union framework. The format of that cooperation is further described in Protocol 10 to the Lisbon Treaty. As was noted by Cremona, 'in a number of ways permanent structured cooperation resembles enhanced cooperation, but agreed in advance by way of a specific Protocol.'[27] The drafters of the Constitutional Treaty and of the Lisbon Treaty took care to define in a rather detailed way the institutional and substantial shape of PESCO, making it into an 'off-the-shelf form of cooperation', which may have facilitated the launch once the political impetus was there. PESCO's main institutional characteristic is the fact that decision-making is entirely situated *within* the EU legal order, namely with the Council and its preparatory bodies.

In fact, despite this appearance of detailed regulation, the PESCO functions very much according to an à la carte model, at two levels.[28] First, at the time of launching, each state could freely choose to participate in the mechanism or not. The 'capability' conditions listed in Art. 42(7) TEU did not really limit that discretion, since all the states had to do at the time of launching was to express a *commitment* to cooperate, rather than meet some quantified criteria for participation. Eventually, twenty-five states (all except the UK, Denmark, and Malta) decided to join the project. Since the participation of Denmark is impeded by its defence opt-out entrenched in the Treaties, the only member state currently staying out of its free will is tiny Malta. The second level of à la carte participation occurs when adopting actual cooperation projects under the PESCO umbrella. Each of the projects approved by the Council is carried out by a different group of countries. So far, none of the twenty-five PESCO members has taken part in all forty-seven projects, and participation to the single projects varies between two and twenty-four states.[29] The 'modular approach' to defence cooperation has been turned into 'a permanent vehicle for opt-outs and exemptions in the area of defence'.[30]

[27] Cremona, 'Enhanced cooperation and the common foreign and security and defence policy', EUI Working Papers LAW 2009/21, p. 14.

[28] For a more detailed discussion of PESCO's institutional regime, see Blockmans, 'The EU's modular approach to defence integration: An inclusive, ambitious and legally binding PESCO?', 55 *Common Market Law Review* (2018), 1785, at 1805–1823.

[29] Missiroli and Lonardo, 'The evolution of enhanced cooperation in the EU: from EnCo to PeSCo (2009–2019)', *Bruges Political Research Papers* 80/2020, p. 28.

[30] Blockmans, *supra* note 28, at 1825.

3. Legal Constraints for the Use of Differentiation Tools

3.1 Legal Constraints for Enhanced Cooperation Projects

As was shown in the first part of this chapter, enhanced cooperation has become a feasible option in the post-Lisbon operation of the European Union. The Treaty text, however, still contains numerous substantive and procedural conditions for launching and running an enhanced cooperation initiative.[31] This makes sense because the participating states get the benefit of using the entire EU institutional system to adopt policies among themselves instead of policies for the whole EU. The Commission (acting in its full composition) supports their initiative, the European Parliament (also acting in its full composition) approves the enhanced cooperation project, and the project, if successful, takes the legal form of an EU regulation, directive, or decision, thus benefiting from the supranational qualities of EU law. Fulfilling certain conditions for engaging in enhanced cooperation is therefore a very reasonable price to pay for obtaining those benefits.

Those conditions, taken together, affect enhanced cooperation's potential use for creating a broad-ranging 'multi-speed Europe'. Indeed, given the rather open-ended formulation of the relevant Treaty articles, it has sometimes been suggested that enhanced cooperation should not be limited to single-project cases, as was the case so far, but could also be used in a systematic way by a group of like-minded member states so as to constitute a true 'pioneer group' that operates together in a whole range of policy areas. This option was even mentioned in the Treaty on Stability, Coordination and Governance (more commonly known as Fiscal Compact). Its Article 10 states that the Parties to that Treaty 'stand ready to make active use, whenever appropriate and necessary, of measures ... of enhanced cooperation ... on matters that are essential for the proper functioning of the euro area, without undermining the internal market'. This statement seems to contain a promise (or threat) of concerted action to multiply the usage of enhanced cooperation as a tool to build a euro area integration project. However, no action of this nature was taken during the eight years since the entry into force of the Fiscal Compact. Rather, the

[31] For a detailed discussion of those conditions, see among others: Wessels and Gerards, *supra* note 7, at 18–23; Peers, 'Enhanced Cooperation: The Cinderella of Differentiated Integration', in De Witte, Ott, and Vos (eds.), *Between Flexibility and Disintegration—The Trajectory of Differentiation in EU Law* (Edward Elgar, 2017), p. 76; Pistoia, *Limiti all'integrazione differenziata dell'Unione europea* (Cacucci Editore, 2018) at 27–30 and 39–53; Miglio, *Integrazione differenziata e principi strutturali dell'ordinamento dell'Unione europea* (Giappichelli Editore, 2020), pp. 85–126; Angelaki, *La différenciation entre les Etats membres de l'Union européenne* (Bruylant, 2020), pp. 121–149.

usages of enhanced cooperation were based, so far, on other fault lines than the one between euro area and non-euro area countries.

In fact, the rules on enhanced cooperation contain a number of legal constraints, making it rather unlikely that this mechanism could serve for the construction of a closed and coherent pioneer group operating across a whole range of policy areas. The conditions and procedures for enhanced cooperation operations are spelled out in detail in the text of the TEU and the TFEU. Because of the hierarchy between primary law (the Treaties) and secondary law (the enhanced cooperation instruments), it is clear that enhanced cooperation can only validly come into being if it respects the constraints imposed by the Treaties. These constraints are judicially enforceable, as was shown when enhanced cooperation in the field of patent law was challenged before the Court of Justice by two non-participating states, Italy and Spain, and when the project for an enhanced cooperation on a financial transaction tax was challenged by the United Kingdom.[32] Those challenges were unsuccessful on the merits, but the Court left no doubt that the Treaty conditions are indeed binding on the states that want to engage in enhanced cooperation.

The first procedural constraint is the 'last resort' rule, which is taken rather seriously since all cases of enhanced cooperation so far were preceded by genuine attempts to achieve the desired result through legislation applicable to all states. A second constraint is that the authorization for launching an enhanced cooperation project must be given by the Council acting by qualified majority, so that any pioneer group initiatives should receive the blessing of a large part of EU membership, as well as the active support of the Commission and the European Parliament. A third constraint is the right for every member state to join an enhanced cooperation project, so that a self-defined pioneer group cannot exclude states that do not form part of the group. Indeed, Article 328(1) TFEU provides that 'the Commission and the member states participating in enhanced cooperation shall ensure that they promote participation by as many Member States as possible.' If one takes together these procedural constraints, it is clear that a self-appointed vanguard cannot engage in a broad cross-policy cooperation project whilst ignoring the other member states. The enhanced cooperation mechanism was, from the start in the 1990s, conceived as antithetical to the core Europe idea, and it remains so today.

Finally, it deserves to be mentioned that enhanced cooperation operates within the existing limits of EU competences: it cannot be used to extend EU competences beyond the domains currently defined by the Treaties. In

[32] ECJ, Case C-209/13, *United Kingdom v Council*, ECLI:EU:C:2014:283.

addition, laws adopted under enhanced cooperation laws cannot modify existing EU legislation, because that would affect the rights of the non-participating states.

What are now the implications of those legal constraints for a future integrative use of enhanced cooperation? The Commission scenario of 'Those who want more do more'[33] lists a number of other areas in which new projects of differentiated integration could be experimented, such as defence, justice and security, taxation, and social policy. For areas such as taxation, migration, and criminal justice, where the TFEU provides clear and rather broad legal bases, enhanced cooperation would seem, indeed, to be an appropriate tool. It would allow for the circumvention of the unanimity requirement where it is still in place (especially for taxation), and more generally would allow like-minded states to take forward their cooperation, using the instruments of EU law and sidelining the acrimonious resistance of other states even where decisions taken by qualified majority vote (QMV) would technically be feasible (as in the field of migration). In the field of social law, the scope for enhanced cooperation is more problematic, as some of the most frequently invoked reform measures, such as the creation of a European minimum wage system, or of a European minimum income benefit, possibly fall outside the scope of EU competences.[34] In that case, the tool of enhanced cooperation would not be available, and the conclusion of a separate international agreement by socially minded states would be the only available option.

3.2 Legal Constraints for À la Carte Differentiation

As was argued before, the EU's defence policy developed into a special domain for the purpose of differentiated integration. Permanent Structured Cooperation (PESCO) was implemented, in practice, as an à la carte cooperation mechanism. All member states seem to be happy with this approach, and it is not likely to change any time soon. However, it is worth noting that this à la carte approach is subject to legal and political constraints, so that the autonomy of the participating states is far from complete. One external

[33] European Commission, *White Paper on the Future of Europe—reflections and scenarios for the EU27 by 2025*, COM(2017) 2025 of 1 March 2017.

[34] The Commission proposed a directive on European minimum wages in October 2020 (COM(2020) 682), but it is met with strong opposition from a number of member states, and with claims that it exceeds the Union's competences. See discussion of the competence question by Aranguiz and Garben, 'Combating income inequality in the EU: A legal assessment of a potential EU minimum wage directive', 46 *European Law Review* (2021), 156.

constraint is the NATO membership of most of the member states and the non-membership of others: this necessarily affects the scope of participation of the various countries, but also the content of the cooperation within PESCO. Also, the institutional design of PESCO is embedded within the EU legal order. The participating states do not have recourse to the instruments of international law. Their projects are embedded in EU law, in that they have to be approved by Council decisions and their governance is set out in EU acts. As a result of those constraints, we saw the emergence of a rival cooperation mechanism that is situated entirely outside the EU legal order, namely the European Intervention Initiative launched by Macron in 2017, that is, at around the same time as PESCO.[35] Apparently, the reason for creating this parallel-to-EU framework was to enable the continuing participation of the UK in defence initiatives, but perhaps also to escape from the strictures of EU decision-making rules.

The conclusion of separate international law agreements between groups of member states is, and will remain, the main route for à la carte cooperation and, thus, for an autonomy-preserving use of differentiated integration. So far, the EU states have made only a limited use of this instrument, but there is a long-standing discussion (dating back to the time the Schengen Convention was adopted) as to whether the member states, or at least some of them, might start making a more systematic use of this instrument and thereby hollow out the EU legal order. In this context, the question arises whether there are legal limits to the enactment of such 'satellite agreements'.

Whereas the legal constraints for enhanced cooperation (as discussed above) are listed in the text of the TEU and the TFEU, the constraints that limit recourse to international agreements cannot be found in the Treaty text; they rather result from the inherent primacy of EU law over the national law of the member states. Indeed, it has always been clear that a group of EU states may not resort to the conclusion of a separate *inter se* treaty in order to escape from their obligations under EU law. Satellite agreements cannot derogate from either primary or secondary EU law. In its case law, the Court of Justice has consistently held that the primacy of EU law extends not only to measures of national law but also to agreements between two or more member states, which must be disapplied by national courts if they are inconsistent with EU law. Similarly, in direct actions for infringement, the Court of Justice does not distinguish between infringements caused by a state acting on its own and infringements caused by a bi- or multilateral agreement concluded between

[35] Zandee and Kruijver, *The European Intervention Initiative—Developing a shared strategic culture for European defence*, Clingendael Report, September 2019.

several member states.[36] This is entirely logical. It would otherwise be easy for the member states to escape from their EU law obligations by concluding a separate treaty with each other.

The practical importance of the principle of primacy of EU law over *inter se* agreements between member states was illustrated by a judgment of the European Court of Justice (ECJ) in 2006. The Court found the application of a Schengen Convention rule to be incompatible with the rights of free movement, which third country nationals who are family members of EU citizens derive from Union law.[37] The Court's finding was facilitated by the fact that Article 134 of the Schengen Convention contained an express conflict rule giving priority to (what was then) Community law, but there is no doubt that the ECJ would come to the same conclusion with regard to an agreement that does not contain such an express EU primacy rule.

Indeed, it did so in the more recent *Achmea* judgment in which it held that a bilateral investment treaty (BIT) between the Netherlands and Slovakia was contrary to EU law.[38] This particular agreement dates from the time that one of the parties (namely Slovakia or, in fact, its predecessor state Czechoslovakia) was not yet a member state of the Union, and it is one among hundreds of similar BITs that were concluded in the 1990s between Western European and Central or Eastern European countries. The incompatibility of those BITs with EU law is not at all obvious from their wording. The Court of Justice rather objected against a structural characteristic of these BITs, namely the fact that they submit investment disputes to a 'neutral' arbitration tribunal rather than to the domestic courts of either of the two states (in this case Slovakia or the Netherlands). Since those arbitration tribunals could, when settling an investment dispute, interpret and apply norms of EU law, this implied that questions of interpretation of EU law would be decided by bodies that are not part of the EU judicial system (which is composed of the ECJ and the national courts of its member states). The rather radical position adopted by the ECJ is a clear reminder that the EU member states are not at all free to engage in à la carte cooperation with each other. They must not only respect the existing *substantive* rules of EU law, but also refrain from agreeing anything that could undermine the *institutional* integrity of the EU legal order. Despite the

[36] See, for a judgment of the Court of Justice in this sense, Case C-546/07, *Commission v Germany*, ECLI:EU:C:2010:25, para 42 to 44.

[37] ECJ, Case C-503/03, *Commission v Spain*, ECLI:EU:C:2006:74, particularly the paras. 33 to 35.

[38] ECJ, Case C-284/16, *Slowakische Republik v Achmea*, ECLI:EU:C:2018:158. Among the many comments of this judgment and of its implications for international investment law, see Fanou, 'Intra-European Union investor-State arbitration post-*Achmea*: RIP?', 26 *Maastricht Journal of European and Comparative Law* (2019).

radical message conveyed by the *Achmea* judgment, the member states diligently complied with it. In a common declaration, adopted after the *Achmea* judgment, they agreed to terminate all the bilateral investment treaties that they had concluded between each other.[39] Complying with the primacy of EU law was probably facilitated, in this case, by the fact that those bilateral agreements between EU member states had lost most of their initial purpose and function.

In addition to the basic rule that EU law has priority over agreements between EU member states, a further legal constraint is discussed in the literature, namely whether enhanced cooperation should have priority over extra-EU agreements. Should a group of member states first try to implement a common project by means of enhanced cooperation before they can engage in extra-EU cooperation? A positive answer to that question could be grounded on the principle of sincere cooperation, contained in Article 4(3) TEU, which requires the member states to 'refrain from any measure which could jeopardise the attainment of the Union's objectives'.[40] To date, the ECJ has never directly addressed that question. In any case, when the enhanced cooperation mechanism was introduced in the text of the Treaties, that innovation was not accompanied by an express prohibition of closer cooperation on EU-related matters outside the EU framework.

There are, in fact, several reasons why such a systematic priority should not be given to enhanced cooperation, and why an international agreement may be preferable to EU legislation in enhanced cooperation mode.[41] One of these reasons is that the international treaty instrument can more easily be opened to third countries who may want to join in a project. For example, when the aim is to develop a system of environmental protection for the Alpine region, this could, in principle, be done through EU legislation, but it makes more sense to involve the non-EU states of the Alpine region by means of an international treaty.[42] Another reason for preferring intergovernmental agreements is that a policy initiative may require funding from the national budgets. This was the

[39] Declaration of the governments of the member states of 15 January 2019 on the legal consequences of the judgment of the Court of Justice in Achmea and on investment protection in the European Union, accessible on the Council's website: https://ec.europa.eu

[40] For the view that priority should indeed be given to enhanced cooperation, see for instance Martínez Capdevila, 'Son los acuerdos *inter se* una alternativa a la cooperación reforzada en la UE? Reflexiones al hilo del Tratado de Prüm', *Revista Española de Derecho Europeon*, 40 (2011), 419. See also Tuori, *European Constitutionalism* (Cambridge University Press, 2015), p. 208: 'a powerful case can be made for Member States not being allowed to resort to international agreements where enhanced cooperation is legally possible.'

[41] See also, for further arguments in the same sense, Angelaki, *supra* note 31, at 211–218.

[42] Alpine Convention, signed in Salzburg, 7 November 1991.

case when the EFSF and later the ESM were created during the sovereign debt crisis: the EU budget did not have enough 'firepower' to stabilize the financial markets, and much larger contributions were needed from the national budgets of the participating states. It made sense to organize such national budget contributions by means of a Treaty between participating states such as the ESM Treaty.

4. Conclusion

This chapter aimed to illustrate the role of the law in affecting the preferences that states and EU institutions have with regard to differentiated integration, including with regard to the choice among different forms of differentiation. The first part of the chapter sketched a contrast between two types of differentiation that coexist in the legal toolbox and have both been widely used in the past decades: the 'orthodox' forms of differentiated integration that are provided for, and partially regulated, by the European Treaties and the 'wilder' à la carte forms of differentiation that preserve the policy discretion and operational control of the participating governments. The second part of the chapter showed that both forms of differentiation face a different set of legal constraints, which affect the conditions for their use and makes one more attractive than the other, depending on, among other things, the policy domain in which they are used.

5

Rather Reduce than Accommodate? Coping with Territorial Diversity in Multilevel Polities

Christian Freudlsperger

1. Introduction

All multilevel polities face the challenge of territorial diversity. The economic, political, and cultural heterogeneity among their constituent units translates into heterogeneous preferences and capacities. This leads to deadlock in decision-making processes, and in some cases, it even instils members of a union with a desire for secession and independence. The EU, as a recurrently gridlocked union of formerly twenty-eight members, is all too familiar with the impact of territorial diversity on its multilevel structure. Yet even federal states need to deal with territorial diversity. Canada and Switzerland are prominent examples, and more homogeneous unions such as the United States have equally developed institutional strategies to cope with territorial diversity. This chapter will demonstrate, however, that there are immense differences in the way that the EU, on one hand, and federal states, on the other, deal with the challenge. The aim of the chapter is to understand why, and to reflect on possible ways forward for the EU.

Multilevel polities have different means of diversity governance at their disposal. This chapter will focus primarily on two such means that are of particular relevance for the EU context. When faced with demands for enhanced self-rule, multilevel systems can either accommodate the heterogeneity among their constituent units or they can (seek to) reduce the heterogeneity among their constituent units. To achieve the former, they decentralize contested policy areas altogether or grant special rights and freedoms to individual constituent units, for instance via policy opt-outs or subgroup cooperation. To achieve the latter, they can use regulatory or redistributive means to promote increased economic, political, and/or cultural homogeneity among

Christian Freudlsperger, *Rather Reduce than Accommodate? Coping with Territorial Diversity in Multilevel Polities.* In: *Autonomy without Collapse in a Better European Union.* Edited by Mark Dawson and Markus Jachtenfuchs, Oxford University Press. © Oxford University Press (2022). DOI: 10.1093/oso/9780192897541.003.0005

their constituent units, for instance via regulatory harmonization or fiscal redistribution.

The EU accommodates diversity more extensively than federal states. Differentiated integration (DI), an extreme variant of accommodation that allows individual constituent units permanent sectoral opt-outs, enjoyed increasing appeal in a post–Maastricht Union marked by increased heterogeneity, a rigid institutional setting, a functional drive towards integration, and a historical dynamic of territorial enlargement.[1] Some federal states have relied on similar strategies.[2] One example is Canada, where Québec and various other provinces have carved out specific rights for themselves. As theorists of federalism[3] and state-building[4] emphasize, asymmetric accommodation enables initial agreement but comes at potential long-term costs, including the democratic costs of complicating accountability structures,[5] the solidarity costs of fluid policy boundaries, and the stability costs of opt-out cascades.[6] Consequently, federal states not on rely less on differentiation than the EU, they also do so in different areas. The EU uses DI primarily in the context of 'core state powers'[7] such as internal and external security policy, monetary, and fiscal policy. Federal states, on the other hand, rely on differentiation primarily in areas that they deem crucial for the preservation of regional cultural identities, among others language, education, and migration policy.

Federal states reduce diversity more extensively than the EU. Multilevel systems can try to reduce territorial diversity over time by regulation, redistribution, or combinations of both. For want of an independent fiscal firepower, the EU relies mostly on relatively rigid regulation in order to approximate

[1] Schimmelfennig and Winzen, *Ever Looser Union? Differentiated European Integration* (Oxford University Press, 2020); Schimmelfennig and Winzen, 'Instrumental and constitutional differentiation in the European Union', 52 *Journal of Common Market Studies* (2014), 354–370; Schimmelfennig, Leuffen, and Rittberger, 'The European Union as a system of differentiated integration: interdependence, politicization and differentiation', 22 *Journal of European Public Policy* (2015), 764–782.

[2] Mcgarry, 'Asymmetry in federations, federacies and unitary states', 6 *Ethnopolitics* (2007), 105–116; Zuber, 'Understanding the multinational game: Toward a theory of asymmetrical federalism', 44 *Comparative Political Studies* (2011), 546–571; Popelier and Sahadžić, *Constitutional Asymmetry in Multinational Federalism: Managing Multinationalism in Multi-tiered Systems* (Palgrave Macmillan, 2019).

[3] Tarlton, 'Symmetry and asymmetry as elements of federalism: A theoretical speculation', 27 *The Journal of Politics* (1965), 861–874.

[4] Bartolini, *Restructuring Europe: Centre Formation, System Building and Political Structuring Between the Nation-State and the European Union* (Oxford University Press, 2005).

[5] Fossum, 'Democracy and differentiation in Europe', 22 *Journal of European Public Policy* (2015), 799–815.

[6] Hvidsten and Hovi, 'Why no twin-track Europe? Unity, discontent, and differentiation in European integration', 16 *European Union Politics* (2015), 3–22; Zuber (2011), *supra* note 2.

[7] Genschel and Jachtenfuchs, *Beyond the Regulatory Polity? The European Integration of Core State Powers* (Oxford University Press, 2014); Genschel and Jachtenfuchs, 'More integration, less federation: The European integration of core state powers', 23 *Journal of European Public Policy* (2016), 42–59.

gradually its member states' economic and political systems. This mode of integration, however, reaches its limits where it breeds resistance due to the constraints it imposes on member states' individual autonomy. In addition to the regulatory build-up of internal markets, virtually all federal states have thus developed extensive equalization or grant schemes to and/or among constituent units[8]. Whereas the EU regulatory polity relies mostly on regulatory intervention, federal states use the power of the federal purse to incentivize rather than force constituent units' loyalty, and to create disincentives for territorial exit.

The chapter's core finding is that the EU has to use permanent differentiation and rigid regulation due to its 'fiscal void',[9] that is, its tightly limited ability to reduce territorial diversity by redistributive means. This mode of integration, however, comes at long-term costs that could further exacerbate the risk of polity collapse. In this view, the EU's recent attempts to gradually build a supranational 'investment state',[10] the latest incarnation of which is the Recovery Instrument that was created during the Covid-19 pandemic in 2020, points in a noticeably novel direction. A build-up of significant redistributive capacities could herald a new stage in the EU's systemic evolution. To safeguard individual autonomy all while avoiding systemic collapse, the EU would complement its current model of a predominantly regulatory state with the nucleus of a redistributive state. This way, it would tackle the very sources of its systemic malaise and seek to reduce excessive economic and political diversity by means of fiscally underwritten incentives.

2. Institutional Strategies to Meet the Challenge of Territorial Diversity

How do multilevel polities cope with territorial diversity, and why does diversity governance differ across polities? In analogy to an expectation formulated by the literature on DI in the EU,[11] the chapter starts from a simple demand–supply model of diversity governance. The necessity for diversity governance

[8] Oates, 'An essay on fiscal federalism', 37 *Journal of Economic Literature* (1999), 1120–1149; Rodden, *Hamilton's Paradox: The Promise and Peril of Fiscal Federalism* (Cambridge University Press, 2006); Yilmaz and Zahir, *Intergovernmental Transfers in Federations* (Edward Elgar, 2020).

[9] Schelkle, 'Fiscal Integration by Default', in Genschel and Jachtenfuchs (eds.), *Beyond the Regulatory Polity?* (Oxford University Press, 2014), p. 105.

[10] Mertens and Thiemann, 'Building a hidden investment state? The European Investment Bank, national development banks and European economic governance', 26 *Journal of European Public Policy* (2019), 23–43.

[11] Schimmelfennig, Leuffen, and Rittberger (2015), *supra* note 1.

stems from individual constituent units' demands for enhanced self-rule. Such demands arise from regional political actors' attempts to politicize a constituent unit's economic, political, and/or cultural distinctness. The supply of diversity governance, in turn, depends on the availability of alternatives to differentiation, and central-level actors' ability to push for these alternatives.

Territorial diversity in multilevel polities has three key dimensions:

- *Political diversity* describes the heterogeneity of state and legal traditions within multilevel polities. Examples include Québec's civil law system inside common law Canada, historical cases of authoritarian enclaves in the deep south of the United States,[12] and recent patterns of 'democratic backsliding' in the European Union.[13]
- *Economic diversity* means territorial inequalities in economic development, in the institutional organization of the economy, and in the types of welfare systems.
- *Cultural diversity* describes territorial differences in identities, based on regional customs, religions, and languages. Evidently, cultural diversity ranks among the highest goods that federalism is supposed to protect, and individual identities in multilevel systems tend to be nested and inclusive. In cases, however, in which the citizens of a given constituent unit hold exclusive regional identities that are irreconcilable with a concomitant attachment to the union, this can complicate the organization of shared rule in a multilevel system.

By increasing the heterogeneity of preferences and capacities within a union, territorial diversity can put a multilevel system under considerable strain. Not only can it lead to deadlock in decision-making processes, it may also inspire individual constituent units to try and leave a union altogether. To be sure, territorial diversity per se provides merely a latent potential for self-rule demands and requires active politicization[14] by regional parties and political actors. Where such a politicizing move takes place, constituent units' perceived distinctness on any of the three abovementioned dimensions can serve as a justification for demands for enhanced self-rule.

[12] Mickey, *Paths Out of Dixie: The Democratization of Authoritarian Enclaves in America's Deep South, 1944–1972* (Princeton University Press, 2015).

[13] Kelemen, 'The European Union's authoritarian equilibrium', 26 *Journal of European Public Policy* (2020), 481–499.

[14] De Wilde and Zürn, 'Can the politicization of European integration be reversed?', 50 *Journal of Common Market Studies* (2012), 137–153.

For instance, both the literatures on federalism and on the EU emphasize a key role for cultural diversity. Constituent units in which territorial and ethnolinguistic boundaries coincide[15] and/or in which identities that exclude an attachment to the union are widespread among the citizenry[16] tend to prefer self-rule in fields they deem crucial for their communal self-determination. An example is Québec, where the 'Quiet Revolution' of the 1960s rendered Québecois' sense of belonging to the Canadian union increasingly precarious. Economic diversity can also act as a driver of regional self-rule demands. The rationale is that richer and more capable constituent units tend to be less dependent on others to engage in specialization and realize economies of scale, inciting regional political actors to form a preference for the liberty of self-rule over the solidarity of shared rule. Both Catalonia in Spain and Flanders in Belgium are examples of regions that are not only culturally distinct but also economically comparatively well off. Lastly, political diversity can equally spur regional demands for self-rule. In the contemporary EU, for instance, the governments of Hungary and Poland demand more or less free reign from EU institutions in their efforts to curb the rule of law and dismantle institutional checks and balances.

Expectation 1: *Demands for enhanced self-rule arise from the politicization of a constituent unit's cultural, economic, and/or political distinctness.*

Which institutional means do multilevel polities have at their disposal to cope with territorial diversity? Scholars of the EU[17] and federal states[18] have frequently employed Hirschman's[19] model of the relationship between an organization and its 'customer-members' when interpreting the dynamic development of multilevel systems and their attempts to strike a balance between self-rule and shared rule. In the context of diversity governance, too, the model can provide a useful starting point. Hirschman's framework famously relies on three central categories: exit, voice, and loyalty. Applied to the realm of

[15] Stepan, 'Federalism and Democracy: Beyond the U.S. Model', in Karmis and Norman (eds.), *Theories of Federalism: A Reader* (Palgrave Macmillan, 1999), pp. 255–268.

[16] Schimmelfennig and Winzen (2020), *supra* note 1.

[17] Bartolini (2005), *supra* note 4; Jachtenfuchs and Kasack, 'Balancing sub-unit autonomy and collective problem-solving by varying exit and voice: An analytical framework', 24 *Journal of European Public Policy* (2017), 598–614.

[18] Benz and Broschek, *Federal Dynamics: Continuity, Change, and the Varieties of Federalism* (Oxford University Press, 2013).

[19] Hirschman, *Exit, Voice, and Loyalty: Responses to Decline in Firms, Organizations, and States* (Harvard University Press, 1970).

multilevel government, 'exit' describes constituent units' non-application of system-wide policies, 'voice' means constituent units' influence on collective decisions, and 'loyalty' means constituent units' readiness to accept union-wide decisions.[20] When reacting to territorial demands for increased self-rule, this chapter argues that multilevel polities can utilize institutional means to manipulate any of these three elements:

- *Accommodating diversity*: Multilevel polities can provide for controlled means of sectoral *exit* that allow for enhanced subfederal autonomy. This enables multilevel systems to avoid secession and avert potential systemic collapse. Territorial diversity can be accommodated asymmetrically by means of opt-outs from polity-wide policies or by subgroup cooperation in the absence of polity-wide policies, or symmetrically by decentralizing certain policy areas altogether.
- *Incorporating diversity*: Multilevel polities can also provide for enhanced subfederal *voice* in polity-wide policymaking. The rationale behind increasing constituent units' voice is to lower their propensity to seek exit.[21] Territorial diversity can be incorporated asymmetrically by facilitating the representation of regional minorities in legislative processes or by prescribing consociational elements[22] in government formation, or symmetrically by increasing constituent units' influence in collective decision-making.
- *Reducing diversity*: Multilevel polities can seek to increase constituent units' *loyalty* to the system and decrease their desire for enhanced self-rule. Loyal members of an organization tend to choose voice over exit. Reducing diversity is tantamount to the attempt of removing the necessity for diversity governance over time. Ideally, strategies of reducing diversity are necessary only temporarily and render themselves redundant in the long run. To reduce economic, political, and/or cultural territorial diversity, multilevel systems can employ either regulatory means, i.e., more or less rigid forms of legal approximation and harmonization, or redistributive means, i.e., fiscal support in the form of grants, or a combination of the two, for instance via earmarked grants.

[20] Freudlsperger, *Trade Policy in Multilevel Government: Organizing Openness* (Oxford University Press, 2020);Jachtenfuchs and Kasack (2017), *supra* note 17.

[21] Freudlsperger, 'More voice, less exit: sub-federal resistance to international procurement liberalization in the European Union, the United States and Canada', 25 *Journal of European Public Policy* (2018), 1686–1705; ibid. Freudlsperger (2020).

[22] Lijphart, 'The Wave of Power-Sharing Democracy' in, *The Architecture of Democracy: Constitutional Design, Conflict Management, and Democracy* (Oxford University Press, 2002), pp. 37–54.

As the EU already incorporates diversity to an extraordinary extent, this chapter focuses on the alternative strategies of accommodating and reducing diversity. Member state executives occupy a central institutional role in both its dual legislature and dual executive,[23] so much so that the EU system is commonly considered one of 'second-chamber governance'.[24] When dealing with territorial diversity, the EU thus disposes of tightly limited scope to increase member states' voice even further. As the chapter is interested in the EU's potentials of systemic development, the remainder of the analysis will focus on the two alternative variants of either accommodating diversity, i.e., allowing for controlled exit, or reducing diversity, i.e., promoting increased homogeneity by either regulatory or redistributive means.

What determines the supply of either of these two types of diversity governance? In line with the literature on asymmetrical federalism,[25] this chapter puts a particular analytical emphasis on the reactions of central-level actors' reactions to constituent units' demands for enhanced self-rule. The literature on DI in the EU is less interested in central-level actors' role simply because their impact on constitutional reform in the EU system is tightly limited, with the member states controlling the division of competencies. The literature on asymmetrical federalism, in turn, emphasizes that central-level actors and other constituent units tend to regard accommodation, and especially permanent asymmetrical differentiation, as a cost borne by the union. Potential cost categories include:

- *Democratic costs*: Central-level actors regard sectoral policy opt-outs as calling into question the representativeness of central-level legislative bodies and as aggravating accountability problems by producing uncertainty among citizens on their legal rights and avenues of democratic expression.[26]
- *Solidarity costs*: Central-level actors regard solid systemic boundaries as the prerequisite of organizing solidarity within a union.[27] If wealthy and capable constituent units can credibly threaten or actually obtain opt-outs once their solidarity is required in a given matter, or if constituents

[23] Fabbrini, *Which European Union?* (Cambridge University Press, 2015).

[24] Hueglin and Fenna, *Comparative Federalism: A systematic inquiry* (University of Toronto Press, 2015), p. 65.

[25] Popelier and Sahadžić 2019, Zuber (2011) supra n 2.

[26] Fossum, 'Democracy and differentiation in Europe', 22 *Journal of European Public Policy* (2015), 799–815.

[27] Bartolini (2005), *supra* note 4.

requesting solidarity can be threatened with expulsion, a system's ability to solve collective action problems is greatly reduced.
- *Stability costs*: Lastly, central-level actors argue horizontal differentiation to undercut the long-term stability of multilevel polities. Granting special rights to one constituent unit, in this view, invites emulation by others. In such cases, the granting of an asymmetrical opt-out to one constituent unit can lead to 'opt-out cascades',[28] causing the wholesale disintegration of a central-level policy, secession, or even the dissolution of a polity.

As a consequence, central-level actors hold an a priori preference against accommodation, seeking to divert constituent units' demands for enhanced self-rule toward alternative types of diversity governance, in this case toward its reduction. Central-level actors' ability to realize this preference depends on two conditions. The first condition is central-level actors' control over the division of competencies. This control can run either through formal processes of constitutional reform[29] or through informal intergovernmental relations (IGR).[30] If central-level institutions control the division of competencies via formal or informal channels, they are likely able to divert self-rule demands towards a reduction of diversity, and vice versa. The second condition is the availability, i.e., primarily the prior institutionalization, of alternatives to accommodation. Many multilevel systems have developed central-level or shared fiscal capacities to organize union-wide risk—and burden-sharing, primarily via equalization or grant schemes to and/or among constituent units.[31] If central-level actors' control (significant parts of) these funds, they are likely able to divert self-rule demands towards a reduction of diversity.

Expectation 2: *The supply of enhanced self-rule depends on central-level actors' control over the division of competencies and the availability of alternative types of diversity governance.*

2.1 Demand Side: Territorial Diversity across Multilevel Systems

The cases selected for comparison are the 'diverse cases'[32] of Canada, Switzerland, and the United States. These federal states have been variously compared

[28] Hvidsten and Hovi (2015), *supra* note 6; Zuber (2011), *supra* note 2.
[29] Benz, *Constitutional Policy in Multilevel Government: The Art of Keeping the Balance* (Oxford University Press, 2016).
[30] Bolleyer, *Intergovernmental Cooperation: rational choices in federal systems and beyond* (Oxford University Press, 2009).
[31] Watts, *Comparing Federal Systems* (McGill-Queen's University Press, 2008).
[32] Gerring, 'Techniques for Choosing Cases', in Gerring (ed.), *Case Study Research* (Cambridge University Press, 2007), pp. 86–150.

to the EU in the past.[33] As the following short vignettes will demonstrate, the four multilevel polities vary with respect to the politicization of territorial diversity, that is, the demand side of diversity governance. For reasons of structural clarity and analytical convenience, the four sections on each polity will also elaborate briefly on central-level actors' control of constitutional reform and intergovernmental relations, which is one aspect of the supply side of diversity governance.

United States: In the US, the politicization of territorial diversity is generally low. There are no states in which territorial and ethnolinguistic boundaries coincide and in which a considerable part of the population holds exclusive identities that are irreconcilable with a dominant attachment to the union. It is hence unsurprising that no significant secession movements have erupted since the end of the Civil War, decreasing the necessity of permanent asymmetric accommodation. In economic terms, there are nonetheless significant differences. According to data for 2018 assembled by the Bureau of Economic Analysis, GDP per capita in the wealthiest state (New York) is 2.3 times as high as in the poorest state (Mississippi).

In the US federal system, central-level actors dominate constitutional reform and union-wide legislation. Core state powers such as defence, border (as a corollary of immigration), monetary, and tax policy rank among the exclusive competencies reserved to the federal order. Even the establishment of redistributive welfare schemes such as Medicaid and Medicare in the 1960s was covered by the federal constitutional ambit. Constituent units play a secondary role in institutional and constitutional reform as the directly elected Senate, which works along party lines, holds a de facto monopoly on the representation of territorial interests. Vertical IGR have only developed in the shadow of congressional control and largely serve the purpose of attracting and allocating federal monies instead of collaborative power-sharing and joint policymaking. Consequently, states rely on informal lobbying outside the constitutionally erected institutional order in their attempts to influence the central government.[34]

Switzerland: The politicization of territorial diversity in the 'multilingual but mono-national'[35] Swiss federation is moderate. Four languages are spoken, with Swiss German spoken by the majority (75 per cent), trailed by the French-speaking (20 per cent), Italian-speaking (4 per cent) and Romansh-speaking minorities (1 per cent). At the same time, the ethnolinguistic and religious cleavages permeating the country do not coincide with cantonal

[33] Freudlsperger (2020), *supra* note 20, at pp. 17–21.
[34] Freudlsperger (2020), *supra* note 20, at pp. 106–7.
[35] Popelier and Sahadžić (2019), *supra* note 2, at p. 3.

politico-administrative borders. Accordingly, since the *Sonderbund* war of 1847, the secession potential among cantons has been generally low. Through the expansion of monolingual mass media, however, citizens' attachment to their respective language community became more politicized in the course of the twentieth century, increasingly providing the main basis of individual identities.[36] In addition, cross cantonal differences in economic and administrative capacities are pronounced. According to data by the Federal Statistics Office for 2016, GDP per capita in Zug was 2.9 times higher than in Uri (Basel-City excluded as an extreme case), spurring demands for territorial redistribution.

In the Swiss federal system, the cantons have considerable influence on constitutional reform and union-wide legislation. Only in defence and external relations, the federation exclusively regulates both policy formulation and implementation. The cantons, in turn, dominate the decentralized fields of justice and police, education, and health.[37] At the same time, the cantons have increasingly regarded the directly elected second chamber, the Council of States, as a deficient device of territorial representation.[38] Horizontal IGR via cantonal conferences and concordats have become an increasingly important vehicle of regional cooperation. Despite this regionalized make-up and the requirement of a cantonal majority for constitutional amendments, the Swiss federation has witnessed some creeping but symmetrical centralization of competencies in fields such as infrastructure, environmental policy, and consumer or data protection.[39]

Canada: Territorial diversity in Canada is highly politicized. Over the twentieth century, the ethnolinguistic differences between the English-speaking majority (60 per cent of the populace) and the French-speaking (20 per cent) as well as indigenous minorities (the 'first nations', 4 per cent) became increasingly politicized. For the largely Catholic, French-speaking Québec, this translated into a realistic path towards sovereign nationhood. In 1980 and 1995, independence referendums resulted in narrow defeats for the sovereigntists. Even so, the politicized distinctness of Québec is a constant bone of contention in the Canadian union, not least through the establishment of sovereigntist parties such as the *Union Nationale* from the 1930s to 1960s, the

[36] Kriesi, 'State Formation and Nation Building in the Swiss Case', in Kriesi et al. (eds.), *Nation and National Identity: The European Experience in Perspective* (Ruegger, 1999).
[37] Kriesi and Trechsel, *The Politics of Switzerland: Continuity and Change in a Consensus Democracy* (Cambridge University Press, 2008).
[38] Bolleyer (2009), *supra* note 30.
[39] Dardanelli and Mueller, 'Dynamic de/centralization in Switzerland, 1848–2010', 49 *Publius* (2019), 138–165.

Parti Québecois since the late 1960s, and the *Coalition Avenir Québec* since the 2010s. While economic heterogeneity among the provinces is less pronounced than in other federations—according to Statistics Canada, Alberta's 2018 GDP per capita was 1.8 times as high as Prince Edward Island's—vast differences in population size and density translate into differing provincial capacities.

In the Canadian federal system, the provinces have considerable influence on constitutional reform and the implementation of union-wide legislation. Although Section 91 of the constitution equips the federal order with exclusive powers in twenty-eight fields such as taxation, defence, foreign, and trade policy, its empowering effect is counteracted by Section 92 that equally enumerates exclusive provincial powers. Sixteen matters are exclusively ascribed to the provinces, among them health, social welfare, education, and, importantly, the control of lands and natural resources. The federal government thus needs to engage systematically in vertical IGR, both through generalist (and highly politicized) First Ministers' conferences and sectoral (and more functional) ministerial councils.[40] In fields falling under their jurisdiction, the provinces also established a formalized system of horizontal IGR via the Council of the Federation and its regional equivalents. The latter allow for flexible subgroup cooperation in cases in which polity-wide consensus is unattainable, for instance through regional trade agreements.[41]

European Union: In the EU, territorial diversity is highly politicized. The Union is a 'coming-together'[42] polity consisting of currently twenty-seven (restrictedly) sovereign nation states in which a panoply of languages is spoken and a variety of creeds is practised. The rise of Eurosceptic challenger parties since the Treaty of Maastricht also indicates that identity-driven dividing lines have emerged as a source of fervent politicization within the EU.[43] Not least the UK's departure, which can be seen as a reaction to both cultural[44] and political[45] distinctness, has demonstrated the brittle legitimacy base of supranational shared rule in the EU, and the secession potential among individual self-rule minded members. In addition, EU member states exhibit a wide variety of economic models and welfare state systems, with economic

[40] Cameron and Simeon, 'Intergovernmental relations in Canada: The emergence of collaborative federalism', 32 *Publius: The Journal of Federalism* (2002), 49–71.

[41] Freudlsperger (2020), *supra* note 20.

[42] Stepan (1999), *supra* note 15.

[43] Hooghe and Marks, 'A postfunctionalist theory of European integration: From permissive consensus to constraining dissensus', 39 *British Journal of Political Science* (2008), 1–23.

[44] Schimmelfennig, 'Brexit: differentiated disintegration in the European Union', 25 *Journal of European Public Policy* (2018), 1154–1173.

[45] Schmidt, 'No match made in heaven: Parliamentary sovereignty, EU over-constitutionalization and Brexit', 27 *Journal of European Public Policy* (2020), 779–794.

differences among them even exacerbated by recent enlargements. According to IMF data for 2017, GDP per capita in Ireland is 3.5 times higher than in Bulgaria (Luxembourg excluded as an extreme small-country case).

Even in comparison with decentralized federations, EU member states have an outsized influence on constitutional reform and Union-wide legislation. Solely in the realm of the 'Community method', that is, mainly in regulatory policies adjacent or attached to the internal market, the member states share their powers with supranational institutions such as the Commission, the Parliament, and the Court. In fields judged sensitive for member state sovereignty, among them foreign and security policy, welfare, and employment as well as fiscal and tax policy,[46] a horizontal logic of intergovernmental decision-making constrains the influence of supranational actors.[47] In reforms of the EU's Treaty-based 'material constitution'[48] too, the member states remain the originators of the Treaties, disposing of an individual veto.

In sum, both the Canadian and the EU multilevel system are characterized by a combination of politicized territorial diversity, which translates into a relatively high demand for enhanced self-rule, and an enormous influence of constituent units on central-level policymaking and constitutional reform. The opposite constellation applies to the US case, where territorial diversity is limited to divergences in economic development and where the states have little clout in federal lawmaking. Lastly, Switzerland is marked by a moderate level of territorial heterogeneity and central-level institutions which rely on cantonal cooperation and collaboration but have nonetheless been able to achieve some centralization over time.

2.2 Supply Side: Diversity Governance across Multilevel Systems

The following section will examine the supply side of diversity governance. Its first part analyses the strategies the four polities have developed to accommodate diversity, while the subsequent segment focuses on the reduction of territorial diversity. Before going into further detail, Table 5.1 summarizes the findings of the analysis. The experience of the four multilevel polities with diversity governance broadly supports the chapter's theoretical argument. Across federal states, the politicization of territorial diversity, the strength of

[46] Genschel and Jachtenfuchs (2014, 2016), *supra* note 7.
[47] Bickerton, Hodson, and Puetter, 'The new intergovernmentalism: European integration in the post-Maastricht era', 53 *Journal of Common Market Studies* (2015), 703–722.
[48] Fabbrini (2015), *supra* note 23, at pp. 66–9.

Table 5.1. Diversity governance in different multilevel polities

Reducing diversity	**Accommodating diversity**
Canada: Extensive vertical redistribution through health and social transfers as well as federal equalization grants to provinces.	*Canada*: Opt-outs for Québec from common law, federal pension system, and Charter of Rights and Freedoms; symmetric decentralization of migration; transitional arrangements for acceding provinces.
EU: Limited regional redistribution; dominance of rigid harmonization alongside flexible framework legislation and soft law.	*EU*: Varying groups of member states opting out of Schengen border regime, euro currency, justice and home affairs; transitional arrangements for accession countries.
Switzerland: Extensive vertical redistribution; flexibility and experimentation in cantonal implementation of federal legislation.	*Switzerland*: No formal differentiation of rights and obligations; systematic cantonal cooperation on devolved competences and policy implementation.
US: Flexibility through setting of minimum standards and practice of waivers; 'coercive federalism' by means of conditional federal grants, but also looser block grants.	*US*: No formal differentiation of rights and obligations; weakly formalized horizontal IGR.

central-level actors, and the prior institutionalization of alternative strategies vary. As does, consequently, their recourse to strategies of either accommodating or reducing diversity.

3. Accommodating Diversity

The EU is probably the most differentiated existing multilevel polity. Before Maastricht, integration had been largely uniform. The exceptions were the European Monetary System after 1979 and transitional arrangements for acceding member states. Around and after Maastricht then, the EU set about both widening and deepening integration. In this context, horizontal differentiation was 'the facilitator—or the price—of dynamic growth in both vertical and horizontal integration.'[49] Consequently, since the mid-1990s, more than half of the policy fields in which the EU is active have witnessed some form

[49] Schimmelfennig, Leuffen, and Rittberger (2015), *supra* note 1, at p. 769.

of differentiation. A share of currently 43 per cent of EU Treaty Articles is formally differentiated in one way or another.[50]

Most DI stems from the Schengen free travel area, the area of freedom, security and justice; the common currency, security and defence policy; and taxation. In such core state power areas, central-level actors and other member states have repeatedly been unable to thwart differing degrees of horizontal differentiation. The EU has developed three primary means of DI. First, it allows groups of constituent units informal intergovernmental contracting outside EU institutions.[51] Second, the EU enables individual member states formal treaty-level opt-outs from or opt-ins into broad areas of EU law. In the various intergovernmental conferences since Maastricht, the EU was repeatedly confronted with member states preferring self-rule over shared rule, accompanied by a high level of politicization in national referendums, ultimately necessitating formal differentiation. Third, the EU also allows for secondary law differentiation through the formalized procedure of 'enhanced cooperation' (Article 20 TEU). Hitherto, this avenue has been used rarely, both for regulatory purposes (e.g., the establishment of a unitary patent and the facilitation of transnational divorces) and to alleviate EU-level capacity building (e.g., the EU public prosecutor's office and permanent structured cooperation in defence).

Constitutional differentiation by means of permanent opt-outs is much rarer in federal states. An exception to the rule is Canada. By the time of the constitution of 1867, the British North America Act, legislators went to great lengths to accommodate grievances among the four founding provinces (Ontario, Québec, Nova Scotia, New Brunswick), establishing asymmetrical arrangements.[52] With respect to Québec, for instance, the constitution stipulated that the province could maintain its civil law system and that its provincial property and civil rights could not be harmonized. In addition, Québec was given specific rights pertaining to the use of the French language and minority education. Upon its accession to the federation in 1870, the latter linguistic and educational rights were extended to the province of Manitoba as well. Transitional arrangements were routinely enshrined in the constitution when provinces joined the union. Until 1930, for instance, resource-rich Manitoba, Alberta (1905), and Saskatchewan (1905) were stripped of the power to control their public lands. Further differential treatments were applied upon

[50] Schimmelfennig and Winzen (2014), *supra* note 1, at p. 358.
[51] de Witte, Chapter 4, this volume.
[52] Watts, 'The Canadian Experience with Asymmetrical Federalism', in Agranoff (ed.), *Accommodating Diversity: Asymmetry in Federal States* (Nomos, 1999), pp. 118–136.

the accession of British Columbia (1871), Prince Edward Island (1873), and Newfoundland (1949). At later instances, too, the Canadian federation used means of accommodation to cope with particularly Québec's reservations vis-à-vis instances of centralization. When, in the 1960s, the 'quiet revolution' in Québec coincided with the federal government's attempt to build a Canadian welfare state, the province received an opt-out from the national pension plan in favour of its own regime (the 'Québec Pension Plan'). In 1982, when the constitution was 'patriated' and supplemented by a Charter of Rights and Freedoms, Québec opposed the latter and refrained from ratifying the Constitution Act.[53] In 1991, the intergovernmental Canada-Québec Accord breathed life into the constitution's denomination of migration policy as a concurrent competence. The agreement allowed Québec significant discretion in steering inward migration from outside the union.

To be sure, differentiation has provided a measure of last resort in the Canadian union. When and where possible, central-level actors avoided asymmetry. Where they could not avoid it, they sought to reduce it over time. At times, federal actors preferred delaying the centralization of a given policy area in order to wait for a permissive preference constellation allowing to integrate Québec. One example is Prime Minister Mackenzie King's decision to delay the introduction of a federal unemployment benefit scheme until 1940, when Québec was no longer ruled by the *Union Nationale*.[54] In other cases, the residual provinces rejected special treatment for Québec and pushed for a general decentralization of policies instead of asymmetrical accommodation. Québec's heightened competencies in controlling inward migration, for instance, have now been extended to most other provinces too.[55] Similarly, after the failed independence referendum in 1995, all provinces were granted a symmetrical decentralization of labour market training.[56] Where opt-outs proved eventually unavoidable, they largely affected areas of significance for cultural and political diversity (language and education; the constitutional and legal system) and important symbolic gestures such as Parliament's recognition in 2006 of Québec as a 'nation' within Canada. Nonetheless, the asymmetrical federalism in Canada even extends to an instrument of horizontal redistribution, that is, the federal pension scheme. Since their inception in the 1960s,

[53] Benz, *Constitutional Policy in Multilevel Government: The Art of Keeping the Balance* (Oxford University Press, 2016), p. 55.

[54] Hooghe *et al.*, *Measuring Regional Authority: A Postfunctionalist Theory of Governance, Volume I* (Oxford University Press, 2016), p. 128.

[55] Paquet, *Province-Building and the Federalization of Immigration in Canada* (University of Toronto Press, 2019).

[56] Watts (1999), *supra* note 52.

however, the pension plans for Québec and Canada have become ever more alike. Contributions and benefits are now largely identical; sharing agreements enable beneficiaries to combine both plans; and pensions from both plans can be drawn anywhere in Canada.[57]

By way of contrast, the US has been described as 'a canonical example of a symmetric federation',[58] and similar arguments have been put forth with respect to Switzerland.[59] In both cases, central-level actors were capable of achieving gradual sectoral centralization without accommodating subfederal diversity by means of horizontal opt-outs. In the Swiss case at least, this came at the price of cumbersome integration processes drawn out over extended periods of time, and relatively low degrees of eventual centralization.[60] One example is the establishment of a Swiss welfare state whose formation, due to repeated challenges in national referendums, extended over decades and whose functioning and financing remains relatively decentralized even nowadays.[61] To manage arising interdependencies in both the implementation of federal policies and in cantonal areas of competence, varying groups of cantons have concluded more than 700 concordats. These pertain primarily to the fields of education, culture, and language, but also internal security.[62] In the US, state governors also form regional and partisan groupings. In comparison to the Swiss cantons, however, the fifty US states show more restraint in horizontal subgroup cooperation. They have concluded roughly 150 interstate compacts, mostly on environmental and education policy, as well as in the areas of justice and border protection.[63]

4. Reducing Diversity

In order to reduce territorial diversity over time, all four multilevel polities under investigation rely upon union-wide regulation in centralized areas of competence. Rigid regulation is the norm in Europe's 'ever tighter Union'.[64]

[57] Béland and Weaver, 'Federalism and the politics of the Canada and Quebec pension plans', 35 *Journal of International and Comparative Social Policy* (2019), 25–40.
[58] Bednar, 'The political science of federalism', 7 *Annual Review of Law and Social Science* (2011), p. 271.
[59] Biaggini, 'Asymmetrien im schweizerischen Bundesstaat?', in Palermo et al. (eds.), *Auf dem Weg zu asymmetrischem Föderalismus?* (Nomos, 2007), pp. 54–64.
[60] Dardanelli and Mueller (2019), *supra* note 39.
[61] Kriesi and Trechsel (2008), *supra* note 37, at pp. 155–71.
[62] Bochsler, 'Neighbours or friends? When Swiss cantonal governments co-operate with each other', 19 *Regional and Federal Studies* (2009), 349–370.
[63] Bolleyer (2009), *supra* note 30, at pp. 124–126.
[64] Matthijs, Parsons, and Toenshoff, 'Ever Tighter Union? Brexit, Grexit, and Frustrated Differentiation in the Single Market and Eurozone', 17 *Comparative European Politics* (2019), 209–30.

In both the internal market (e.g., on the cross-border provision of services, the mutual recognition of professional certificates or public contracting)[65] and in core state powers (e.g., on the extent to which the EU regulates member states' budgetary expenditure), the EU relies on fine-grained regulation to a comparatively high degree. The level of regulatory detail imposed by EU directives, supported by the Commission's surveillance of member state compliance and enforced by the Court of Justice's binding jurisdiction, all contribute to the comparatively rigid regulatory polity that is the EU. At the same time, all multilevel polities have developed some tools to introduce flexibility in regulation. Soft law,[66] for instance, has become an important element in the EU's regulatory toolbox. The US federal level, too, endows states with leeway in implementation. In some fields of concurrent competencies such as environmental policy, states are able to set higher regulatory standards than the federal level prescribes, even where these hinder the free movement of goods and services. Congress also incorporates provisions for flexible implementation in most of its acts. These enable the federal government to grant individual 'waivers' to state, county, and municipal governments, exempting them fully or partially from a given act. Such waivers are particularly frequent in health policy.[67]

In contrast to the EU, which seeks to approximate member states' political and economic systems near exclusively by regulatory means, federal states tend to combine regulation with extensive fiscal incentives. Most multilevel polities have developed schemes of territorial redistribution. Constituent units often depend on these schemes to a considerable extent. According to IMF data for 2019, Canadian provinces and territories generated 19.2 per cent of their overall revenues through grants from the federal government; the figures for the US states and Swiss cantons stood at 20.4 and 25.3 per cent, respectively.[68] Subfederal dependence on grants endows the central level with significant leverage in the pursuit of national policy objectives:

- The US federal government has not established a formalized fiscal equalization scheme. Nevertheless, in what scholars have described as a system

[65] Egan, *Single Markets: Economic Integration in Europe and the United States* (Oxford University Press, 2015).

[66] Falkner et al., *Complying with Europe: EU Harmonisation and Soft Law in the Member States* (Cambridge University Press, 2005).

[67] Hueglin and Fenna (2015), *supra* note 24, at p. 250.

[68] International Monetary Fund, Government Finance Statistics (2021).

of 'coercive federalism',[69] the federal government uses categorical grants-in-aid for its own political ends. Categorical grants are awarded for narrowly defined purposes, for instance to provide nutrition to certain vulnerable groups, to hire additional police in cities, or for specified infrastructure projects. Block grants, by contrast, provide states with more leeway, as their use is specified in solely general terms. The largest current 'block grants' are the 'Temporary Assistance for Needy Families', the 'Child Care and Development Block Grant', and the 'Community Development Block Grant'.[70]

- The formal federal equalization scheme in Switzerland, in turn, has currently two major components. Revenue equalization is to reduce the differentials in fiscal capacity among the cantons, and to guarantee cantons a minimum level of financial resources. Expenditure needs equalization, on the other hand, is based on sociodemographic characteristics of the resident population such as poverty, old age, and the presence of third-country nationals; and the geo-topographic variables of either mountainous and remote or urban and densely populated areas[71].
- In Canada, federal grants proved particularly instrumental in the creation of a redistributive welfare system since the mid-1950s. At the time, 'cooperative federalism'[72] relied largely on the issuing of conditional grants in exchange for the provinces implementing nationwide social security programs.[73] This legacy lives on in the contemporary Canada Health Transfer, which contains relatively broad conditionality requirements, and the Canada Social Transfer, which stipulates that social assistance must be provided without a minimum residency requirement. The formal equalization scheme was introduced in the 1950s and aims to provide a comparable level of public services across the union.[74] As Québec has long profited to a relatively high degree, equalization payments tend to be highly politicized across the union, criticized especially by the Western provinces as a type of 'separatist blackmail'.[75]

[69] Kincaid, 'Contemporary US federalism: Coercive change with cooperative continuity', 4 *Revista d'estudis autonòmics i federals* (2008), 10–36.

[70] Dilger and Boyd, *Block Grants: Perspectives and Controversies* (Congressional Research Service, 2014).

[71] Dafflon, 'Revenue and Expenditure Needs Equalization: The Swiss Answer', in Yilmaz and Zahir (eds.), *Intergovernmental Transfers in Federations* (Edward Elgar, 2020), pp. 134–162.

[72] Cameron and Simeon (2002), *supra* note 40.

[73] Hueglin and Fenna (2015), *supra* note 24, at p. 251.

[74] Béland et al., *Fiscal Federalism and Equalization Policy in Canada* (University of Toronto Press, 2017).

[75] Hueglin and Fenna (2015), *supra* note 24, at p. 186.

The EU uses various channels for territorial redistribution. In comparison with federal states, however, its fiscal firepower is tightly limited. The conventional route goes via the EU's multiannual budget and particularly its cohesion policy. While a handful of member states depend on cohesion monies to a surprisingly high degree, the EU's annual budget merely accounts for roughly half the federal budget of the Federal Republic of Germany and a mere one per cent of overall EU GDP. According to the European Commission, EU cohesion policy financed 8.5 per cent of public investment in EU member states in the years between 2015 and 2017. This figure, however, includes member states' co-financing obligations.[76] Aside from the conventional budgetary route, the EU also draws on other instruments such as the European Fund for Strategic Investments (the so-called 'Juncker Fund'), which mobilizes both public and private money to invest in strategic infrastructure such as broadband networks and renewable energy. In 2020 then, the EU reacted to the Covid pandemic by setting up a debt funded Recovery Instrument on top of the multiannual budget. Between 2021 and 2023, the fund will funnel an overall amount of 750 billion euros in grants and loans into member states to kick-start their economic recoveries. To receive these EU monies, member states submit so-called Recovery and Resilience Plans that need to be coordinated with the European Commission and greenlighted by the Council of Ministers.

5. Comparative Findings and Conclusion

This chapter examined how different multilevel polities cope with the challenge of territorial diversity. With an eye toward the EU's potentials for systemic development, the chapter was particularly interested in two types of diversity governance, defined as either accommodating or reducing diversity. In line with the former type, multilevel polities react to the economic, political, and/or cultural diversity among their constituent units, primarily by allowing for controlled exit via sectoral opt-outs. In keeping with the latter type, multilevel polities react to demands for enhanced self-rule by seeking to enhance constituent units' loyalty to the union, via either regulatory or redistributive means to increase territorial homogeneity over time. The chapter postulated that multilevel polities' fundamental choice between either accommodating

[76] European Commission, *My Region, My Europe, Our Future: Seventh Report on Economic, Social and Territorial Cohesion* (2017).

or reducing diversity is determined, on the demand side, by the politicization of territorial heterogeneity and, on the supply side, by the strength of central-level actors and the prior institutionalization of different types of diversity governance. The preceding analysis of Canada, the EU, Switzerland, and the US traced these demand and supply factors of diversity governance. In comparison, four findings stand out.

First, federal states accommodate diversity less than the EU. Across the four analysed polities, central-level actors expect asymmetric accommodation to undermine the problem-solving capacity, democratic legitimacy, and overall stability of a polity. Despite their historical thrust toward gradual centralization, Switzerland and the US have thus remained largely symmetric federations. This is also due to their generally moderate levels of mostly economic diversity. In the more heterogeneous Canadian and European unions, politicized regional self-rule demands and a relatively weak institutional position of central-level actors resulted in a more systematic recourse to accommodation. Even in comparison to the highly decentralized Canadian federation, however, the EU relies on differentiation to an extraordinary degree.

Second, when federal states accommodate diversity, they do so in other domains than the EU. Asymmetries in federal states occur primarily in identity-sensitive areas deemed vital for the preservation of cultural diversity in a union, e.g., language, education, culture, and migration policy. DI in the EU arises mostly in core state powers. These fields require central-level capacity-building to realize either explicit solidarity or implicit risk-sharing among constituent units. The possibility of differentiation, however, undermines multilevel polities' ability to organize solidarity and risk-sharing. In federal states, redistributive core state policies are thus either assigned uniformly to the federal level, or they are only centralized once all constituent units' consent. The protracted establishment of the—still highly devolved—Swiss welfare state provides a case in point. In Canada, central-level actors could not avoid initial differentiation in redistributive areas, in the establishment of the national pensions system, and the control of inward migration. They could, however, contain the adverse effects of asymmetry by means of long-term regulatory realignment.

Third, in place of asymmetric accommodation, federal states prefer to rely on the regulatory and redistributive reduction of territorial diversity. In this vein, federal states tend to combine union-wide regulation with extensive fiscal incentives. While the US government has not established a formalized fiscal equalization scheme, it relies heavily on categorical grants-in-aid to incentivize the states to comply with national policy objectives. Ultimately, its combined recourse to the regulatory and redistributive reduction of territorial diversity has set the US federal system on a long-term path towards enhanced stability. Both Switzerland and Canada, in turn, have established formalized equalization schemes that are supposed to ensure a comparable level of public service provision throughout both unions. In Canada especially, fiscal equalization has provided an important means at the union's disposal to contain regional demands for self-rule.

Fourth, it is due to its limited fiscal capacity that the EU has to rely on a combination of differentiation and rigid regulation. The Canadian case shows that extreme territorial diversity and weak central-level institutions alone cannot fully account for the extent and nature of the EU's extraordinary recourse to differentiation. Were the EU able to equip itself with the fiscal capacities necessary to tackle the root cause of its systemic malaise, i.e., the extreme economic and political diversity among its member states, it could loosen its regulatory grip of the internal market and the euro area, cut differentiation in core state powers, and avoid the dysfunctionalities that both these modes of integration entail. In this perspective, the 2020 Corona Recovery Instrument might point toward a novel stage in the EU's systemic development. In its quest to safeguard individual autonomy all while avoiding systemic collapse, will the EU be able to shift gradually from its current model of a rigid regulatory state to the more flexible model of a redistributive state that is able to reduce excessive territorial diversity by means of fiscally underwritten incentives?

PART 3

REVISITING THE EU'S CONSTITUTIONAL FOUNDATIONS

6

Governing by Judicial Fiat? Over-Constitutionalization and Its Constraints on EU Legislation

Susanne K. Schmidt

1. Introduction

In 2018, the reform of the posted workers directive (2018/957) was acclaimed a victory for social Europe, finally promising equal pay for equal work. But the important political achievement quickly looked imperilled, when Hungary and Poland, having lost out in the legislative negotiations, initiated an annulment procedure against the directive. The reform of posted workers, both member states argued among other things, infringed the freedom to provide services of the Treaty.

In late 2020, the European Court of Justice (ECJ) judged against both member states and accorded the EU legislature 'broad discretion' to reform the directive. This instance puts a spotlight on the little-explored relationship of the parallel venues of legislative and judicial policymaking in the EU. Political science analyses typically focus on the Court with view to enforcement, but rarely analyse how the status quo of the ECJ's case law impacts the legislative process. Also in the national context, legislation faces the constraints of judicial review. However, in the EU, the relationship between the ECJ and the legislature is much closer, given that the Court has a much broader mandate than that of national constitutional courts. The latter watch the national legislative process with a focus on the competences of the different institutions and individuals' fundamental rights. The different EU Treaties defining the ECJ's mandate, however, are policy-rich, they include different policy aims, such as the four freedoms. After its rulings established the Treaty's direct effect and supremacy in 1963/4, the ECJ could shape policy directly through its case law, for which the single market programme's reliance on the *Cassis* ruling

Susanne K. Schmidt, *Governing by Judicial Fiat? Over-Constitutionalization and Its Constraints on EU Legislation.*
In: *Autonomy without Collapse in a Better European Union.* Edited by Mark Dawson and Markus Jachtenfuchs,
Oxford University Press. © Oxford University Press (2022). DOI: 10.1093/oso/9780192897541.003.0006

is the best example. Grimm argues the EU to be over-constitutionalized, as policymaking can proceed without legislative majorities.[1]

In political science, the implications of over-constitutionalization for policymaking are predominantly discussed as a bias in favour of negative integration.[2] While the Court can unilaterally liberalize markets, re-regulation requires action by the EU legislature under demanding decision rules. Beyond, European integration research has paid little attention to the role of the Court in the policy process.[3] In EU law, there is increasing attention on the constraints that case law imposes on the integration process.[4] But interestingly, so far, legal scholarship has come to mixed results on how the Court's interpretation of the Treaty constrains subsequent policymaking of the EU legislature. Some authors deny any scope to deviate in legislation from the Court's Treaty interpretation, while others assume more leeway for the legislature.[5] The 'broad discretion', which the ECJ recently accorded, was all but common sense.

In an EU being faced with the need to grant more autonomy to deter collapse,[6] attention to the implications of over-constitutionalization seems particularly relevant. On the one hand, it is plausible to connect the populist challenge with the dominance of non-majoritarian decision-making in the EU,[7] of which the Court is a long-standing and important proponent. On the other hand, the lack of flexibility of EU governance is rooted in its judicial regime. Calls for decentralization and subsidiarity must fail in the light of the ECJ's extensive interpretation of free movement rights, of competition law, or citizenship. Accumulating case law on constitutional provisions implies rigidities, which neither the Court through jurisprudential about-turns nor member states via a revision of a Treaty can easily change. In this article, I analyse the interaction between judicial and legislative policymaking, drawing on different case studies from the case law on the freedom to provide services, free movement of workers, and citizenship.

[1] Grimm, *The Constitution of European Democracy* (Oxford University Press, 2017).

[2] Scharpf, 'Negative and positive integration in the political economy of European welfare states', in Gary Marks (ed.), *Governance in the European Union* (Sage, 1996).

[3] Schmidt, *The European Court of Justice and the Policy Process: The Shadow of Case Law* (Oxford University Press, 2018).

[4] Horsley, *The Court of Justice of the European Union as an Institutional Actor* (Cambridge University Press, 2018); Davies, 'Legislative control of the European Court of Justice', 51 *CMLR* (2014), 1579; Garben, 'Confronting the competence conundrum: Democratising the European Union through an expansion of its legislative powers', 35 *Oxford Journal of Legal Studies* (2014), 55.

[5] Höpner and Schmidt, 'Can we make the European fundamental freedoms less constraining? A literature review', 22 *Cambridge Yearbook of European Legal Studies* (2020), 182.

[6] Dawson and Jachtenfuchs, Chapter 1, this volume.

[7] Manow, *Die Politische Ökonomie des Populismus* (1st ed., Suhrkamp Verlag, 2018).

In the following, I start by elucidating where the ECJ's case law enters the EU legislative process, asking how the literature assesses the means of the legislature to override the Court. On this basis, I analyse in greater detail different forms of interaction between judicial and legislative policymaking, constructing a typology. Over-constitutionalization facilitated the progress of European integration; but analysing the interaction of case law and legislation shows drawbacks of continued legal uncertainty, waiting for judicial fiat. These consequences have been little recognized by political science and legal scholarship alike.

2. Beyond Negative Integration: Case Law and the EU's Legislative Process

Although the Court's importance for the integration process is widely acknowledged,[8] there is little attention to the relevance of its case law in the EU's legislative process. When analysing legislation, attention to the Court is paid mainly with view to the enforcement of legislative decisions.[9] While there is much recognition of the peculiarity of the EU's political system, with the Commission's formal monopoly of initiative,[10] there is little discussion of the role of the judicial branch. The Commission acts as the guardian of the Treaty, and will base its legislative proposals on case law as it stands. The legal service of the Commission is a powerful internal veto player when it comes to Commission proposals.[11] The European Parliament and the Council are similarly advised by their internal legal services on the feasibility of policy proposals given existing case law.

The bias of the Treaty towards free movement and competition law favours negative integration institutionally over positive integration.[12] If private actors can successfully claim in court that member states' market regulations hamper their transborder activities, even if only potentially or indirectly, EU law

[8] Weiler, 'The transformation of Europe', 100 *The Yale Law Journal* (1991), 2402; Pollack, 'Delegation, agency, and agenda setting in the European community', 51 *IO* (1997), 99; Alter, 'Who are the "masters of the treaty"?: European governments and the European Court of Justice', 52 *IO* (1998), 121.

[9] Börzel, Hofmann, and Panke, 'Caving in or sitting it out? Longitudinal patterns of non-compliance in the European Union', 16 *JEPP* (2012), 454.

[10] Kreppel and Oztas, 'Leading the band or just playing the tune? Reassessing the agenda-setting powers of the European Commission', 50 *CPS* (2016), 1118.

[11] Rasmussen, 'Establishing a constitutional practice of European law: the history of the legal service of the European executive, 1952–65', 21 *Contemporary European History* (2012), 375; Hartlapp, Metz, and Rauh, *Which Policy for Europe? Power and Conflict Inside the European Commission* (Oxford University Press, 2014).

[12] Scharpf, 'The joint-decision trap revisited', 44 *JCMS* (2006), 845.

may find a violation of the proportionality principle. In the 1970s, the Court established in the case *Dassonville* (case 8/74) that the free movement of goods has to be interpreted as prohibiting restrictions of this freedom, and this broad interpretation was subsequently applied to the other freedoms.[13] Whenever member states differ in their regulation of markets, private actors may be able to choose the most favourable regulatory setting, long discussed as the danger of a race to the bottom.[14] Regulatory competition also gives incentives for re-regulation (and positive integration) at the European level.

The former German constitutional judge Dieter Grimm coined the term 'over-constitutionalization' to capture the power of the Court in the EU.[15] Discussing the legitimation deficit of the EU polity, he emphasizes that the constitutionalization of material policy allows a non-majoritarian institution to substitute for majoritarian decision-making. The concomitant lack of voice within the EU system is reflected in populist challenges as well as in Brexit, showing the close connection to the danger of collapse. Before it is possible to discuss how over-constitutionalization impacts EU legislation, however, it is necessary to regard whether case law does not itself closely follow member states' political preferences, as some of the literature argues. Then it would not be much of a constraint for the legislature.

3. Reining in the Court? Member States' Influence over the Court

Direct effect and supremacy allow the ECJ to play the role of a constitutional court. It interprets the 'law of the land'. As with any constitutional court, the interpretation of the constitution adds onto the constitution's meaning.[16] The hierarchy of norms implies that secondary law cannot overrule primary law. If constitutional courts interpret the constitution in a way the legislature and the executive disagree with, two possibilities exist: changing the constitution (constitutional override)[17] or hoping that the constitutional court aligns its jurisprudence in the face of political contention.

[13] Tryfonidou, 'Further steps on the road to convergence among the market freedoms', 35 *ELR* (2010), 36; Schmidt (2018), *supra* note 4.

[14] Sun and Pelkmans, 'Regulatory competition in the single market', 33 *JCMS* (1995), 67.

[15] Grimm (2017), *supra* note 2.

[16] Kranenpohl, 'Die Bedeutung von Interpretationsmethoden und Dogmatik in der Entscheidungspraxis des Bundesverfassungsgerichts', 48 *Der Staat* (2009), 387.

[17] Larsson, 'Political and constitutional overrides: The case of the Court of Justice of European Union', 27 *JEPP* (2020), 1.

Constitutional courts also depend on the willingness of the other branches of government to follow their rulings.[18] Though political interests in the rule of law mean that even politically contentious judgments stand a good chance at implementation, any court has to be careful not to become too controversial. Political actors can adjust how they implement case law, and substitute sweeping legislative changes with 'justice contained'.[19] Already when courts encounter silent, let alone vocal, opposition to their rulings, this has the potential to undermine their legitimacy. Why turn to a court as litigant, if rulings show little effect? This dependence of the independent judiciary on the political branches applies to domestic and international courts alike, as Staton and Moore argue.[20]

In the EU context, broadly two literatures exist, one emphasizing the dependence, and one emphasizing the independence of the ECJ. Should over-constitutionalization result in constraints for the EU legislature, as I argue, this would point towards independence. It is therefore useful to present the counterfactual of such an analysis and focus on the literature emphasizing the Court's dependence on member states.[21] Predominantly, this dependence is analysed either with view to the influence of member states' preferences on the Court's jurisprudence (here the Court anticipates opposition), or by their means overriding Court decisions (the effect of such opposition).

Political science research lends empirical support to the view that the Court is attentive to member states' preferences, which these can make known via their submissions to the Court. Thus, Larsson and Naurin[22] find that rulings correspond to the position of member states in the integration dimension in 57 per cent of cases. This compares to 75 per cent correspondence with the Commission's position, a finding also supported by Carrubba and Gabel.[23] The match is explained with a separation of powers model, where the Court anticipates legislative override. Following Alter,[24] one could say that the findings

[18] Maravall, 'The Rule of Law as a Political Weapon', in Przeworski and Maravall (eds.), *Democracy and the Rule of Law* (Cambridge Studies in the Theory of Democracy, Cambridge University Press, 2003); Vanberg, 'Constitutional Courts in comparative perspective: A theoretical assessment', 18 *Annual Review of Political Science* (2015), 167.

[19] Conant, *Justice Contained. Law and Politics in the European Union* (Cornell University Press, 2002).

[20] Staton and Moore, 'Judicial power in domestic and international politics', 65 *International Organization* (2011), 553.

[21] Fearon, 'Counterfactuals and hypothesis testing in political science', 43 *World Politics* (1991), 169.

[22] Larsson and Naurin, 'Judicial independence and political uncertainty: how the risk of override impacts on the Court of Justice of the EU', 70 *IO* (2016), 1, at fn. 82.

[23] Carrubba and Gabel, *International Courts and the Performance of International Agreements: A General Theory with Evidence from the European Union* (Cambridge University Press, 2014), p. 134.

[24] Alter, *The New Terrain of International Law: Courts, Politics, Rights* (Princeton University Press, 2014), p. 338.

represent quite some disagreement with member states, as there is no reason to assume that courts consistently divert from member states' preferences.

Other research, including qualitative works, focuses directly on the possibility of member states to override ECJ decisions. Thus, Dorte Martinsen[25] analysed different cases of social policy legislation, arguing that European integration research overestimates the power of the Court. Distinguishing codification, modification, non-adoption, and override as strategies with which the EU legislator can react to the Court, she finds the intermediate reactions (modification and non-adoption) to be dominant. However, she combines cases where the Treaty is directly relevant (the freedom to provide services for patient mobility and posted workers) with an attempted reform of the Court's interpretation of secondary law (the working-time directive). The possible impact of over-constitutionalization is therefore not captured.

Larsson[26] argues that the discussion of override has conceptual flaws by not differentiating constitutional from political override. Under constitutional override, he suggests to analyse cases where the Court's mandate is altered in response, for which there are hardly any examples. Political overrides are those, where the policy implications of the Court are countered, happen more frequently. I agree that it is necessary to draw this distinction, but would argue, similar to my remark towards Martinsen, that it is crucial to distinguish whether the legislature attempts to override case law on secondary or on primary law. Larsson refers to the finding of Fjelstul[27] that only 33 per cent of the Court's rulings refer to Treaty articles, so that secondary law makes up the bulk in preliminary cases. But 33 per cent can hardly be dismissed, when the resulting case law may become relevant as precedent. One ruling like *Dassonville* or *Cassis de Dijon* (112/78) goes a long way, making a huge difference to European policies.

To summarize, over-constitutionalization allows the Court to impose (constitutional) constraints on EU policymaking that are absent at the national level. The Court cannot develop case law in total oblivion of political preferences, having to be careful that its rulings are being followed as well as anticipating potential override. But given the constitutional status of important case law development, the attention to member states' preferences does not tell us much about the Court's longer-term impact on policymaking. The difficulty of reacting via legislation will be analysed now.

[25] Martinsen, *An Ever More Powerful Court? The Political Constraints of Legal Integration in the European Union* (Oxford University Press, 2015).

[26] Larsson (2020), *supra* note 18.

[27] Fjelstul, 'The evolution of European Union law: A new data set on the Acquis Communautaire', 20 *EUP* (2019), 670, 685.

4. Legislating in the Shadow of Case Law

Case law interpreting the Treaty imposes constraints on subsequent legislation. Overrule, in this perspective of taking over-constitutionalization seriously, faces three types of difficulties: political, procedural, and legal.

Political difficulties are the ones most prominently discussed in the literature: whether or not constitutional aspects of case law are in focus, sufficient majorities for legislation are required for altering the status quo. Because it is always easier to keep than to change the status quo, there is a 'ratchet effect'.[28] Changes through case law are more likely to stay than to be altered again; this matters in particular when these changes would not have had the political majorities for their enactment in the first place.

Procedural difficulties are discussed less frequently. The Commission has the formal monopoly of initiative. In particular, when legislating in areas directly rooted in Treaty provisions, the Commission will follow the jurisprudence, which its legal service monitors and upholds. Often, the extent to which proposals are rooted in the case law is non-transparent as the Commission does not make explicit references to case law, this being deemed 'bad practice'.[29] The opinions of the legal services are not published.[30] Having the initiative allows the Commission to inscribe its interpretation of case law into the legislative proposals.

Last, but not least, there is the legal question of whether secondary law can overrule primary law. As mentioned in the introduction, EU law scholars come to mixed conclusions on the leeway of the EU legislature.[31] The 'broad discretion' accorded in the annulment case of the posted workers directive was a very welcome clarification that should inspire the EU legislator to feel less bound by previous case law: if the Commission presents a proposal and if there are political majorities.

Considering further the constraints of case law, it is important to take into account the multilevel character of the judicial–legislative dialogue taking place.[32] At the national level, courts interpret rules decided by legislatures, with

[28] Pollack, *The Engines of European Integration—Delegation, Agency, and Agenda Setting in the EU* (Oxford University Press, 2003).

[29] Lubow and Schmidt, 'A hidden champion? The European Court of Justice as an agenda-setter in the case of posted workers', *PA* (2020), 1, 10.

[30] Menéndez, 'The Strange Case of the Publicity of Brexit Legal Advice', *Verfassungsblog*, 12 December 2018. https://verfassungsblog.de/the-strange-case-of-the-publicity-of-the-brexit-legal-advice/ (accessed 4 April 2021).

[31] Höpner and Schmidt, *supra* note 6, at p. 9.

[32] I thank Fritz Scharpf for pointing me to this.

the latter often refining rules in response.[33] In the EU, it is rare that there is such a direct dialogue between the ECJ and the EU legislature. Rather, the Court responds to member states' courts interpreting national rules. The results of this case law then feed into the EU legislative process. Different institutional conditions in the member states make it difficult to assess the general implications of these rulings. The accumulating case law of the ECJ defining the Treaty poses the danger of judicially closing the available zone of agreement and of possible compromises for the EU legislature, constraining options for European secondary law. After enlargement, member states' preferences have become more heterogeneous. In the rare cases of direct interaction, the ECJ typically allows the EU legislature more leeway than it does towards national rules.[34]

5. Parallel Judicial and Legislative Policymaking

Over-constitutionalization allows parallel venues for EU policymaking. What does this interaction mean for governance at the EU level?[35] The focus will be on citizenship, individual free movement rights, and the services freedom. These areas of case law developed since the late 1990s in a very dynamic way, resulting in everyday repercussions as individuals are targeted. The interaction could similarly be analysed in other areas of EU law, for instance in competition law and procurement.[36] But note that in some areas of European law, the ECJ shows greater deference to the will of the member states, as Thym[37] analyses for migration policy, where case law hardly interferes with legislation.

I will analyse the interaction between case law and legislation in a temporal dimension, distinguishing several different cases that can form the basis for a typology. Typologies stand in the descriptive research tradition,[38] allowing

[33] Blauberger and Schmidt, 'Free movement, the welfare state, and the European Union's over-constitutionalization: administrating contradictions', 95 *PA* (2017), 437.

[34] Sørensen, 'Reconciling secondary legislation and the treaty rights of free movement', 36 *ELR* (2011) 339, 347.

[35] A focus on the member-state level would analyse the direct implementation of case law through national administrative practice and/or legislation.

[36] Blauberger and Weiss, '"If you can't beat me, join me!" How the commission pushed and pulled member states into legislating defence procurement', 20 *JEPP* (2013), 1120; Bovis, 'Developing public procurement regulation: jurisprudence and its influence on law making', 43 *CMLR* (2006), 461.

[37] Thym, 'Rolle des EuGH in der Migrationspolitik: zwischen "Verwaltungsethos" und "Verfassungsimagination"', 53 *Europarecht* (2018), 672.

[38] Gerring, 'Mere description', 42 *British Journal of Political Science* (2012), 721.

us to determine 'What is this a case of?'[39] Only then is it possible to engage in comparison, and thus in explanation.[40] In light of what was said about over-constitutionalization and the (in-)dependence of courts, much depends on the sequence of case law vis-à-vis legislation, so that this will be taken as basis for categorization. To start, (1) if the Court moved first, established case law principles may make legislation virtually impossible in an area; even if common rules were desirable (*foreclosure*). (2) The legislature may want to clarify the rules in a field but be reluctant to fully endorse the Court's case law, resulting in *regulatory gaps* between existing case law and the following secondary law. (3) The Court may be second to move and enter an area where secondary law already exists, but divert from it and create a parallel policy (*duplication*). (4) Finally, over-constitutionalization impacts the relationship between different pieces of legislation. It implies a greater likelihood of treaty principles determining the course of things as *lex superior*. Clarification between contradictory rules can then only be settled by the Court (*judicial fiat*), while in a national setting other rules of conflict are available. Table 6.1 depicts this typology based on sequence.

Table 6.1 The impact of over-constitutionalization on legislation

Type	First mover	Second mover	Third mover	Result
1) Foreclosure	Court	–	–	No legislation on desirable rules
2) Gaps	Court	Legislation without full codification		Legal uncertainty as to the precise reach of case law—legislation
3) Duplication	Legislature	Court establishes new regime	Legislature codifies case law	Two separate regimes regulate an area
4) Judicial fiat	Legislature	Legislature	Court has to determine relationship	Long-term legal uncertainty

[39] Bennett and Elman, 'Case study methods in the international relations subfield', 40 *Comparative Political Studies* (2007), 170, 181.

[40] Lieberson, 'Small N's and Big Conclusions: An Examination of the Reasoning in Comparative Studies Based on a Small Number of Cases', 70 *Social Forces* (1991), 307.

The interaction between legislatures and the judiciary is all but unusual. Laws will never be able to provide rules for all circumstances, they are incomplete contracts, which courts have to interpret, thereby developing the legislation's meaning.[41] Before analysing the different types of interaction, it is therefore useful to shortly address how we normally expect this dialogue to be.

6. A Standard Account of Legislative–Judicial Interaction

Does over-constitutionalization really lead to a special situation in the EU? As a backdrop, let us consider an example of how the interaction takes place at the national level. I will discuss below under 'gaps' and 'judicial fiat' that for several years it was unclear whether economically inactive EU citizens have the right to social benefits before having resided legally for five years in a member state. This is the context of the following example. After the ECJ finally gave a restrictive interpretation of the access to social benefits, the German Federal Social Court ruled in late 2015 that social support after six months of residence followed from German law (B 4 AS 44/15 R). In an unusual move, many lower social courts did not follow. Politicians at the municipal level much criticized the judgment's fiscal burden. The Federal Ministry of Labour responded within a year with a law that reinstated the five-year residence requirement.[42]

The case of the failed annulment procedure against the posted workers directive, referred to in the introduction, appears similar. The ECJ accorded the EU legislator broad discretion in shaping the posted workers regime and redressing social repercussions. However, in 2015 in a case originating from Finland (C-396/13), the ECJ had already ruled that minimum pay under the 1996 directive had to include elements such as travelling time, paving the way for the concept of remuneration in the reform directive. Just as the original directive was much influenced by case law (*Rush Portuguesa* C-113/89), it is thus not entirely clear how much discretion from case the EU legislator claimed for itself.[43]

[41] Stone Sweet, 'The European Court of Justice and the judicialization of EU governance', 5 *LREG* (2010), 1.
[42] Blauberger and Schmidt (2017), *supra* note 34, at pp. 446–447.
[43] Lubow and Schmidt (2010), *supra* note 30.

6.1 Foreclosing Legislation

When confronted with existing case law interpreting the Treaty, the EU legislature faces the political, procedural, and legal problems for legislating noted above. The status quo of case law is therefore likely to persist.[44] Any legislative compromise not reflecting constitutionalized case law as the default condition risks judicial challenges. Moreover, there is the risk for legislation being interpreted by the Court or member states' courts in the light of earlier case law.

As a thought experiment, one may consider what would happen were the EU legislature to define the term 'worker' in secondary legislation. Being a worker under EU law grants important privileges, for instance to economically inactive EU citizens that are.[45] In the case *Levin* (53/81), the Court argued that a worker is someone in 'pursuit of effective and genuine activities, to the exclusion of activities on such a small scale as to be regarded as purely marginal and ancillary'. In *Genc* (C-14/09) the Court accorded worker privileges, where only five hours weekly were worked.[46] The most recent ruling, C-483/17 *Tarola*, dealing with the worker status and access to unemployment benefits after a two-week contract, exemplifies ongoing open issues regarding the definition of workers.

Given economic heterogeneity and increasing labour mobility in the enlarged union, it may become politically important to define the threshold of the worker status more explicitly. But member states are affected in very different ways by the existing case law definition, given asymmetric movements and different structures of welfare states. Larsson notes that the citizenship directive 2004/38/EC of 2004 overruled the case *Ninni-Orasche* (C-413/01) by requiring a one-year employment for unlimited worker status.[47] Heterogeneous preferences between sending and receiving countries make such successful political settlement increasingly unlikely. Existing case law implies foreclosure. The Brexit discussion elucidated how much policy reforms of the Union are constrained by over-constitutionalization. After the compromise of the European Council on a 'new settlement' with the UK before the

[44] Scharpf (2006), *supra* note 13.

[45] Maas, 'European citizenship and free movement after Brexit', in Greer and Laible (eds.), *The European Union after Brexit* (Manchester University Press, 2020); Menéndez and Olsen, *Challenging European Citizenship: Ideas and Realities in Contrast* (Palgrave Pivot, 2020).

[46] O'Brien, Spaventa, and De Coninck, *Comparative Report 2015—The concept of worker under Article 45 TFEU and certain non-standard forms of employment* (European Commission, 2016), p. 16.

[47] Larsson (2020), *supra* note 18.

referendum,[48] there was much discussion whether the concessions were legal under the Treaty and could stand up to the Court.[49] Brexit, of course, illustrates at the same time the possible consequences of the lack of voice that over-constitutionalization implies; exit, and therefore collapse become more attractive.

6.2 Regulatory Gaps: The Citizenship Directive

The parallelism of judicial and legislative policymaking always risks that there are no political majorities in the EU legislature to follow and codify case law. Regulatory gaps result. A case in point is the citizenship directive that was agreed shortly before Eastern enlargement.[50] The directive establishes a gradual system of rights of EU citizens: for the first three months, EU citizens are free to settle anywhere in the Union, with no right to social assistance in the host member state. After five years of legal residence, EU citizens have equal rights. Between three months and five years of stay, EU citizens need to have sufficient financial resources and a comprehensive sickness insurance. However, financial assistance may not automatically end the right of residence (Article 14.3). This directly reflects the ruling in *Grzelczyk* (C-184/99, No. 43), which was issued in the midst of legislative negotiations in September 2001 and granted assistance already after three years. In the legislative process, member states were unwilling to follow the Court and to grant equal rights before five years of legal residence, but they could hardly fall behind *Grzelczyk* where the Court had demanded solidarity after three years, as long as this is not 'an unreasonable burden on the public finances of the host Member State' (No. 6).

Consequently, in a central aspect the directive could not provide clear guidelines on the rights of EU citizens. It took until 2014 and the *Dano* case (C-333/13) before the Court clearly followed the directive and the member states' interests in more restrictive access to benefits.[51] It is seen as a turning

[48] European Council, 'Conclusions—18 and 19 February 2016, EU/CO 16', February 2016. http://data.consilium.europa.eu/doc/document/ST-1-2016-INIT/en/pdf (accessed June 2021).

[49] Pulvirenti, 'A new settlement for the United Kingdom in the European Union: A new challenge to EU citizens' social benefits and freedom of movement?' 1 *EP* (2016), 727.

[50] Wasserfallen, 'The judiciary as legislator? How the European Court of Justice shapes policy-making in the European Union', 17 *JEPP* (2010), 1128.

[51] Thym, 'The Judicial Deconstruction of Union Citizenship', in Thym (ed.), *Questioning EU Citizenship Judges and the Limits of Free Movement and Solidarity in the EU* (Hart Publishing, 2017); van den Brink, 'EU citizenship and (fundamental) rights: Empirical, normative, and conceptual problems', 25 *European Law Journal* (2019), 21; Wollenschläger, 'Consolidating Union Citizenship: Residence

point. But was it that the ECJ only had the opportunity in 2014 to acknowledge these limits decided by the EU legislator? In earlier cases, such as *Vatsouras* (C-22-23/08), the Court appeared to disrespect the directive by classifying financial benefits not as 'social assistance' in the meaning of Article 24.2 of the directive but as easing the access of EU citizens to the labour market.[52] In *Brey* (C-140/12), the Court had demanded an individual assessment before denying the Austrian supplementary pension, a social assistance. *Dano* could thus reflect the increasingly politically controversial nature of far-reaching rights of economically inactive EU citizens,[53] or indicate the length of time needed for a case reaching the Court to clarify the interplay between the directive and Treaty obligations.

For a long time, a closely related question was whether access to social benefits in the host state could cover the required financial self-sufficiency. Here, rights under regulations 883/2004 and 987/2009 on the coordination of social security overlap with the citizenship directive, and I discuss this as an example of judicial fiat below.

6.3 Parallel Venues: Duplication in Patient Mobility

The parallel venues of judicial and legislative policymaking are not necessarily synchronized. In the citizenship directive as in many other important pieces of legislation, the EU legislature was confronted with existing case law. It moved too late. Given over-constitutionalization, however, the Court need not follow the first-moving legislator.

A well-known example is patient mobility. Starting in 1998, the ECJ interpreted patient mobility as being subject to the passive use of the services freedom, i.e., the freedom to consume services (C-120/95 *Kohll*), although regulation 1408/71 coordinating social security required a prior authorization. The Court simply stated that adhering to EU secondary law 'does not have the effect of removing that measure from the scope of the provisions of the Treaty' (No. 25), and went on to apply the services freedom. Other cases followed (C-157/99 *Smits/Peerbooms*, C-368/98 *Vanbraekel*, C-385/99 *Müller-Fauré & Van Riet*, C-372/04 *Watts*), putting member states

and Solidarity Rights for Jobseekers and the Economically Inactive in the Post-Dano Era', in Thym, op. cit.

[52] Barnard, *The Substantive Law of the EU: The Four Freedoms* (3rd ed., Oxford University Press, 2010), p. 285.

[53] Blauberger et al., 'ECJ Judges read the morning papers. Explaining the turnaround of European citizenship jurisprudence', 25 *JEPP* (2018), 1422.

increasingly under pressure of having to liberalize part of their health sectors.[54] Thus, although there was legislation on cross-border treatment, the Court chose to establish an alternative regime of realizing cross-border healthcare building on the Treaty.

Member states were interested in codifying this case law for several reasons. It allowed them to signal their preferences to the Court, and they felt pressured not to leave this instance of 'social Europe' to the Court.[55] Interestingly, there was no critical discussion that the Court had simply disregarded existing secondary law.[56] Codification was successful in 2011 with directive 2011/24/EU, but cross-border treatment faces several contradictions now, depending on whether it is based on the coordination regulations or on this directive.[57] The regulation requires ex-ante authorization and covers all cost, the directive covers only the cost of the equivalent treatment in the home country, thereby confusing cross-border patients.

'The existence of different routes of reimbursement has created complexity and confusion, not only for patients but also for providers and national administrations. Patients just want to access cross-border healthcare and be reimbursed. They do not understand the complexity of the current routes that require them to make choices.'[58]

The monitoring of the directive shows the large variation among member states in taking up the rules. Of the 157,063 outgoing patients without prior authorization (data from Germany lacking), 69,321 patients moved from France to Germany, Spain, and Italy.[59] This shows a very uneven impact after high costs of rule-making and implementation.

So far, I have discussed the interaction of judicial and legislative policymaking with view to the legislature being the second to move, leading to 'foreclosure' or 'gaps'. In 'duplication' the legislature moves first, but the Court constructs an alternative regulatory regime directly out of the Treaty. My final

[54] Kloka and Schmidt, 'Legislative and judicial politics in the post-Maastricht era', in Bickerton, Hodson, and Puetter (eds.), *The New Intergovernmentalism: States and Supranational Actors in the Post-Maastricht Era* (1st ed., Oxford University Press, 2015).

[55] Schmidt (2018), *supra* note 4, at p. 148.

[56] Kloka and Schmidt (2015), *supra* note 55, at p. 242.

[57] European Commission, 'REPORT FROM THE COMMISSION TO THE COUNCIL AND THE EUROPEAN PARLIAMENT compliant with the obligations foreseen under Article 20(3) of Directive 2011/24/EU of the European Parliament and of the Council of 9 March 2011 on the application of patients' rights in cross-border healthcare', February 2014. https://eur-lex.europa.eu/LexUriServ/LexUriServ.do?uri=COM:2014:0044:FIN:EN:PDF (accessed June 2021).

[58] Strban et al., *FreSsco Analytical Report 2016. Access to healthcare in cross-border situations* (European Commission, 2017), p. 50.

[59] Wilson and Andoulsi, 'European member state data cross-border patient flows based on Directive 2011/24/EU Year 2016', p. 15. https://ec.europa.eu/health/sites/health/files/cross_border_care/docs/ev_20171019_co01_en.pdf (accessed December 2020).

example of the problems resulting from over-constitutionalization concerns contradictions between different pieces of secondary law. When policy follows from the Treaty, only the Court can decide which rule to follow.

6.4 Contradictory Rules: Requiring Judicial Fiat

The rule of law and legal certainty require that different legislative acts coexist without contradiction. Every so often, such contradictions cannot be prevented. In the national context, conflict rules give direction as to which rule to apply under which circumstances: *lex specialis*, *lex posterior*, and *lex superior*. To my knowledge, it has not been discussed for the European polity whether over-constitutionalization does not prolong legal uncertainty regarding conflicts between legislative acts, because Treaty provisions are relevant so often, meaning *lex superior* is relevant. In an over-constitutionalized setting, how rules relate to each other therefore depends on judicial fiat.

I will give two examples of legal uncertainty linked to this *problematique*, both concerning how the citizenship directive 2004/38 and the regulation for the coordination of social security 883/2004 relate to each other. Both acts were adopted by the Council on the same day in 2004. The citizenship directive requires equal rights after five years having been financially self-sufficient and having comprehensive sickness insurance. The regulation determines the responsible member state for social security, on the basis, firstly, of *lex loci laboris*, the place of work, and secondly of the place of habitual residence. It is important to note that social assistance is excluded and left under exclusive national purview.[60]

These principles of social coordination led to the question of whether economically inactive EU citizens could rely on social security of the host state to cover the financial self-sufficiency requirement of the directive. This is the first example. The regulation gives the responsibility for the so-called SNCBs, special non-contributory benefits (tax financed social benefits complementing social security) to the country of residence. SNCBs cannot be exported to other member states.[61] This was agreed in council regulation 1247/92, after the Court had repeatedly lifted national restrictions on SNCBs. 'After 1992, it was no longer necessary to prove that the person claiming

[60] Martinsen (2015), *supra* note 26, at p. 88.

[61] Cornelissen, 'EU Regulations on the Coordination of Social Security Systems and Special Non-Contributory Benefits: A Source of Never-Ending Controversy', in Guild, Carrera, and Eisele (eds.), *Social Benefits and Migration: A Contested Relationship and Policy Challenge in the EU* (Centre for European Policy Studies (CEPS), 2013), p. 92.

the "special non-contributory" benefit in the member states of residence had previously worked there; he was entitled to be treated in the same way as nationals of the host state.'[62] Based on this view, social benefits of the host country could cover the directive's financial self-sufficiency requirement. The social security regulations were regarded as *lex specialis* to the directive (please note that regulation 883/2004 reformed 1408/71):

> This seems to be logical. Any other conclusion would make this special coordination system meaningless. If a person first had to prove that her or his residence in the host State is in line with the subsistence requirement under Directive 2004/38/EC before s/he could even claim a minimum subsistence benefit under Regulation 1408/71, it would never be possible for him/her to do so.[63]

The Commission shared this view.[64] Thus, the host state was assumed to grant social benefits (under the regulation), thereby assuring the financial self-sufficiency of economically inactive EU citizens, which the directive in Article 7.1b required to protect the finances of the same host state: 'not to become a burden on the social assistance system of the host Member State'.

Finally, different Court rulings (*Brey* C-140/12, *Dano* C-333/13, *Alimanovic* C-67/14, and *Garcia Nieto* C-299/14) settled the relationship of both pieces of legislation from 2013 onwards and gave priority to the restrictions of the directive. My argument is that over-constitutionalization requires the Court's interpretation of the *lex superior* more frequently than is the case in the national context. When policy is subject to secondary law only, conflicts can be settled with recourse to *lex specialis* or *posterior*. Legal uncertainty is a side effect of the dynamic interpretation of the EU Treaties by the ECJ, resulting in grave individual consequences in the case of economically inactive EU citizens.[65]

The Brexit process exemplified these very negative repercussions, which is my second example. Article 7 of the citizenship directive requires EU citizens to have a comprehensive sickness insurance (CSI) as a precondition for legal residence. The UK government considered that health cover through the NHS did not meet this requirement; after all, the rule was meant to protect the

[62] Cornelissen (2013), p. 104.

[63] Coucheir et al., *trESS think tank report 2008. The relationship and interaction between the coordination regulations and Directive 2004/38/EC* (Ghent University, 2008), p. 32.

[64] European Commission, *Explanatory Notes on Modernised Social Security Coordination. Regulations (EC) No 883/2004 & No 897/2009* (European Commission, 2011).

[65] Schmidt (2018), *supra* note 4.

public finances of the host state. But the Commission regarded access to the NHS as following from residence under the coordination regulations,[66] sending a reasoned opinion as part of an infringement procedure in 2012.[67] Access to healthcare in this view was part of the prohibition to discriminate along national lines.[68]

Because EU citizens could easily access the NHS, it was only when clarifying their long-term legal residence after the Brexit decision that many EU citizens learned about failing the requirement. Based on ordinary residence, access to the NHS was possible under the regulation. But the lack of a self-financed CSI implied that the five years of legal residence under the directive could not be met, even by EU citizens who had spent many more years living in the UK.[69]

While the UK agreed to lift this restriction for settled status after some time of political contention,[70] the saga of CSI appears ongoing for those EU citizens seeking naturalization.[71] The issue remains relevant for the EU after Brexit, with preliminary proceedings from Latvia (C-535/19), as well as from Northern Ireland (C-247/20) regarding access to healthcare. In the EU, the Court can still settle the matter by judicial fiat. For EU citizens in the UK, it would have been preferable had it been possible to settle the relationship between the regulation and the directive earlier. Were it not possible to draw so many rights directly from the over-constitutionalized Treaty, an earlier settlement of the question would have had a greater likelihood of success, I argue.

7. Conclusion

Case law is ever changing, and the relationship between the ECJ and the legislature is in constant flux. The ECJ that just recently accorded broad discretion to the EU legislator is the same that for long constructed an alternative health

[66] European Commission, *Explanatory Notes on Modernised Social Security Coordination. Regulations (EC) No 883/2004 & No 897/2009* (Brussels 2011), p. 5, at fn. 8. ec.europa.eu/social/BlobServlet?docId=6481&langId=en (accessed June 2021).

[67] European Commission, 'Free movement: Commission asks the UK to uphold EU citizens' rights', European Commission, 26 April 2012. https://ec.europa.eu/commission/presscorner/detail/en/IP_12_417 (accessed June 2021).

[68] Strban et al., *supra* note 59.

[69] Herbeć, 'The Scandal of CSI, the Little-Known Loophole Used to Deny EU Citizens Permanent Residency', LSE blog, 17 March 2017.

[70] Department of Health United Kingdom, *Guidance on Implementing the Overseas Visitor Hospital Charging Regulations 2015. Ways in which People Can Be Lawfully Resident in the UK* (Department of Health United Kingdom, 2016).

[71] McIndoe (Latitude Law), 'Naturalisation for EU citizens: comprehensive sickness insurance, the elephant in the room', electronic immigration network, 19 August 2020. https://www.ein.org.uk/blog/naturalisation-eu-citizens-comprehensive-sickness-insurance-elephant-room (accessed December 2020).

regime out of the Treaty, bypassing existing secondary law. At the national level, this would be highly unlikely, as the reaction to the German Federal Social Court exemplified. Over-constitutionalization implies that the Court's jurisprudence assures not only the implementation of agreed cooperation, but redefines the content of this cooperation, or indeed establishes alternative policy regimes via its case law. By interpreting laws, courts necessarily add on to their meaning. But many rules enjoy constitutional protection in the EU that are secondary law nationally. Thus, the legislature can hardly react to the Court with override. Being subject to few political checks and balances, judicial interpretation needs to be changed judicially.

With accumulating case law, much is already decided at the level of the EU's constitution, also implying a judicial closure of zones of agreement for legislative political compromises in a very heterogeneous EU. Under conditions of preference heterogeneity in a widened EU, over-constitutionalization may protect the 'deepened' integration, but Brexit shows how much it may also be a destabilizing force.

Focusing on the parallelism of judicial and legislative policymaking in a temporal dimension, I have distinguished several different types of how this interaction takes place, using examples from the area of citizenship and free movement. This allows a typology of this interaction. Case law of the Court may effectively *foreclose* subsequent legislation, though such rules would be politically beneficial. If there are no legislative majorities to codify already existing case law, there may be *regulatory gaps* left open, as can be seen with the citizenship directive. But even if there is secondary law, the Court may interpret rights directly out of the Treaty, leading to *duplication*, as happened with patient mobility. Finally, over-constitutionalization implies that in many policy areas the Court has to decide by judicial fiat how different rules relate to each other. Once over-constitutionalization gives relevance to *lex superior*, other conflict rules can no longer give direction. For individual beneficiaries of rights, extended periods of legal uncertainty while waiting for judicial fiat may well prove more disadvantageous than less far-reaching rights being known from the beginning.

Can my findings be generalized? I have mentioned that the level of influence the Court has over policymaking varies across policy fields. That the interaction leads to a duplication of policies as found in patient mobility is probably rare. But the other types are likely to be present in different areas in the broad context of the single market, and possibly also beyond.

The European Union is facing many crises and the threat of collapse. Among the many problems, over-constitutionalization receives little attention, though the dominance of non-majoritarian decision-making is intricately linked to the long-standing democracy deficit,[72] the more recent Brexit,[73] and rising populism. Different ideas exist how to de-constitutionalize the EU.[74] Supremacy and direct effect should imply that the substantive policy goals in the Treaty (four freedoms, EU citizenship, competition law) are exempted from this constitutional status in order to leave scope for majoritarian decision-making. Treaty changes are difficult to achieve, but incremental options appear feasible. The reform of the posted workers directive is an example of redefining the limits to the freedom to provide services to some extent: at least sufficiently far-reaching to lead Hungary and Poland to address the ECJ with an annulment procedure. That the Court accorded broad discretion to the EU legislature is a positive sign and one to keep in mind, when legislative proposals of the Commission simply aim at codifying case law, taking rulings of the ECJ to be set as much in stone as the Treaty itself. Integration has to be shaped by political majorities, in order to be better able to protect the autonomy of its members and to avoid collapse.[75]

[72] Grimm (2017), *supra* note 2.

[73] Menéndez and Olsen (2020), *supra* note 46.

[74] Höpner and Schmidt (2020), *supra* note 6.

[75] The research for this paper was originally financed by Norface, *Welfare State Futures*. Project Transjudfare (DFG: SCHM 2404/1-1), and subsequently by project B04 of the CRC 1342 (374666841). I would like to thank Fritz Scharpf for comments on a preliminary early draft. I benefited from comments on several occasions: the ECPR SGEU conference 2018 in Paris, EUSA 2019 in Denver, the Verbund 'Europäische Wirtschafts—und Sozialintegration' in 2021, notably Maximilian Kiecker, as well the Better Union project, in particular Mark Dawson.

7

Interpretative Pluralism and the Constitutionalization of the EU Legal Order

Gareth Davies

1. Resistance and the Search for Balance

The phenomenon of national resistance to transnational constitution-building has been growing in importance and attracting increasing scholarly attention.[1] It is the product of divided societies, a resurgence of local and national identity politics in the face of globalization, and a weakening of the idea that law and courts are in some sense outside of politics. This phenomenon is perhaps most richly and complexly displayed within the EU, where robust and deeply embedded ideologies, institutions, and laws exist at both national and European level, pulling towards the centre and away from it. The scene is set for a contest over the proper locus and degree of constitutionalization in which neither the optimal nor the actual outcome is a priori predictable, but it is beyond any reasonable doubt that the conflicts involved will be multiple and many-sided.

However, this framing in terms of oppositions should not lead to the conclusion that the final outcome is necessarily a win for one side. On the contrary, the centre and the decentral, the EU and the national, each have their own merits, whether economic, social, or political, and there is no reason to think that constitutionalization—the legitimate legal ordering of European space—will or should entail the subordination of one to the other in any clear-cut and generalized way. Rather, as with the *trias politica* and the concept of division of powers, it would seem more plausible to expect a move towards a nuanced and interactive system of balancing, of non-domination, in which domination of one locus in a specific sense is balanced by a capacity for subversion or alternative domination of the other. The European project is surely not an attempt to create an unassailable focus of power.

[1] Hirschl, 'Opting-out of "global constitutionalism"', 12 *Law and Ethics of Human Rights* (2018), 1; Hofmann, 'Resistance against the Court of Justice of the EU' (2018) iCourts Working Paper No 121.

Gareth Davies, *Interpretative Pluralism and the Constitutionalization of the EU Legal Order*. In: *Autonomy without Collapse in a Better European Union*. Edited by Mark Dawson and Markus Jachtenfuchs, Oxford University Press. © Oxford University Press (2022). DOI: 10.1093/oso/9780192897541.003.0007

The law is, however, sometimes thought to be different from politics: in law there is an attraction to simplicity, and to the idea of hierarchy, and even to the idea of the final court—a body that truly does have the last word and is, in that sense, itself above the law. Yet even while this state of affairs sometimes seems to exist within a given jurisdiction, the formal truths of the legal system usually give—as ever—a misleading picture of the actual distribution of legal power. For one thing, supreme courts are typically balanced by a legislature, that can steer, challenge, and, some scholars like to suggest, even override unwelcome judicial decisions.[2] For another, disagreement between judges is a part of every legal system, if not a part of every legal textbook, as is complexity and case-specificity. A powerful ruling by a supreme court does not generally suffice to wipe out the capacity of other courts to avoid, subvert, or even ignore the supreme court view. De facto, law is certainly created by courts, but it is created by them collectively, such that no supreme court acting alone and without lower court sympathies can create the state of law in society that corresponds to its pronounced doctrine.[3]

This is not a bug—it is a feature. Certainly, lower courts running rampant and ignoring higher jurisprudence would represent a problematic situation of legal uncertainty. However, lower courts that did no more than implement higher decisions in a state of unthinking loyalty would represent a state of over-centralized judicial dictatorship, a situation in which the legislature and executive powers were balanced not by the judiciary, or the legal system, but by a handful of men and women appointed for life and beyond control or accountability.[4] Their dependence on the support of lower courts is a legitimating factor within the legal system.[5] That constitutional descriptions sometimes work with an ideal type of uncontaminated hierarchy is not because of the normative force of that model, but because of its descriptive simplicity. It is the legal equivalent of models of human behaviour used by economists; necessary simplifications that can help us model the architecture of a system but can also deceive us about that architecture if we start to believe they are true.

[2] Davies, 'Legislative control of the European Court of Justice', 51 *CMLRev* (2004), 1579; Dawson, 'Constitutional dialogue between courts and legislatures in the European Union: Prospects and limits', 19 *European Public Law* (2013), 2; Larsson and Naurin, 'Judicial Independence and political uncertainty: How the risk of override affects the Court of Justice of the EU', 70 *International Organization* (2016), 377.

[3] Hirschl (2018), *supra* note 1; Hofmann (2018), *supra* note 1; Murphy, 'Lower court checks on Supreme Court power', 53 *The American Political Science Review* (1959), 1017.

[4] Stith, 'Securing the rule of law through interpretative pluralism: An argument from comparative law', 35 *Hastings Constitutional Law Quarterly* (2018), 401.

[5] Rosenfeld, 'Comparing constitutional review by the European Court of Justice and the US Supreme Court', 4 *International Journal of Constitutional Law* (2006), 618.

The ideal state, and indeed the actual state, of legal power structures is thus one of permanent compromise. One should not wish for the final elimination of the pull in one direction, nor even for a stable balance, for what is optimal in one moment of history may not be optimal in another. For this same reason, one should not perhaps even hope for a stable process of balancing, for process is itself part of politics, and the way in which the levels, directions, and actors of politics and law interact must surely itself be a product of context and so of the age. In short, unless the world stops changing, there seems little sense in hoping that any aspect of the legal system can be carved in stone, and where that is attempted, it will merely create tensions and obstacles.

However, not all change is equally fast. The rhythm of the pendulum swing between centralization and decentralization might be measured in decades, but the rhythm of the changes in how we interact and think about institutions may be somewhat slower. There may have been a time, and it may come again, when mechanisms for dialogue between loci of power will seem inadequate and inappropriate, and the way that power balance is achieved will have to change. However, as long as the EU exists, it would seem to be arguably a premise that there is a prevailing willingness to engage between the European and national levels, and to do so in a way that seeks common ground rather than merely seeking to achieve primacy. To that extent, one may suggest that for the moment it is desirable to find a frame and a mechanism that allows courts at national and European level to communicate effectively, in a way that stimulates and facilitates response to the concerns and views of the other, and in a way that allows for change and dynamism without this becoming destructive of the legal order.[6]

2. Autonomy without Collapse

That search belongs in the wider context of the tension that this book addresses: between national autonomy and European collapse. There is a widespread recognition that national autonomy serves many goals, and not just the obvious local identitarian and communitarian ones.[7] Above all, it facilitates diversity and experiment in the social and economic sphere.[8] Policies adapted to the peculiarities of individual member states contribute

[6] Bobić, 'Constructive versus destructive conflict: Taking stock of the recent constitutional jurisprudence in the EU', 22 *Cambridge Yearbook of European Legal Studies* (2020), 60.

[7] Davies, 'Subsidiarity: The wrong idea, in the wrong place, at the wrong time', 43 *Common Market Law Review* (2006), 63.

[8] Van den Bergh, 'Subsidiarity as an economic demarcation principle and the emergence of European private law', 5(2) *Maastricht Journal of European and Comparative Law* (1998), 129.

to efficiency and effectiveness. A range of different policies within the EU contributes to mutual learning and progress, while allowing for specialization and increasing synergies between the member states.[9] A well-functioning EU is not a uniform one. At the same time, diversity of rules and policies between member states creates problems for movement and interaction, hinders cooperation, and reduces efficiency and well-being which that cooperation might have enhanced. This then in turn encourages fragmentation and alienation. If member states are entirely free, they will drift, or break, apart.[10] Finding the right compromise is a perennial challenge for the EU, particularly urgent in a time of widespread dissatisfaction.

Constitutional law, in its broadest sense, is a normative frame that may be superimposed on all these issues of societal well-being. Constitutional or supreme courts have thus played an important role in describing the tensions inherent in integration and in explaining the norms applicable to the management of those tensions. Drawing on their own constitutions primarily, but also on their understanding of EU law, they have set out their own limits to EU policies and laws, and to the authority of the European Court of Justice.[11] These judgments, many of them famous, have a role that is both conservative and destabilizing. On the one hand, they draw lines around the EU, protecting member states from interference beyond what they consider legally legitimate. This is the conservative function. However, they also, in doing this, nudge the EU into change, sometimes incremental and sometimes significant.[12] The EU's internal human rights doctrine has its origin in a need to overcome resistance by the German Federal Constitutional Court (FCC), while the approach of the European Central Bank (ECB) to bond-buying and the European Court of Justice's (ECJ's) understanding of the right to be forgotten are both currently being nudged by that same obstinate FCC.[13] Finally, the limit-setting judgments of courts such as the FCC also create domestic change, perhaps

[9] Deakin, 'Legal diversity and regulatory competition: Which model for Europe?' 12 *European Law Journal* (2006), 440.

[10] Davies, 'European Union citizenship and the sorting of Europe', 43(1) *Journal of European Integration* (2021), 49.

[11] Bobić, 'Constitutional pluralism is not dead: An analysis of interactions between constitutional courts of member states and the European Court of Justice', 18 *German Law Journal* (2017), 1395.

[12] Fasone, 'Constitutional amendments' theory and troubles at supranational level: Constitutional change in the EU from the perspective of Richard Albert's analysis', 7(3) *Revista de Investigações Constitucionais* (2020), 707.

[13] Tzanakopoulos, 'Judicial Dialogue in Multi-Level Governance: The Impact of the Solange Argument', in Fauchald and Nollkaemper (eds.), *The Practice Of International And National Courts And The (De-)Fragmentation Of International Law* (Hart, 2012), p. 185; Petric, 'Methodological Solange, or the Spirit of PSPP', Europeanlawblog.eu, 18 June 2020; Bobić, 'Developments in The EU-German judicial love story: The right to be forgotten II', 21 *German Law Journal* (2020), 31.

less obviously, but no less importantly. In drawing their lines, they create new interpretations of their own constitutions, and indeed of their national identities and values.[14] While resistance judgments may be presented as a defence of the national constitutional status quo, they are inevitably also an amendment of it, and may even be more than that, perhaps even a dismemberment of it.[15] For the demands of EU law can be considerable, and are typically outside of the conventional concerns envisaged in a traditional constitution. In offering a constitutional interpretation which reasonably accommodates but also constrains European institutions—for most national supreme courts have not engaged in unmitigated hostility, but in compromise and negotiation with the ECJ—constitutional courts go into novel terrain, and if they manage to stick to some of their constitutional values, they almost inevitably do so at the cost of others. This is inevitable because EU integration is a process of adapting to the choices made by peoples and institutions that do not belong to the nation, whereas constitutions, even if, like the German one, they contain EU clauses, are in most of their provisions aimed at reflecting, preserving, and embodying the nation. Constitutional resistance, in all but its most extreme and closed forms, is also constitutional reinvention.

3. Framing Judicial Resistance in Europe

Normative analysis of the stand-offs and tensions between the European Court of Justice and national supreme and constitutional courts typically revolves around a handful of interrelated, overlapping, and almost aspirational concepts: democracy, legitimacy, identity, legality, and, for some, efficiency.[16] Wielding these does not tell us who should get their way in any given conflict, but it provides a frame for that question which appears unexceptionable: it shows the goods to be measured and the issues that have to be addressed. The concepts delineate a more or less common normative core.[17]

[14] Dani, 'National constitutional courts in supranational litigation: A contextual analysis', 23 *ELJ* (2017), 189.

[15] Fasone (2020), *supra* note 12.

[16] Kumm, 'The jurisprudence of constitutional cConflict', 11 *ELJ* (2005), 262; Maduro, 'Three Claims of Constitutional Pluralism', in Avbelj and Komárek (eds.), *Constitutional Pluralism in the European Union and Beyond* (Hart, 2012), p. 67.

[17] Bobić (2020), *supra* note 6; Lawrence, 'Constitutional pluralism's unspoken normative core', 21 *Cambridge Yearbook of European Legal Studies* (2019), 24; Eijsbouts and Besselink, '"The Law of Laws"—Overcoming Pluralism', 4(3) *EuConst* (2008), 395.

The fact that this core leaves ample space for substantive disagreement could be experienced as unsatisfying, however, and might encourage a dive into the concepts in greater depth, to try and establish what is more democratic, or who is more legitimate, and so on: to take sides. Instead, the thrust of most recent scholarship has been to avoid this question, and model a kind of adaptive, heterarchical constitutionalism, for which the conventional name is now pluralism.[18] They embrace the idea of differing opinions at the highest level not as an obstacle on the way to a constitutionally optimal legal order, but as a part of one. The inability of either the European Court of Justice or national constitutional courts to effectively subdue and dominate the other is not seen as a failure of either side, but as a triumph of their composite whole.[19]

However, there is an element of President Johnson's philosophy of camping in pluralism.[20] It brings the conflict into the tent. While that may be advantageous, it also, in doing so, gives that conflict a central place in what may be a limited constitutional space. Thinking about ECJ and national constitutional court relations has become, to quite a large extent, an institutional question of who prevails. For those who move beyond the person to the law, the focus has been on which law prevails, the constitution or the Treaties, these texts being a proxy for their respective courts, and vice versa.[21] This follows naturally, since it is largely taken as self-evident that the highest court of each legal order owns the texts of that order; at least in relation to courts of other orders, if perhaps not in relation to the legislature. The constitution is the kingdom on behalf of which the judge-princes go to war. There is a border between legal orders, and while peace treaties may be signed, they remain ultimately other. This is the oppositional, somewhat macho way of thinking about inter-court relations to which constitutional pluralism offers its high-functioning Cold War solution.[22]

[18] E.g. Walker, 'The idea of constitutional pluralism', 65 *The Modern Law Review* (2002), 317; Maduro (2012), *supra* note 16; Kumm (2005), *supra* note 16; Fichera, 'Securing the European project: From self-referentiality to heterarchy', 21 *Cambridge Yearbook of European Legal Studies* (2019), 273.

[19] Ibid. Maduro; ibid. Fichera. Although, cf., e.g., Somek, 'Monism: A Tale of the Undead', *U Iowa Legal Studies Research Paper* (2010) No. 10-22; Kelemen, 'On the unsustainability of constitutional pluralism', 23 *Maastricht Journal of European and Comparative Law* (2016), 136; Eleftheriadis, 'Pluralism and Integrity', 23 *Ratio Juris* (2010), 365.

[20] See Halberstam, 'The Vantage Point Perspectives of the Presidency 1963–1969. By Lyndon Baines Johnson. Illustrated. 636 pp. New York: Holt, Rinehart and Winston. $15.', *New York Times*, 31 October 1971.

[21] Davies, 'Does the Court of Justice own the Treaties? Interpretative pluralism as a solution to over-constitutionalisation', 24 *ELJ* (2018), 358.

[22] Davies, 'Interpretative Pluralism within EU Law', in Davies and Avbelj (eds.), *Research Handbook on Legal Pluralism and EU Law* (Edward Elgar, 2018), p. 323; Goldoni, 'Constitutional pluralism and the question of the European common good', 18 *European Law Journal* (2012), 38.

4. Interpretative Pluralism

Disagreements between courts cannot of course simply be wished away. The substantive difference in viewpoints needs to be identified, and if we are scholars, discussed, or for policymakers, addressed. However, it can be helpful not to lose sight of what is also agreed upon, or could be agreed upon, both from the point of view of understanding the conflict and in order to manage it. Interpretative pluralism tries to see judicial disagreements in terms of different views of a shared body of law, rather than in terms of two bodies of law each put forward as a candidate for primacy.[23]

It rests on a few premises. One is that both EU law and national constitutions are part of a shared legal order and the legitimacy of both should be accepted by EU and national courts. Another is that there is almost never, perhaps never, any need for a conflict between these two bodies of higher law, as they are sufficiently open-textured and value-laden that they can be read to be compatible with each other. The third is that this reconciliation of the texts is to a great extent the task of national constitutional courts. While the ECJ should certainly show respect for national constitutions, these are less accessible to it, each being rooted in a specific national context. By contrast, EU law belongs to all the courts of the EU, and is fully accessible to national constitutional courts, who should be involved in its formation and development.

These three premises lead to a conclusion on how conflicts should be approached. It can nevertheless happen that the ECJ and, for example, the FCC, fundamentally disagree on how a situation should be resolved. Their sense of constitutional values and priorities may lead them to different conclusions. It would be somewhat artificial to say that these disagreements are the product of the law, as all forms of higher law leave so much space to the court that they are vehicles for decisions rather than generators of them. A constitutional decision is an expression of values in the language of constitutional principles. Not all courts balance and assess values in the same way.

Thus, in such a situation of value conflict, a court such as the FCC should, rather than holding up its constitution to defend its views against the Treaties, start from the premise that both the constitution and EU law are legitimate and binding, and should read them in a way that reconciles them and preserves the

[23] Stith, 'Securing the Rule of Law through Interpretative Pluralism: An Argument from Comparative Law', 35 *Hastings Constitutional Law Quarterly* (2008), 401; Davies (2018), *supra* note 21; Goldoni, 'The Pluralist Turn and its Political Discontents', in Priban (ed.), *The Self-Constitution of European Society* (Routledge, 2016), p. 116; Habermas, 'Some comments on "Interpretative Pluralism"', 16 *Ratio Juris* (2003), 187.

values that they consider essential. This may indeed lead them to reject the view of the ECJ, but what they will be rejecting is not the application of EU law, or the validity of EU law, but rather the particular interpretation offered from Luxembourg. The texts will not be in issue, but the two highest courts will disagree on their meaning.

The novelty of this idea, if novelty there be, is that it rejects the idea that only the ECJ can interpret EU law, or that its interpretations are definitive and binding on all other courts.[24] It embraces the idea that national constitutional courts are co-owners of EU law. It suggests that there is a single, composite, legal system with multiple supreme courts. That is not entirely unlike the case in many member states, which have separate highest courts for civil and constitutional matters, who also often bicker similarly about outcomes in a multi-step game kind of way.

I have argued elsewhere that interpretative pluralism is constitutionally more satisfying than the alternatives.[25] In this chapter, I suggest that it also helps bring coherence, and indeed legitimacy, to the preliminary reference procedure and to the mechanics of inter-court relations.

However, before making that argument, it should be noted that it is both a normative and a descriptive 'theory'. It is normative in the sense that I argue that this is how courts *should* behave and *should* look at EU law and at disagreements with the ECJ. The 'should', the normative claim, is based on accepted ideas about what courts do, and their legitimacy and proper limits, as well as on the desire to achieve constructive and well-being–enhancing European integration. If one accepts those normative premises, then I suggest it leads to interpretative, rather than constitutional, pluralism.

It is descriptive in that, to some extent, this is what courts already do. That extent varies between courts, over time, and from case to case. However, there is no doubt that one can see, at times, a significant engagement with the substance of EU law by national courts, most strikingly perhaps in the recent *Weiss* and *Right to Be Forgotten* judgments by the FCC.[26] National constitutional courts sometimes just push EU law away when they don't like it, but sometimes they engage with it seriously, and thinking in terms of interpretative pluralism

[24] See Case C-446/98 *Fazenda Pubblica* ECLI:EU:C:2000:691; Case C-69/85 *Wünsche* ECLI:EU:C:1986:104; Case C-445/05 *Haderer* ECLI:EU:C:2007:344; Schilling, 'The autonomy of the community legal order: An analysis of possible foundations', 37 *Harvard International Law Journal* (1996), 389.

[25] Davies (2018) *supra* note 21.

[26] BVerfG, Judgment of the Second Senate of 5 May 2020–2 BvR 859/15, ECLI:DE:BVerfG:2020:rs20200505.2bvr085915; BVerfG, Order of the First Senate of 6 November 2019–1 BvR 276/17, ECLI:DE:BVerfG:2019:rs20191106.1bvr027617.

helps us see the distinction between those situations. Lawyers should not treat cases where a national court says 'our constitution won't allow that—EU law cannot apply' as analytically similar to cases where they say to the ECJ 'your interpretation of EU law is unacceptable—here is a better one.' Politically, there may be a similarity, in terms of the institutional opposition and the sporting question of who will win in the case, but legally they represent different situations, and the scholarship does not distinguish between them with adequate clarity. Law is not just about outcomes: it is also about arguments and process.

5. The Problems of Preliminary References

The reference procedure is a central part of the construction and maintenance of EU law, and it is hard to see how it could be replaced or removed. An EU court brings obvious added value to a legal system that would otherwise be radically fragmented, and the only immediately apparent alternative way for it to interact with national courts, via appeals, is as unacceptable now as it was when it was rejected in the 1950s.[27] It is not just a question of the pride of national final courts that prevents them subordinating themselves to the ECJ, but a question of the relative legitimacy of the national and European levels of governance. As the FCC noted early on, a full absorption of the state within a hierarchically superior European order does not have a sufficient social basis for it to be democratically legitimate, with as a necessary consequence that the courts of the national order also cannot be placed in a position of simple subordination.[28] Yet the opposing alternative, a simple subordination of the EU to national constitutional courts, is no more than a rejection of the contract of membership, and facile in the extreme: we'll follow the rules unless we really don't want to.[29] A more complex, and almost certainly ambiguous, solution is inevitably required.[30]

Interpretative pluralism thus rejects the Court's view that its answers are definitive and binding on all courts, even national apex courts, and override even national constitutions. That would amount to a legal revolution, the

[27] European Commission 'Report by the Working Party on the Future of the European Communities' Court System' (Jan 2000), in Dashwood and Johnston (eds.), *the Future of the Judicial System of the European Union* (Hart, 2001), p. 1.

[28] Solange I—Internationale Handelsgesellschaft von Einfuhr—und Vorratsstelle für Getreide und Futtermittel, decision of 29 May 1974, BVerfGE 37, 271 [1974] CMLR 540.

[29] Davies, 'Constitutional Disagreement in Europe and the Search for Pluralism', in Komarek and Avbelj (eds.), *Constitutional Pluralism in the European Union and Beyond* (Hart, 2012), p. 269.

[30] Dani, 'National constitutional courts in supranational litigation: A contextual analysis', 23 *ELJ* (2017), 189;

creation of a fully-fledged legal order, but one arising by judicial fiat rather than political process. It would also be a violation of the principle of conferral, since no organization limited to conferred powers can also have *kompetenz-komptenz*, which is what final interpretative authority would amount to.[31] The Court's view of its own authority, and of the authority of EU law, is constitutionally repugnant.

Yet interpretative pluralism also rejects the approach taken by many national apex courts that their own constitutions offer a viable and legitimate means of resistance to unwelcome incursions of EU law. This is incompatible with the binding nature of a Treaty obligation. Admittedly the national identity article of the TEU, Article 4 TEU, requires a respect for the constitutional particularities of each member state, but the fact that this article is in the Treaty shows that this respect is to be a negotiated process in which the EU is involved.[32] It is not recognizing a pre-existing opt-out, which would be done via a declaration, but creating one, and in that sense it is a step towards the harmonization of constitutional values; that which the EU wishes to Europeanize, it first makes a derogation.[33]

The middle way that interpretative pluralism offers is that both Treaties and constitutions are legitimate and binding law which must be read as a coherent whole, reflecting the composite values of both.[34] This is primarily the task of national constitutional courts, but they are obliged to refer questions of EU law to the ECJ because it can provide a uniquely positioned understanding of the EU interests and EU law as a whole. The ECJ is genuinely cooperating with and assisting the national court in achieving a result, not simply dictating to it. Instead of two courts laying down their respective, and non-comparable, red lines, interpretative pluralism allows them to engage in discussion of a shared law.

One merit of this approach is its constitutional coherence, as mentioned above and discussed elsewhere.[35] Another is its realism: it reflects the actual and desirable relationship of these texts and courts: coexistence and mutual influence, not hierarchy.[36] Another is that it invites national constitutional

[31] Beck, 'The Lisbon Judgment of the German Constitutional Court, the primacy of EU law and the problem of Kompetenz-Kompetenz: A conflict between right and right in which there is no praetor', 17 *ELJ* (2011), 470; *Lisbon* judgment of the BverfG, 2 BvE, 2/08, 30 June 2009, ECLI:DE:BVerfG:2009:es20090630.2bve000208; Schilling (1996) *supra* note 24; *Honeywell* judgment of the BverfG, 2 BvR 2661/06, 6 July 2010, ECLI:DE:BVerfG:2010:rs20100706.2bvr266106.

[32] Martinico, 'The "polemical" spirit of European constitutional law: On the importance of conflicts in EU Law', 16 *German Law Journal* (2015), 1343.

[33] Case C-260/89 *Elliniki Radiophonia Tiléorassi* ECLI:EU:C:1991:254.

[34] Similarly, Eleftheriadis (2010), *supra* note 19; Maduro (2012), *supra* note 16.

[35] Davies (2018), *supra* note 21.

[36] Rossi, 'The Principle of Equality Among Member States of the European Union', in Rossi and Casolari (eds.), *The Principle of Equality in EU Law* (Springer, 2017), p. 10; Maduro (2012), *supra* note

courts to seriously think about the meaning of the Treaties and of European integration, rather than only about the meaning of their national constitutions. This expansion of the horizon of national apex courts is surely an essential step in the Europeanization of national legal orders; in the integration of Europe. Finally, it has the potential to improve the quality of communication between the ECJ and national apex courts. If they swap views on the meaning of a text they share, their interaction is more transparent, more constructive, and more satisfyingly deliberative than if they present their standpoints as outside the competence of the other.[37] The ECJ changed the meaning of EU law in response to the FCC's interpretation of its constitution in the *Solange* saga. It would have been a discursively richer exchange if their respective views had been anchored in common texts, if the FCC had suggested that surely the Treaties must be read to contain a human rights doctrine, and the Court had agreed.

However, despite all these conciliatory merits, interpretative pluralism runs up against the traditional fear of the non-binding reference. This is something that the Court has always been wary of, for fear that the uniformity of EU law, as well as its own status, would be undermined if judicial underlings disagreed with it.[38] On a more macro level, it is widely accepted that the binding quality of ECJ judgments is important to the uniformity of EU law, and without that uniformity not just the coherence of the legal order but its political sustainability would be in danger.[39] It is, after all, a deal, and everyone needs to have the same terms.[40] The fear is that autonomy of interpretation would lead to legal and political collapse.

6. What Makes EU Law Uniform?

There would still be some mechanisms for enforcing a central interpretation of EU law. The direct action against a member state would allow the EU to sue member states whose courts adopted interpretations that it considered fundamentally at odds with the Treaty, and in this case the Court of Justice would

16; Kirchhof, 'The balance of powers between national and European institutions', 5 *European Law Journal* (1999), 225.

[37] Habermas, 'Democracy in Europe', 21 *European Law Journal* (2015), 546; Ghavanini, 'Power talk: Effects of inter-court disagreement on legal reasoning in the preliminary reference procedure', 5 *European Papers* (2020), 887.

[38] See, e.g., Krommendijk, 'Wide open and unguarded stand our gates: The CJEU and references for a preliminary ruling in purely internal situations', 18 *German Law Journal* (2017), 1359.

[39] Lenaerts, Maselis, and Gutman, *EU Procedural Law* (Oxford University Press, 2014), p. 245.

[40] Phelan, *In Place of Inter-State Retaliation. The European Union's Rejection of WTO-Style Trade Sanctions and Trade Remedies* (Oxford University Press, 2015)

have the last word.[41] However, as in any legal system, the limited resources of highest courts mean that not all deviant lower ones can be called to order. Just as not all cases are appealed, even where they might be, not all interpretations can be brought before the ECJ.

In that sense, interpretative pluralism relies on goodwill. It works if national apex courts take their obligations to the EU seriously, and take the ECJ seriously, and do not merely wallow in the national constitutional status quo. That seems weak, particularly in a time where national identity politics is resurgent. Yet it is less different from the current situation than one might think. For one thing, this chapter confines itself to highest courts, the situation of lower courts may be more nuanced, and in any case, if the national apex court is on board then they are likely to follow.[42] But then, we see that the current claim that national apex courts are bound is not backed by reality anyway: the ECJ cannot compel them to follow it, and sometimes they do not.[43] Even under the doctrine as it is, the direct influence of the ECJ on national apex courts works by appeal to their judicial integrity and acceptance of EU law. It would not really be such a big change to acknowledge a capacity to deviate that they already robustly assert and use. The real difference would be that this capacity would be steered into a different form; instead of the rejection of EU law in favour of the constitution, they would be encouraged towards a reinterpretation of it.

As well as the communicative merits discussed above, this raises the question of what we mean by the uniformity of EU law. For in a situation of interpretative pluralism it is a premise that the text is accepted by all parties. The law, in its formal sense, is uniform—unlike the current situation, where national constitutions limit EU law to varying extents and thus create a variable scope of its application. It is only interpretations that vary.

To a common lawyer that might seem like sophism, since the interpretation is, in a practical sense, the rule. However, in civil law countries it is not unusual to assert the interpretative independence of the judiciary, and to treat the law as consisting in legislation, not in judicial decisions.

Certainly, that can lead to diversity of outcomes, where apparently analytically similar situations are adjudged differently in different courtrooms. Yet this happens in all legal systems to some degree. Judges vary. Provided the judiciary is honest and trained, and there is the possibility of appeal, such variation

[41] Davies (2018), *supra* note 21.

[42] Alter, 'The European Court's political power', 19 *West European Politics* (1996), 458; Golub 'The politics of judicial discretion: Rethinking the interaction between national courts and the European Court of Justice', 19 *West European Politics* (1996), 360.

[43] Somek (2010), *supra* note 19.

can be kept within socially acceptable bounds, and can even be an asset, as it allows for legal change and development.[44] It is quite common for long-term and systematic differences to exist between how certain courts decide certain kinds of cases; say between regions, or levels of court, or branches of the judiciary. Eventually, sometimes, something gives, and a higher doctrine is adapted to lower pressure, or a disobedient lower branch is brought into line.

The mere fact of judicial variation is not a problem. It only becomes one when it becomes excessive. The fact that too much autonomy may lead to collapse is not a persuasive argument against autonomy as such, but merely for its effective management.

A shared text is a powerful binding and even integrative factor.[45] It creates legal uniformity in a very meaningful sense. From the point of view of symbolism, and creating a common commitment and sense of belonging, it may be more important than ensuring uniform interpretations, for interpretation in a given case is often a slippery and complex thing, and the possibilities for distinguishing each fact set are endless. It is the shared framing principles, combined with a belief in the honesty of those who apply them, which create constitutional loyalty. Interpretative pluralism, in placing the text much more centrally than the individual decision, offers a chance to give powerful meaning to the idea of a shared EU law; to strengthen the very idea that it could be accused of weakening.

Another way of putting this, is to say that the sense of commitment to EU law, for which uniformity is considered so important, can be increased by increasing a sense of ownership of that law. This, in turn, can be stimulated by focusing on the principles which the Treaties proclaim, and encouraging, demanding, that national apex courts engage fully with these, and give them meaning. Only when they can interpret the law will it be theirs.

7. Brexit, Exit, and Voice

The management of diversity has become particularly relevant as a result of Brexit. While the UK experience is hardly inspiring to others at the moment, they have shown that leaving genuinely is possible, and is no longer something that can be laughed away. It may not seem an attractive option, but an option

44 Lasser, 'Anticipating three models of judicial control, debate and legitimacy: the European Court of Justice, the Cour de cassation and the United States Supreme Court,' NYU Jean Monnet Working Paper No. 1/03 (2003).

45 Grimm, 'Integration by constitution', 3 *International Journal of Constitutional Law* (2005), 193.

it is. That raises frightening new prospects for the fragmentation and collapse of the EU and creates an extra imperative to manage the tensions within it.

Yet the lessons which it offers for courts and law pull in different directions. On the one hand, the possibility of leaving reduces the justification for blunt constitutional resistance to the Court. If a state feels that the EU is at odds with its most fundamental values, the honest thing to do is to leave. If it chooses to be in, it should obey the rules.[46] Constitutional resistance is at its most legitimate when membership is seen as something irreversible, as a destiny.[47] If we have to be here, then surely we have the right to fight for a space within that fits us. Post-Brexit, one could argue that constitutional courts should tone down their rhetoric.

Yet this is not an entirely convincing argument, because leaving is all or nothing. It allows no response to the smaller, but still important, constitutional incursions, ones which do not justify an exit but are too important to be ignored. Precisely these are the matters which come before constitutional courts.

In any case, 'if you don't like it you can leave' is hardly an attractive argument for the EU itself, which does not want more member states to follow the British. In its own interest, Brexit provides an encouragement to be more responsive to genuinely felt concerns. Now is not the time to scold deviants, but to let them be heard. Collapse can come from suppression of autonomy as well as its excess.[48] Interpretative pluralism—in that it is a participatory approach to law, and by encouraging the expression of national concerns in the language of EU law helps them to be recognized and integrated—is a doctrine for a more empathetic post-Brexit age.

8. The FCC's Turn to EU Law

The discussions of the actual relations between national constitutional courts and the ECJ are extensive.[49] Nevertheless, the fact that both sides have been consistent in their claims to definitive authority, but neither fully engages with the legal position of the other, has led scholars to understandably focus

[46] Kelemen (2016), *supra* note 19.

[47] Klabbers, 'On Babies, Bathwater and the Three Musketeers, or the Beginning of the End of European Integration', in Heiskanen and Kulovesi (eds.), *Function and Future of European Law* (Helsinki: Helsinki University Press, 1999), p. 275.

[48] See discussion in Delavalle, '"Top-down" vs. "bottom-up": A dichotomy of paradigms for the legitimation of public power in the EU', 9 *Perspectives on Federalism* (2017), 18.

[49] E.g. Bobić (2017), *supra* note 11; Martinico (2015), *supra* note 32; Dani (2017), *supra* note 14; Komárek, 'The place of constitutional courts in the EU', 9 *Eur Const L Rev* (2013), 420.

on meta-analysis of the stand-off rather than on the nuances of each court's reasoning towards its standpoint. When an apex court takes a stand and will not be moved—cannot be moved—then this standpoint can come to seem like a legal fact that must be accepted, and the 'why' becomes less urgent than the 'what'.

However, reasoning can change even while decisions remain apparently the same. A reason to look at those nuances is because it is here that one can see movement, of a potentially important kind. Taking the FCC as an example—as the ECJ's leading interlocutor—it has not wavered an inch since its first *Solange* cases on the question of relative institutional authority. It claimed and claims the authority to overrule the ECJ, as does that European court vice versa.[50] When the FCC moved to a looser supervision of human rights in EU law, it did not do so because it was conceding limits to its powers, but as a question of *noblesse oblige*; it considered the ECJ was doing a sufficiently good job that it could be given some freedom, which freedom would only be curtailed by the FCC if it was misused.[51] The underlying hierarchy was robustly present in this delegatory gesture, just as it is in the recent cases on EMU and the euro.

However, in the early *Solange* cases it was the constitution that was the FCC's sole crutch. It rested on the values and authority deriving from this to justify the potential exclusion of EU law from application in Germany. The reasoning was clear and simple, in as much as any FCC judgment can ever be described in those terms: EU law has force in Germany only on condition that complies with the constitution.[52] On the question of what EU law was, the FCC claimed no authority. Inherent in the logic of the warning that without sufficient human rights protection EU law would not be applied was, firstly, acceptance that the ECJ was the court to determine the proper meaning of EU law, and secondly, acceptance that EU law could, potentially, have a meaning that conflicted with the constitution. These are both perfectly logical conclusions if EU law is treated as an essentially alien law, a jurisdiction to which Germany is connected, but with which it is not fully integrated.[53]

[50] Case C-399/11 *Melloni* ECLI:EU:C:2013:107; Kumm, 'Rebel without a good cause: Karlsruhe's misguided attempt to draw the CJEU into a game of "chicken" and what the CJEU might do about it', 15 *German Law Journal* (2014), 203.

[51] *Re Wünsche Handelsgesellschaft* (Solange II), judgment of 22 October 1986, BVerfGE 73, 339, 2 BvR 197/83, 3 C.M.L.R. 225 (1987).

[52] Kumm (2014), *supra* note 50.

[53] See also Goldoni, 'Constitutional pluralism and the question of the European common good', 18 *European Law Journal* (2012), 38.

The development of its *ultra vires* case law, some years later, shows a shift.[54] On the one hand, the basis for the FCC's limits to EU powers was still constitutional: EU powers beyond this cannot be accepted because they violate constitutional norms. In that sense it relies on the same logic as the *Solange* cases. However, the use of the term *ultra vires* implies change. The FCC is not just saying that a certain exercise of power would violate the constitution, but also saying that such an exercise would violate EU law's own terms, in that it would be *ultra vires*. While the reasoning is constitutional,[55] one could argue that the decision by the FCC to speak about what the Treaty itself properly allows, and not just what the constitution allows, represents the beginning of a shift towards claiming interpretative jurisdiction over EU law itself.[56]

That comes to a degree of fruition in more recent cases. The *Right to Be Forgotten* judgments of the FCC have attracted attention for the interpretation of that right which they put forward. They accept the application of the *Right to Be Forgotten*, but suggest an understanding of it which is not quite the same as that which the ECJ put forward. Most importantly, they seek to integrate the Charter of Fundamental Rights into the German Constitutional Frame, on the one hand showing openness to EU law, but also, in doing so, bringing it within their interpretative jurisdiction.[57]

However, a more dramatic step towards engagement with EU law came in *Weiss*, the recent FCC judgment on price stability. There has been plenty written about the substance of the case, which will not be addressed here.[58] However, the FCC was distinctly upset about the ECB's 'whatever it takes' approach to achieving monetary policy goals, which it regarded as allowing the ECB to act beyond its proper powers. It asked the ECJ to consider the matter, but the ECJ came to the conclusion that the ECB's actions were lawful and not—using the concept which came to be central—disproportionate.[59]

[54] Möllers, 'German Federal Constitutional Court: Constitutional ultra vires review of European acts only under exceptional circumstances; decision of 6 July 2010, 2 BvR 2661/06, Honeywell', 7 *European Constitutional Law Review* (2011), 161.

[55] Craig, 'The ECJ and ultra vires action: A conceptual analysis', 48 *Common Market Law Review* (2011), 395.

[56] Ibid.

[57] Rauchegger, 'National Constitutional Courts as guardians of the charter: A comparative appraisal of the German federal Constitutional Court's right to be forgotten judgments', 22 *Cambridge Yearbook of European Legal Studies* (2020), 258; Friedl, 'A new European fundamental rights court: The German Constitutional Court on the right to be forgotten', 5(1) *European Papers* (2020), 447; Thym, 'Friendly takeover, or: the power of the "first word". The German Constitutional Court embraces the Charter of Fundamental Rights as a standard of domestic judicial review', 16 *European Constitutional Law Review* (2020), 2.

[58] See, e.g., contributions to 'Special Section: "The German Federal Constitutional Court's PSPP Judgment"', 21 *German Law Journal* (2020); References and discussion in Bobić (2020), *supra* note 6.

[59] Davies, 'The German Constitutional Court Decides Price Stability May Not Be Worth Its Price', Europeanlawblog.eu, 21 May 2020; See also *supra* note 58.

The FCC decided to reject this, and to state that if the ECB did not show persuasively that its measures were proportionate, and that it had taken into account the proper considerations in reaching this conclusion, then it—the FCC—would prevent German institutions from taking part in the relevant policy structures.[60]

The important part is not, ultimately, the threat, which came to nothing. The FCC chose to make a procedural demand, and such demands are not terribly hard to meet; one considers all the factors that one has been asked to consider, with all due care, and then comes to the same conclusion. Thus, although the FCC chose a highly confrontational tone, its attack must be understood as more to do with the ECJ than the ECB. The Public Sector Purchasing Programme was barely disturbed. It is the ECJ that, for the first time, was actually rebuffed by the FCC in specific case, and told that its view of EU law was wrong.

That decision was only possible because the FCC engaged with EU law. It could have followed its familiar constitutional arguments, and to be fair, it did, resorting to democracy and the self-rule of the German people and so on. But it also went beyond this. Rather than just subjecting the ECJ's reading of the Treaties to a constitutional test, it also considered whether it was a correct interpretation of EU law and came to the conclusion that it was not. The FCC engaged in a lengthy consideration of proportionality as a matter of EU law and came to the conclusion that the ECJ's understanding of it was untenable and must be rejected.[61] There was thus no question of unacceptable EU law. Rather, there was a question of institutions not correctly complying with EU law as a result of the ECJ misunderstanding it.

The FCC has not attracted much support for its view of EU law. While it accused the ECJ of being incomprehensible, most readers will find it considerably less so than the FCC's judgment was. However, where FCC deserves credit, is that it ventured beyond its constitutional safe zone, and engaged substantively with the meaning of EU law. It did not walk away when things got difficult—when EU law got constitutionally difficult—but tried to make them better.

As part of an integrated Europe, Germany is part of the European legal order, and EU law is part of the German legal order. The highest court of the land in every member state has the responsibility to contribute to the harmonization and integration of its constitution and the EU Treaties, by explaining how they can be read to fit. If it just sticks to its constitution, and leaves the

[60] Ibid.
[61] Ibid.

Treaties to the ECJ, then there is no body providing the holistic thinking that a European legal order needs. If national constitutional interpretation of EU law is done arrogantly, without respect for the distinctive EU nature of that law, it will not contribute much.[62] But in *Weiss*, despite the lengthy bombast, and a not terribly precise or coherent style of argument, the FCC did express an important and legitimate critique of how proportionality was understood by the ECJ, offering a different and more conservative reading. Even its procedural approach can be seen as constructive: it allows its understanding of proportionality to be integrated into the law of the ECB without this having any disruptive consequences, thereby softening the blow.

That is not to say that the ECJ will accept the FCC's interpretation. It may simply ignore it, or take small conciliatory steps over the coming years. There is likely to be quite a voyage ahead before an interpretative consensus is reached. However, for the first time in the two courts' decades of negotiation, they are talking directly and explicitly about the same thing, not just arguing past each other, but with each other. If one wants to build a European constitutional order, that can surely be seen as a step on the way.

[62] Cloots, 'Germs of pluralist adjudication: *Advocaten Voor De Wereld* and other references from the Belgian Constitutional Court', 47(3) *Common Market Law Review* (2010), 645.

8

Forging Identity-Based Constructive Constitutional Conflict in the European Union

Ana Bobić

1. Introduction

Both the 'national identity' clause reflected in today's Article 4(2) TEU and the economic and monetary union (EMU) were first introduced in the Maastricht Treaty in 1992.[1] The national identity clause lies at the intersection between the inclination towards integration, while preserving national particularities and interests. In EU's economic governance, the tension translates to the relationship between member states' preservation of national budgetary autonomy embedded in the no-bailout clause and the prohibition of monetary financing, in opposition to the need to manage a shared currency area through a common central bank. In other words, this set-up is reflective of the autonomy preserving tendencies of member states. Yet, placing the national identity clause in the Treaties allows for a constitutional treatment of the issue and its placement within the judicial realm, allowing for constitutional interpretation in solving demands for national autonomy and avoiding the possibility of collapse or disintegration that might ensue following the lack of sufficient agreement in the political realm. Accordingly, this contribution aims to present the ways in which this tension materializes itself in constitutional conflict in the monetary field.

The analysis will be based on the premise that the EU's constitutional set-up is characterized by a permanent, regular presence of constitutional conflict: it is not a bug, but a feature of the system's functioning. However, this does not

[1] See also, de Witte, 'The Lisbon Treaty and National Constitutions: More or Less Europeanisation?', in Closa (ed.), *The Lisbon Treaty and National Constitutions: Europeanisation and Democratic Implications* (Oslo: Centre for European Studies, 2009), p. 34.

Ana Bobić, *Forging Identity-Based Constructive Constitutional Conflict in the European Union.* In: *Autonomy without Collapse in a Better European Union.* Edited by Mark Dawson and Markus Jachtenfuchs. Oxford University Press.
 DOI: 10.1093/oso/9780192897541.003.0008

mean that every instance of conflict is a feature of the system, as it also exceptionally experiences bugs: the analysis employed will thus test the boundary between conflict that is constructive and one that is destructive for the EU's monetary field, and the EU's constitutional space more broadly. Placed in the framework of autonomy demands from the national level, it will be shown that some constitutional conflicts cannot be mediated through constitutional interpretation and may lead to collapse. Such destructive conflicts are exceptionally rare, however, and only occur in the event of a severe disregard of the basic constitutional values that all the member states share with the EU, codified in Article 2 TEU.

Constitutional conflicts in the EU materialize themselves in three main areas: competence control (*ultra vires* review), fundamental rights review, and identity review.[2] In this context, in this chapter I will focus on constitutional conflicts stemming from the national reliance on the national identity clause in Article 4(2) TEU and analyse their constructive or destructive potential. While the literature emphasizes that identity review carries dangers to integration and is inherently autonomy-conducive,[3] I argue that the use of Article 4(2) TEU as a limit to the application of primacy of EU law does not lead to collapse in the pursuit of national autonomy. Rather, it creates a Union-wide procedure for determining the use of Article 4(2) TEU and enables member states to invoke each other's case law and practice in order to reinforce the national identity clause. Understood in this way, a proper implementation of the national identity clause and conducting identity review can in fact contribute to a further connection between national constitutional jurisdictions throughout the EU. This is so because it acknowledges national constitutional demands for autonomy, while at the same time granting them constitutional relevance and a platform for reasonable disagreement through a number of interpretative methods at the EU level. This ensures that national constitutional concerns are given proper consideration at the EU level, while at the same time preventing an escalation in the way they are interpreted and applied. That is to say, the principles guiding judicial interactions will in the majority of cases lead to an outcome that prevents destructive conflict and the ensuing collapse.

[2] Bobić, *The Jurisprudence of Constitutional Conflict in the European Union* (Oxford University Press, 2022).

[3] Most prominently Kelemen and Pech, 'The uses and abuses of constitutional pluralism: Undermining the rule of law in the name of constitutional identity in Hungary and Poland', 21 *Cambridge Yearbook of European Legal Studies* (2019), 59.

In what follows, I will first explore the EU's constitutional structure and the characteristics that render it prone to constitutional conflict (section 2). Taking into account the contested nature of the EU's constitutional authority from the national level, specifically enhanced by the national identity clause in Article 4(2) TEU, I will set out the concepts of constructive and destructive conflict. The third section will explore in more detail the way that conflicts unfold in the area of identity review. This section will also underline the destructive potential of conflicts rooted in identity-based contestation from the national level. Next, the fourth section will offer a broad-brush proposal on managing identity conflicts within the confines of constructive conflict. I will then turn to the examination of constitutional conflict in the monetary field, namely the conflict between national identity and the prohibition of monetary financing as interpreted by the Court of Justice (section 5). The concluding section will summarize the lessons learned from identity-based conflicts in the monetary field to be applied to the broader relationship between national autonomy demands and integration.

2. EU's Constitutional Structure and Its Contested Nature

The failure of the Constitutional Treaty in 2000 may have prevented the EU from acquiring a formal, written constitution, but this hardly resulted in permanently depriving the EU from developing constitutional features, and more generally, a small 'c' constitution in the broad sense of the term,[4] one that regulates the main features of the polity.[5] In my understanding, a definition of the 'constitutional' in the European Union includes both what the Court of Justice calls 'essential characteristics of EU law',[6] but also contributions from the national constitutional spheres of twenty-seven member states. Accordingly, and crucially for understanding the challenges the EU is currently facing and its capacity to address them, contestation from the national level is considered

[4] The Court of Justice called the system of the Treaties the EU's 'constitutional charter' in Case 294/83, *Les Verts*, EU:C:1986:166, para 23. For Lenaerts, this was an undisputed fact back in 1990. Lenaerts, 'Constitutionalism and the many faces of federalism', 38(2) *American Journal of Comparative Law* (1990), 205, 210. See also, Stein, 'Lawyers, judges, and the making of a transnational constitution', 75(1) *American Journal of International Law* (1981), 1.

[5] On the written/unwritten, as well as political/legal understanding of the concept of the constitution, see Pek, 'Things better left unwritten?: Constitutional text and the rule of law', 83 *New York University Law Review* (2008), 1979.

[6] Case C-284/16, *Achmea*, EU:C:2018:158, para 33; Case C-621/18, *Wightman*, EU:C:2018:999, para 45.

the permanent condition and feature of the EU's constitutional structure.[7] I will therefore explore the basic structure of the EU as a shared constitutional space and the types of conflicts that shape its development. In addition, I will also address what content found in the EU's constitutional sphere cannot be done away with for the system to function.

Recalling Maduro's work on principles of contrapunctual law, the EU's constitutional essentials include those values and principles that 'make it possible for the processes of justification of national and European decisions to be based on different arguments while their actual application leads to compatible decisions'.[8] He continues, 'it is however necessary to create a set of rules that is shared by the different legal systems in putting forward and applying their different claims of authority.'[9] In ascertaining this set of rules in the EU's constitutional sphere, the case law of the Court of Justice is instructive, as it develops in more detail the autonomy of EU law and its essential characteristics. In *Achmea*, the Court gives an outline of the EU's idiosyncratic constitutional frame:

> EU law is characterised by the fact that it stems from an independent source of law, the Treaties, by its primacy over the laws of the Member States, and by the direct effect of a whole series of provisions which are applicable to their nationals and to the Member States themselves. Those characteristics have given rise to a structured network of principles, rules and mutually interdependent legal relations binding the European Union and its Member States reciprocally as well as binding its Member States to each other.[10]

For these principles and values to actually apply, the Court of Justice underlined the centrality of judicial enforcement of EU law to individuals, in cooperation with national courts.[11] In that sense, EU citizens are, in addition to member states, the beneficiaries and direct addressees of EU law. The Court of Justice has, since the early days of European integration, established the so-called '*Simmenthal* mandate', according to which each national court must apply EU law to cases within their jurisdiction and protect the rights

[7] Stone Sweet, 'A cosmopolitan legal order: Constitutional pluralism and rights adjudication in Europe', 1(1) *Global Constitutionalism* (2012), p. 53.

[8] Maduro, 'Contrapunctual Law: Europe's Constitutional Pluralism in Action' in Walker (ed.), *Sovereignty in Transition* (Hart Publishing, 2003), p. 524.

[9] Ibid., p. 525.

[10] Case C-284/16 *Achmea, supra* note 6, para 33.

[11] Ibid., para 36.

that it accords to citizens in their entirety.[12] This set-up created an idiosyncratic constitutional space shared by EU and national constitutional law, and by extension, the Court of Justice and national (constitutional) courts. It is well established, empirically, that what we can thus observe is a heterarchical relationship between different loci of constitutional authority. More specifically, this means there is no predetermined hierarchy, but each of the sites of constitutional authority possesses the ability to be ranked in a number of different ways in different points in time.[13] I have argued elsewhere that the courts taking part in these interactions are aware of this constellation, and that this is normatively desirable for the incremental development of the EU's constitution, broadly defined.[14]

Furthermore, the definition of the EU's essential constitutional characteristics is impossible to spell out without emphasizing its interconnectedness with member states, and their own structures which form a constitutional network of mutual reciprocity, all grounded in the principle of sincere cooperation.[15] Having described the relationship between the different sources of constitutional authority, the Court of Justice also provided the content that is shared and reciprocally applicable between them:

> EU law is thus based on the fundamental premiss that each Member State shares with all the other Member States, and recognises that they share with it, a set of common values on which the EU is founded, as stated in Article 2 TEU.[16]

The shared nature of EU constitutionalism therefore inevitably includes the contributions from the national level, which translates also to the obligation of the EU to respect national identities of its member states. In my earlier work, I have distinguished two types of constitutional conflicts that are taking place in the EU: constructive and destructive. The operation of the system of constitutional pluralism provides insight into how this distinction works: the 'constitutional' determines the basis that cannot be questioned by different sites of ultimate authority. The shared basis of the constitutional in the

[12] Claes, *The National Courts' Mandate in the European Constitution* (Hart Publishing, 2006), p. 108.

[13] See, on heterarchy more generally, Crumley, 'Heterarchy and the analysis of complex societies', 6 *Archaeological Papers of the American Anthropological Association* (1995) 1, 3.

[14] Bobić, 'Constitutional pluralism is not dead: An analysis of interactions between the European Court of Justice and constitutional courts of Member States', 18(6) *German Law Journal* (2017), 1395, 1423. See also the contribution of Gareth Davies in Chapter 7 of this volume.

[15] Case C-284/16, *Achmea, supra* note 6, para 34.

[16] Ibid., para 34.

EU is codified in Article 2 TEU which, as mentioned above, lists the values common to all member states, forming the basis of their membership. These values operate as the normative ideal of constitutional pluralism, without resulting in an ultimately monist solution. As the text of the provision itself states, the values listed therein are common to all member states, and represent the basis for EU membership, in the same way as a geographical link to the European continent, satisfying certain economic criteria, etc. This does not lead to homogenization of national constitutions and their content, but rather serves as a codification and a common denominator of their shared values and reduces the incommensurability of constitutional concepts in substance.[17]

In addition, the 'pluralist' element tells us how far reasonable disagreement concerning the 'constitutional' can go in order to remain within the realm of a constructive conflict, as oppose to turning into one of a destructive nature. In other words, we may not be in agreement as to the precise extent of, for example, the rule of law, or how it influences judicial independence in one or another constitutional and institutional context, but we can be in agreement what falls *outside* its borders. In this process, Maduro stresses the importance of the discursive element between different sites of constitutional authority, who jointly and coherently strive to create the shared European legal space.[18] The next section zooms in on identity-based conflicts more specifically.

3. Identity-Based Constitutional Conflicts

The national identity clause in Article 4(2) TEU, introduced first in the Maastricht Treaty in 1992, lies at the intersection between the essential characteristics of EU law demanding primacy of EU law over the laws of member states, and the supremacy of national constitutions in sovereign member states. Reliance on the clause by the Court of Justice has been limited, confined mainly to its use as a public policy justification of a member state's failure to respect EU law obligations.[19] In essence, Article 4(2) TEU is a substantive expression of autonomy demands in the form of national constitutional

[17] Christiansen and Reh, *Constitutionalizing the European Union* (Macmillan International, 2009), p. 27. See also Lenaerts and Wójcik, 'Judges Should Be Fully Insulated from Any Sort of Pressure', Verfassungsblog (2020), https://verfassungsblog.de/judges-should-be-fully-insulated-from-any-sort-of-pressure (all sites last accessed 21 May 2021).

[18] Maduro *supra* note 8, pp. 513–14, 518.

[19] Representative of this logic is the recent decision of the Court of Justice concerning the recognition of same-sex marriages in Romania. Case C-673/16, *Coman*, EU:C:2018:385.

concerns[20] and its aim is to minimize future constitutional, as well as institutional, conflicts.

Beyond the formal expression in the Lisbon Treaty, in the wider constitutional dialogue of the EU, the terms 'national' and 'constitutional' identity have been used as synonyms.[21] However, in its first preliminary reference to the Court of Justice, the *Bundesverfassungsgericht* stated that the terms were not interchangeable, and, more importantly, that the protection of constitutional identity of a member state falls within exclusive national jurisdiction.[22] Constitutional identity is thus a concept developed by national constitutional courts in the process of identity review, as one of the heads of review in the area of constitutional conflict. Constitutional adjudicators have referred to constitutional identity with the aim of determining constitutional limits to the primacy of Union law, and have thus reasserted their own position in the judicial triangle between ordinary national courts and the Court of Justice.

On the EU level, the Court of Justice has not, in interpreting Article 4(2) TEU, declared national identity an autonomous concept of EU law. In situations where a certain concept in EU law requires interpretation, and no reference is made to national law, the Court of Justice grants it an autonomous interpretation to be uniformly applied in all member states.[23] Advocate General Maduro argued that national identity is a legal concept shared between the EU and the national level, given that its content is to be defined by the national level (this will predominantly be constitutional courts),[24] while the Court of Justice controls the compliance with fundamental rights and the objectives of EU law.[25] Article 4(2) TEU does indeed make reference to national constitutional structures, and it would be counterintuitive to define it as an

[20] For an analysis of the introduction of national constitutional concepts in the Constitutional Treaty, see Ziller, 'National constitutional concepts in the new Constitution for Europe', 1(2) *EuConst* (2005), 247.

[21] Opinion of Advocate General Maduro in Case C-53/04, *Marrosu*, EU:C:2006:569, para 40. See also Besselink, 'National and constitutional identity before and after Lisbon', 6(3) *ULRev* (2010), 36, 37; Rodin, 'National identity and market freedoms after the Treaty of Lisbon', 7 *CYELP* (2011), 11; von Bogdandy and Schill, 'Overcoming absolute primacy: respect for national identity under the Lisbon Treaty', 48 *CMLRev* (2011), 1417, 1435; van der Schyff, 'The constitutional relationship between the European Union and its Member States: the role of national identity in article 4(2) TEU', 37(5) *ELRev* (2012), 563, 568.

[22] Case 2 BvR 2728/13 *Gauweiler*, Order of 14 January 2014, para 29.

[23] See, for example, Case C-516/19, *NMI Technologietransfer GmbH v EuroNorm GmbH*, EU:C:2020:754, para 45. For a broader analysis concerning autonomous concepts of EU law, see Mancano, 'Judicial harmonisation through autonomous concepts of European Union Law: The example of the European Arrest Warrant Framework decision', 43(1) *ELRev* (2018), 69.

[24] He stated that: 'Those authorities are best placed to define the constitutional identity of the Member States which the European Union has undertaken to respect.' Opinion of Advocate General Maduro in *Marrosu*, *supra* note 21, para 40.

[25] Ibid.

autonomous concept of EU law with identical meaning in all member states.[26] Rather, it is inherent in the purpose of this provision that it accounts for the diverse constitutional structures across member states. Importantly, this also means that the provision concerns the structural constitutional solutions, rather than substantive values.[27]

Fabbrini has argued that the principle of primacy must be applied without exceptions to all member states, so as to preserve the multilateral, rather than a bilateral, framework of the Union constitutional order.[28] In contrast, I argue that the use of Article 4(2) TEU as an exception to the primacy of EU law would not reduce the EU's constitutional order to bilateral relations between individual countries and the EU. It would create a Union-wide procedure for determining the limits to Article 4(2) TEU, and member states would be able to invoke each other's case law and practice in order to reinforce the national identity clause. Understood in this way, a proper implementation of the national identity clause and identity review can in fact contribute to a further connection between national constitutional jurisdictions throughout the EU.

The concept of constitutional identity is therefore intrinsically heterarchical, as it does not impose an overarching European value over specific national values. In that respect, constitutional identity is in itself a contributing element to the nature of EU constitutionalism as permanently contested, endorsing an equal position of a variety of national specificity claims.[29] Such a view in my opinion outweighs the proposal of Advocate General Cruz Villalón in *Gauweiler*[30] who argued in favour of a converging European identity in a *Solange*-like trend.[31] There are two reasons to support this claim. First, the application of the Advocate General's view would create a hierarchical relationship between identity claims on the EU and the national level, thus increasing the possibility of constitutional conflict. A clear statement of hierarchy does not appear as something that national constitutional adjudicators

[26] In that sense, see also van der Schyff, 'Member States of the European Union, Constitutions, and Identity', in Calliess and van der Schyff (eds.), *Constitutional Identity in a Europe of Multilevel Constitutionalism* (Cambridge University Press, 2019), p. 328.

[27] de Witte, *supra* note 1, p. 34.

[28] Fabbrini, 'After the *OMT* case: the supremacy of EU law as the guarantee of the equality of the Member States', 16(4) *German Law Journal* (2015), 1003, 1005.

[29] To quote the Polish *Trybunał Konstytucyjny* from a different era: 'confirming one's national identity in solidarity with other nations, and not against them'. *Treaty of Lisbon*, K 32/09, Judgment of 24 November 2010, para 2.1.

[30] Opinion of Advocate General Cruz Villalón in Case C-62/14 *Gauweiler*, EU:C:2015:7, para 61.

[31] Lord Mance in fact used the argument of the Advocate General against him—in *Pham* he stated: 'This recognises, perhaps, that Europe has not yet reached a situation where it is axiomatic that there is constitutional identity between the Union and its Members.' Case *Pham* [2015] UKSC 19, para 79.

would welcome, as their jurisprudence revolves around the reconciliation between the primacy of EU law and the supremacy of national constitutions in their own territory.[32] Second, from an institutional point of view, respecting national particularities contributes to mutual respect and cooperation between constitutional adjudicators and the Court of Justice, which would be jeopardized if a converging European identity were to replace the current understanding of the identity clause. In essence, the national identity clause in its heterarchical operation accommodates autonomy demands, without exacerbating the disintegrative elements that accompany such demands on the political level. Its interpretative outcomes are also less visible than differentiated integration solutions, given that accommodations of national identity claims take place for individual member states in isolation from the more general legislative/integration agenda.[33]

Identity-based limits to the principle of primacy have thus resulted in a permanently contested nature of the EU constitutional sphere. As Lenaerts and Gutiérrez-Fons explain in the context of general principles of EU law, which have often been at the centre of conflict with national constitutions:

> [General] principles leave some room for constitutional values that differ from one Member State to another. ... In this view, the ECJ cannot rely on general principles of EU law, particularly fundamental rights, as an unstoppable centripetal force that would ensure uniformity while destroying constitutional diversity.[34]

Therefore, both the EU and the national level are in a permanent relation of mutual influence, developing and changing incrementally through their interactions. In that sense, the famous statement that member states are the 'Masters of the Treaties' is no longer accurate; rather, in some sense, the Treaties no longer have a clear master as once found in the international law sphere. The Court of Justice has famously taken to expanding the self-referential system of the Treaties.[35] However, while member states would in principle be at full liberty to do so, it is almost impossible to imagine a Treaty reform doing away

[32] See Spanish *Tribunal Constitucional* case *Constitutional Treaty*, DTC 1/2004, Declaration of 13 December 2004, Ground 4; Polish *Trybunał Konstytucyjny* case *Accession Treaty*, K 18/04, Judgment of 11 May 2005, para 12.

[33] Although it must be appreciated that the recent review of the *Bundesverfassungsgericht* in the monetary field does come at a time when further economic integration is gaining momentum. For a further analysis of this point, see below section 5.

[34] Lenaerts and Gutiérez-Fons, 'The constitutional allocation of powers and general principles of EU Law', 47(6) *CMLRev* (2010), 1629, 1662–1663.

[35] Lenaerts concludes that the Court of Justice has 'a constitutional mandate in a self-referential and, in that sense, autonomous legal order'. Lenaerts, 'The Court's Outer and Inner Selves: Exploring the

with the cornerstone principles of EU law introduced by the Court of Justice. The same goes for national constitutions: the entrenchment of EU integration clauses therein[36] significantly restricts the extent to which constitutional review is conducted.[37]

Constructive conflict is therefore characterized by the differing interpretation of shared values across member states. Still, so long as the national level interprets the 'constitutional', expressed through the values in Article 2 TEU, coherently within the limits of mutual respect and sincere cooperation, as well as by an independent judiciary, we can speak of constructive conflict, conducive to the dynamic development of the EU's constitutional sphere. The '*Simmenthal* mandate' established by the Court of Justice requires that national courts apply EU law to cases within their jurisdiction and protect the rights accorded to citizens in their entirety.[38] The reliance on judicial independence for ensuring the rights of individuals is thus at the centre of EU membership and the shared values in Article 2 TEU. However, it is not the case that judicial independence is merely a requirement for compliance with EU law, but rather, it is the very essence of membership to be observed regardless of the applicability of EU law in a particular case.[39] This means that in effect, autonomy demands by constitutional courts that are in the realm of constructive conflict should always operate based on sincere cooperation, in order to preserve the shared common denominator contained in Article 2 TEU. In that respect, a large number of national constitutional courts approach EU law demands with a self-imposed obligation of an EU-friendly interpretation,[40] at times also backed up by a self-imposed obligation to submit a preliminary

External and Internal Legitimacy of the Court of Justice', in Adams, de Waele, Meeusen, and Straetmans (eds.), *Judging Europe's Judges. The Legitimacy of the Case Law of the European Court of Justice* (Hart Publishing, 2015), p. 15.

[36] Claes, 'Constitutionalizing Europe at its source: The "European clauses" in the national constitutions: evolution and typology', 24(1) *Yearbook of European Law* (2005), 81.

[37] Millet points to different constitutional amendments that several member states undertook in order to accommodate the implementation of the European Arrest Warrant. See Millet, 'How Much Lenience for How Much Cooperation? On the First Preliminary Reference of the French Constitutional Council to the Court of Justice', 51 *CMLRev* (2014), 195–196. Moreover, the Spanish Constitutional Tribunal accepted the necessary changes in its *Melloni* decision (*Melloni*, Judgment 26/2014 of 13 February 2014), after receiving a response to the preliminary reference submitted to the Court of Justice in Case C-399/11, *Melloni*, EU:C:2013:107.

[38] Claes, *supra* note 12, p. 108.

[39] Opinion of Advocate General Bobek, Joined Cases C-748/19 to C-754/19, *W.B. and Others*, EU:C:2021:403, para 136.

[40] For example: Italian *Corte Costituzionale*, Case 170/84, *Granital*, paras 7–3; German *Bundesverfassungsgericht*, Case 2BvR 2661/06, *Honeywell*, para 100; Polish *Trybunał Konstytucyjny* Case K 32/09 *Treaty of Lisbon*, Judgment of 24 November 2010, http://trybunal.gov.pl/fileadmin/content/omowienia/K_32_09_EN.pdf, para 3.1. For further references, see Bobić, *supra* note 14, p. 1417, fn. 114.

reference to the Court of Justice.[41] Conversely, destructive conflict is one where the system's entire existence is being put into question by the national level, by disregarding the interpretation of Article 2 TEU that forms part of the basic common denominator shared by the EU and all member states.

For example, in fundamental rights review, the reservations put in place by the German and Italian constitutional courts as regards the satisfactory level of fundamental rights protection pushed the Court of Justice to introduce the concept of 'common constitutional traditions' as the source for protection of fundamental rights.[42] This process arguably led to the German initiative for a formal fundamental rights catalogue, resulting in the Charter of fundamental rights.[43] In that sense, constructive conflict is contributing to acknowledging the contributions from the national level without leading to a demand for autonomy (e.g., over fundamental rights protection) and by extension without undermining the integration process. Another contribution of constructive conflict that manifests itself specifically in identity conflicts can be found in the acknowledgement of national constitutional specificities (autonomy demands) and their accommodation within the EU's broader constitutional frame.[44] Finally, such conflicts contribute to stabilizing the tensions between EU and national law demands, as national courts take part in increasing the control that the Court of Justice exerts over EU institutions, as will become visible in section 5 concerning the EMU.

Contrary to constructive conflicts, an example of destructive conflict can be found in the recent decision of the Disciplinary Chamber of the captured Polish Supreme Court,[45] where a disciplined prosecutor sought the applicability of the decisions of the Court of Justice concerning judicial independence in the proceedings. Strikingly, the Disciplinary Chamber stated that 'this application did not deserve to be taken into account on substance.'[46] No standard of review has been introduced or presented. The Disciplinary Chamber then had the opportunity to consider the judicial independence of a Supreme Court Chamber of Labour and Social Security that submitted the relevant preliminary reference to the Court of Justice. Here the standard of impartiality set

[41] Case 2BvR 2661/06, *Honeywell*, *supra* note 40, paras 60–61; Portuguese Constitutional Tribunal, Acórdão N.º 422/2020, http://www.tribunalconstitucional.pt/tc/acordaos/20200422.html, para 2.6.2.2.
[42] Bobić, *The Jurisprudence of Constitutional Conflict in the European Union*, *supra* note 2.
[43] de Búrca, 'The drafting of the European Union Charter of Fundamental Rights', 26(2) *ELRev* (2001), 126.
[44] This advantage of constructive conflict will become particularly visible in the discussion of the decision of the Court of Justice in *Sayn-Wittgenstein* in the following section.
[45] Available at https://ruleoflaw.pl/wp-content/uploads/2020/10/Case-II-DO-52-20.pdf>.
[46] Ibid., p. 3.

out was that 'any external observer will easily see the court's lack of neutrality with regards to the interests in the dispute.'[47] Finally, when assessing the validity of the proceedings carried out by said Chamber of Labour and Social Security, including the preliminary reference, the Disciplinary Chamber concluded that 'since the invalidity concerns the entire proceedings, a preliminary ruling of the CJEU which was obtained in such invalid proceedings cannot be valid either.'[48] Finding standards of review in this judgment is a perplexing task, even more so if one attempts to find any safeguards for sustaining mutual respect and sincere cooperation in the EU judicial space.

Destructive constitutional conflict is thus of such a grave nature that the member state engaging in it no longer meets the basic EU membership criteria,[49] resulting in a need for a solution on both the legal and political levels. In *Republikka*, the Court of Justice connected the compliance with Article 2 TEU values to membership of the Union, and as a consequence stated that member states cannot legislate in a manner that reduces its basic protections, specifically protections of the rule of law.[50] This decision of the Court comes in response to the consistent refusal of the Polish government to cooperate with the Commission and abide by numerous judgments of the Court of Justice concerning judicial independence.[51] The Court of Justice has also issued an order for an interim measure, requesting Poland to suspend the operation of the abovementioned Disciplinary Chamber of the Supreme Court.[52] In its earlier decision,[53] the Court of Justice found the said Chamber to lack judicial independence, however, Poland has continued its operation. The Court of Justice also found that the amendments concerning the appointment procedure to the National Council of the Judiciary are contrary to the rule of law and judicial independence.[54] The decision went so far as to state that the referring court, which has in the meantime been deprived of its jurisdiction to hear the case that was the occasion of the preliminary reference, should continue to assume jurisdiction and, if needed, to apply the provisions of national law that were in force prior to the relevant amendments.[55] Judicial accommodation cannot remedy such systemic deficiencies of rule of law. Rather, maintaining

[47] Ibid., p. 6.

[48] Ibid.

[49] See also, von Bogdandy, 'Principles of a systemic deficiencies doctrine: how to protect checks and balances in the Member States', 57(3) *CMLRev* (2020), 705, 710, 733.

[50] Case C-869/19, *Republikka*, EU:C:2021:311, paras 62–64.

[51] European Commission, Press Release of 31 March 2021, https://ec.europa.eu/commission/presscorner/detail/en/ip_21_1524

[52] Case C-791/19 R, *Commission v Poland*, EU:C:2020:277.

[53] Joined Cases C-585/18, C-624/18 and C-625/18, *A.K. and Others*, EU:C:2019:982.

[54] Case C-824/18, *A.B. and Others*, EU:C:2021:153.

[55] Ibid., paras 149 and 166.

such conflicts in the realm of judicial interactions would legitimize the contestation by the national level and reduce the standards of the 'constitutional' for all members.[56]

The Polish situation thus exemplifies an autonomy demand that leads to collapse, given that it does not allow for judicial balancing of the values in Article 2 TEU, nor does it open up space for reasonable disagreements. In other words, it leaves no space for constitutional principles to address and possibly remedy this demand for autonomy; should all participants in the EU's constitutional space follow suit, we would certainly be witnessing a collapse of the Union. Destructive conflicts nevertheless make up for an extreme exception in the management of interactions between the EU and national levels of constitutional authority, and should not, in my view, overshadow the immense benefits that constructive conflicts bring about to the EU constitutional space.

Destructive constitutional conflicts demonstrate the gravity of the disagreement between a member state and the EU to such an extent that a judicial resolution of the situation is not sufficient in itself to put a halt to the persistent breaches of the rule of law. In this respect, a coherent political and legal action, both top-down (the EU acting vis-à-vis the member state), but also importantly, bottom-up (sourced in the member state itself) is needed to impose an overhaul to the anti-rule of law developments. Protecting the rule of law can only be successful if both processes are in place: isolated EU action, precisely due to the heterarchical nature of the EU's constitutional space, would result in a hierarchical imposition of EU values over national ones, resulting in a reduced legitimacy and an increased contestation from the national level. Bottom-up activity, however, has the advantage of creating a contribution to the EU's constitution more broadly conceived, but also promotes its cosmopolitan character. The myriad preliminary references submitted by Polish judges attempting to protect their independence in the face of political intervention is only possible due to the individual enforcement character of EU law that no longer depends on the willingness of political actors to negotiate it and explicitly implement it.

4. Managing Constructive Conflict in Identity Review

Constructive conflict thus serves the purpose of acknowledging autonomy demands of national constitutional authority and makes use of judicial interactions and constitutional interpretation to manage them without descending

[56] von Bogdandy, *supra* note 49, p. 717.

into collapse. When it comes to identity-based constructive conflicts, it is possible, in the EU's constitutional space, to discern two different views of identity review, one conducted at the national level, and the other by the Court of Justice. According to the former, there are essentially two sets of constitutional values: those underpinning national 'fundamental structures, political and constitutional' as set out in Article 4(2) TEU; and the core constitutional values that represent the national constitutional identity and, in the view of constitutional adjudicators, lie beyond the reach of the primacy of EU law. The latter line of interpretation endorses a more homogeneous understanding of Article 4(2) TEU, according to which the concept of fundamental political and constitutional structures encompasses core constitutional values of member states, leaving no national provision of principle outside its scope.

The first line of interpretation singles out national constitutional provisions that have a higher degree of constitutional entrenchment, such as provisions on the basic principles of state organization, sovereignty, the principle of democracy, and human dignity.[57] From an institutional point of view, it represents an area of primacy for constitutional adjudicators, where their interpretative jurisdiction remains intact. However, constitutional courts that have introduced some form of identity review have themselves imposed limits to such review, grounded in the principles of EU friendly interpretation and self-restraint.[58]

It is difficult to imagine the Court of Justice subscribing to an understanding of Article 4(2) TEU which would seriously undermine its decades long jurisprudence on the primacy of Union law over all sources of national law, including national constitutions. At the same time, the Court of Justice has not been particularly proactive in interpreting the scope of the national identity clause. Advocates General have been more elaborate in proposing a comprehensive interpretation of the notion, which has only exceptionally found its way into the judgments of the Court.

In order to understand how constructive identity conflict works, it is necessary to distinguish between *institutional* and *substantive* balancing.[59] Institutional balancing is closely linked to the use of self-restraint and is the first

[57] von Bogdandy and Schill, *supra* note 21, p. 1432.

[58] The limits can be placed on a spectrum from a seemingly uncompromising identity review (Germany), to a position whereby the Court of Justice is trusted to be the one protecting the national identity on the EU level (Spain). See also, Spieker, 'Framing and managing constitutional identity conflicts: How to stabilize the modus vivendi between the Court of Justice and National Constitutional Courts', 57(2) *CMLRev* (2020), 361.

[59] See also Maduro, 'Three Claims of Constitutional Pluralism', in Avbelj and Komárek (eds.), *Constitutional Pluralism in the European Union and Beyond* (Hart Publishing, 2012), p. 80.

step to be taken once a national constitutional limit is invoked in a particular case. If the specific case is being heard before the Court of Justice, the use of institutional balancing will mean rendering a decision on which court is to take the final decision. Such an approach is well known in the case law of the Court and, as Tridimas explains, the Court of Justice employs it regularly in what he calls 'guidance' and 'deference' cases.[60] In particular, the Court of Justice either gives guidance to the national court that is then finally to decide (guidance cases), or it leaves it entirely up to the national court to decide (deference cases). In deciding whether to rule on a certain issue itself, or leave it to the national court, the Court of Justice will be driven by taking into account the sensitivity of the case, which will condition the extent of self-restraint to be applied.[61] By contrast, when a case takes place before a national constitutional court, regardless of the fact whether the court submitted a preliminary reference or not, national instances will be wary of a possible constitutional conflict. In addition, any situation of a constitutional conflict is to be approached with great self-restraint and in a manner open to European integration.

The decision by the German *Bundesverfassungsgericht* concerning the execution of a European Arrest Warrant (EAW) is an excellent example:[62] the German Court did not refer the case to the Court of Justice for a further interpretation of the EAW but has instead decided the case itself. Nevertheless, it stated that any situation of a constitutional conflict is to be approached with great self-restraint and in a manner open to European integration.[63] More importantly, it underlined that any conflict which might take place would not undermine the uniform application of EU law in Germany as a whole, confirming incrementalism as one of the main features characterizing the EU's constitutional space.

The substantive step takes place after the institutional balancing (the determination of which instance will ultimately decide the case, as explained in the preceding paragraphs), and includes the balancing of values in opposition in the particular case.[64] Surely, the result of the institutional balancing will serve

[60] Tridimas, 'Constitutional review of member state action: The virtues and vices of an incomplete jurisdiction', 9(3–4) *ICON* (2011), 737, 739.

[61] As was done in, for example, Case C-438/14, *Bogendorff von Wolffersdorff*, EU:C:2016:401, para 80, where the Court of Justice acknowledged the importance of abolishing nobility titles when assessing a possible restriction on free movement. See also Huber, 'The Federal Constitutional Court and European integration', 21 *European Public Law* (2015), 83, 107, who emphasizes how the principle of cooperation among courts in the European judicial space needs to work in both directions.

[62] Case 2 BvR 2735/14, *Mr. R*, Order of 15 December 2015.

[63] Ibid., Key considerations, para 1.b.

[64] See Lenaerts and Gutiérrez-Fons, *supra* note 34, at pp. 1649–1653 for a detailed analysis on how the balancing exercise is to be carried out in order to achieve the rule of law.

as a strong indicator as to the extent of the substantive balancing that a particular court is to exhibit. In essence, when the Court of Justice defers to the national court on the ultimate decision, this undoubtedly means an endorsement for that court to protect the national value in question. This argument ensures that judicial cooperation and the ability of individuals to enforce their rights before national courts, as the normative priority, will necessarily trump bad faith readings of constitutional identity that put judicial independence at risk, and hence assuage the dangers of its abuse.

The proposed interpretation of the identity clause is thus twofold: (1) the national identity clause is to serve as an exception to accommodate national particularities in the application of EU law on the national level, while the role of the Court of Justice is to apply a uniform method in determining the limits to this exception through the application of the principle of proportionality;[65] (2) the proportionality analysis will highlight issues of jurisdictional and constitutional conflict, both between the EU and national level, but potentially also conflicts within the member state, and the balancing of these issues will determine the extent of self-restraint that is to be applied in a particular case. In addition, the Court of Justice will, in taking into account national identity concerns, undertake a balancing exercise in reaching its final judgment. The Court of Justice should carry out this balancing carefully, taking into account the historical underpinnings of a particular constitutional principle, as was done, for example, in *Sayn-Wittgenstein*.[66] There, the principle of equality as provided by the Austrian constitution could be placed within the scope of reasonable disagreement in interpreting the principle of equality found in Article 2 TEU, and the Court of Justice stated that while this interpretation pertains specifically to the Austrian context,[67] it does not undermine the principle of equality more generally. Such a division of interpretative tasks between national and EU judiciaries is in line with the essential characteristic of the EU's constitutional space that operates under conditions of permanent mutual contestation.

From an institutional point of view, respecting national particularities contributes to the mutual respect and cooperation between constitutional adjudicators and the Court of Justice, which would be jeopardized if a converging European identity were to replace the current understanding of the identity

[65] Case C-420/07, *Apostolides*, EU:C:2009:271, para 57. See also Besselink, *supra* note 21, p. 46; Lenaerts, 'La Vie Après l'Avis: Exploring the principle of mutual (yet not blind) trust', 54(3) *CMLRev* (2017), 805, 822.

[66] Case C-208/09, *Sayn-Wittgenstein*, EU:C:2010:806.

[67] Ibid., paras 82–83.

clause. Respect for national specificities, subject to the principle of proportionality, reinforces the role of the Court of Justice in ensuring the uniform application of Union law through providing a common method of determining the limit(s) to Article 4(2) TEU. At the same time, national autonomy demands are to be determined by national constitutional courts and provided with procedural tools, such as the use of the preliminary reference procedure or the application of interpretative principles such as EU-friendly interpretation or sincere cooperation, which ensures that the conflict remains within the bounds of the 'constructive'.

Furthermore, through incrementalism, the development of the case law in this area will create a common approach to the substantive issues connected to the national identity clause,[68] as it can be expected that recourse to Article 4(2) TEU will become more frequent over time. However, for sensitive issues (for example of same-sex marriage or abortion) answers are limited to the single case and do not draw on wider implications that this could have on all the member states.[69]

In essence, the national identity clause should be interpreted so as to follow the main characteristics of the EU's permanently contested constitutional order. In this process, Maduro stresses the importance of the discursive element between different sites of constitutional authority, who jointly and coherently strive to create the shared European legal space.[70] In the same vein, Cloots lists a number of interpretative guidelines to both national courts with constitutional jurisdiction and the Court of Justice, in order to not only contain conflict, but also resolve it in a manner that will be respectful of the values, and ultimately constitutional orders, in balance.[71] Besselink and Ejisbouts explain that the judge faced with situations of constitutional conflict should not address it by 'mere reference to the autonomy or the supremacy of his own legal order, nor by reference to legal hierarchy. He shall do so by reference to fundamental substantive norms valid in the wider circumscription.'[72]

[68] A common approach to substantive issues does not mean a convergence of values towards a European identity, as proposed by Advocate General Cruz Villalón. Instead, it means that the sheer volume of cases that will arise over time will establish a unified jurisprudence of the Court of Justice and create expectations on behalf of national authorities as regards the extent to which a particular national value can be protected.

[69] In support of this view, see also Thym, 'Separation versus fusion—or: how to accommodate national autonomy and the Charter? Diverging visions of the German Constitutional Court and the European Court of Justice', 9(3) *EuConst* (2013), 391, 419; Lenaerts and Gutiérrez-Fons, *supra* note 58, p. 1663 (discussing 'value diversity' that the Court of Justice appreciates and strives to protect).

[70] Maduro *supra* note 8, pp. 513–514, 518.

[71] Cloots, 'Germs of pluralist adjudication: *Advocaten Voor De Wereld* and other references from the Belgian Constitutional Court', 47(3) *Common Market Law Review* (2010), 645, 668.

[72] Ejisbouts and Besselink, *supra* note 60, p. 397.

Finally, the EU's constitutional system aims to contain conflict and maintain its constructive nature, both from the perspective of constitutional adjudicators and the Court of Justice. The protection of national identity through Article 4(2) TEU is necessarily multilateral in its nature. Its implementation shows an institutional awareness of the big picture in the everyday work of the courts under analysis, as they are conscious of the need for a balanced relationship among all constitutional jurisdictions in the EU.[73] Finally, as a consequence, in order for the clause to work for everyone, and not against anyone,[74] it is the role of the Court of Justice to set common limits through the application of a careful balancing exercise.[75] This means that sometimes, national particularities will prevail, while other times it will be the primacy of Union law. This ultimately renders the question of the final arbiter immaterial, as the system is one of a clear-cut heterarchy: one where there are no predetermined winners and losers, but rather, different courts will have the final say at different times.

5. The Prohibition of Monetary Financing and Identity Review

The back-and-forth interactions between the Court of Justice and the *Bundesverfassungsgericht* concerning the limits to the ECB mandate have, due to their omnipresence and relevance for the development of the EMU, overwhelmed our constitutional imagination and strained our ability to see positive consequences stemming from constitutional conflict. According to van der Schyff, constitutional identity is understood as the 'core fundamental values or elements of a particular state's constitutional order as the expression of its individuality'.[76] How is the law of the EMU then concerned with identity review? As of yet, not very much. However, the German court has used precisely the monetary policy area to buttress the distinction between the concept of national identity as covered by Article 4(2) TEU and the German constitutional identity that lies beyond it and cannot be subject to European integration.[77] This section will take a look at the incremental developments in

[73] Perhaps the best example of this is the vast number of cross-references among constitutional jurisdictions in the EU in their jurisprudence on national identity. See, for example, United Kingdom Supreme Court Case *Pham*, cited *supra* note 8; German *Bundesverfassungsgericht* Case *Gauweiler*, *supra* note 22; Polish *Trybunał Konstytucyjny* Case K 18/04 *Accession Treaty*, *supra* note 32.

[74] See *supra* note 29.

[75] See, in that sense, Weiler, *The Constitution of Europe. 'Do the new clothes have an emperor?' and other essays on European integration* (Cambridge University Press, 1999), p. 122.

[76] van der Schyff, *supra* note 26, p. 326.

[77] German *Bundesverfassungsgericht* Order in *Gauweiler*, *supra* note 22.

this judicial interaction with the aim of shedding further light on how likely it is that the developments in EU budgetary framework might stumble upon doors locked by constitutional identity.

A brief look into the *Lisbon Treaty* judgment will serve as a starting point here, given that this judgment marks the birth of identity review in Germany. Importantly, while instituting identity review, the German Court was fairly benevolent, stating that 'the guarantee of national constitutional identity under constitutional and under Union law go hand in hand in the European legal area.'[78] The legal solutions to numerous Euro-crisis challenges resulted in the *Bundesverfassungsgericht* reviewing the aid to Greece and the European Financial Stability Facility (the precursor to the European Stability Mechanism). In the resulting decision, the *Bundesverfassungsgericht* added budgetary autonomy to the list of areas that fall in the scope of constitutional identity.[79] More specifically, if the expenditure related to supranational integration results in the Bundestag losing its ability to individually authorize every instance of large amount spending, this would result in breaching the principle of democracy and by extension the core of the identity of the constitution.[80]

This expansion of constitutional identity is what brings us to monetary policy specifically and how it became an identity issue. In the interpretation of the *Bundesverfassungsgericht*, encroachments into the economic policy mandate of member states by breaching the prohibition of monetary financing engages identity review. It is here that the *Bundesverfassungsgericht* departed from seeing German constitutional identity as going hand in hand with the Union concept of national identity, by stating that core constitutional values represent national constitutional identity and lie beyond the reach of EU law. The main difference between the two is that the latter are not subject to European integration and the *Bundesverfassungsgericht* has exclusive jurisdiction to interpret them.[81] Furthermore, the Court stated that the values representing constitutional identity cannot be subject to any kind of balancing exercise and must be unconditionally protected by the *Bundesverfassungsgericht*.[82] Such a distinction between constitutional and national identity is at odds with the reasoning employed in its *Lisbon Treaty* decision. In particular, it seems the

78 Case 2 BVerfG 2/08 *Lisbon Treaty*, Judgment of 30 June 2009, para 240. See also, Halberstam and Möllers, 'The German Constitutional Court says "Ja zu Deutschland!"', 10(8) *German Law Journal* (2009), 1241, 1247.
79 Case 2 BVerfG 987/10 *Aids for Greece and EFSF*, Judgment of 7 September 2011, paras 125–128.
80 Ibid., para 127.
81 German *Bundesverfassungsgericht* Order in *Gauweiler*, *supra* note 22, para 29.
82 Ibid.

German court has abandoned its view that the two notions go 'hand in hand' and clearly outlined a *domaine réservé* for itself. This move increased the likelihood of constitutional conflict and reduced the ability of its accommodation, given that there is no space for compromise in the areas touted as constitutional identity.

Finally, in the decision concerning the Public Sector Purchase Programme (PSPP) of the ECB, where the *Bundesverfassungsgericht* found that the ECB acted in excess of its monetary policy powers, we see identity-based arguments being used in a way that detracts from the balancing between constitutional and EU law demands and is possibly absolute, unilateral, and thus destructive. The *Bundesverfassungsgericht*'s initial worry in *Gauwiler* concerned the possibility that quantitative easing may involve unforeseeable risks for national budgets beyond those directly approved by the Bundestag. It took into account the assurances of the Court of Justice that the Outright Monetary Transactions (OMT) programme entails safeguards preventing such an outcome.[83] The same concern was raised in relation to the PSPP, where the Court of Justice dismissed the question about risk-sharing as hypothetical.[84] The *Bundesverfassungsgericht* took this to mean that the Treaties prohibit risk-sharing as such and added that this would also be contrary to Germany's constitutional identity protected by Article 23(1) and 79(3) of the Basic Law.[85] In that sense, identity review is a weapon of a strength incomparable to that of *ultra vires* review: while the latter allows for the situation to be remedied by an action of the Bundestag, the former is embedded in an unamendable characteristic of the Basic Law and does not allow for any departures.[86]

The good news is that the *Bundesverfassungsgericht* seems to use identity review in a self-restrained manner and is abiding by its well-established self-imposed obligation of an EU-friendly interpretation.[87] In other words, although statements of an uncompromising protection of constitutional identity now feature more prominently in the text of the judgments, in effect, quantitative easing programmes of the ECB are nevertheless accepted when

[83] Case C-62/14 *Gauweiler*, EU:C:2015:400, paras 123–126, accepted by the *Bundesverfassungsgericht* in Case 2 BvR 2728/13 *Gauweiler*, Judgment of 21 June 2016, paras 218–219.

[84] Case C-493/17, *Weiss*, EU:C:2018:1000, paras 165–166.

[85] Cases 2 BvR 859/15, 2 BvR 980/16, 2 BvR 2006/15, 2 BvR 1651/15, *Weiss II*, Judgment of 5 May 2020, paras 227–228.

[86] *Gauweiler* (Judgment), *supra* note 79, para 29.

[87] See *supra* note 40. In addition, this approach may also be seen as confirming interpretative pluralism: 'In offering a constitutional interpretation which reasonably accommodates but also constrains European institutions ... constitutional courts go into novel terrain, and if they manage to stick to some of their constitutional values they almost inevitably do so at the cost of others.' Davies, Chapter 7, this volume, p. 124.

it comes to their compliance with the prohibition of monetary financing. And this is so although each new programme departs further from the original conditions of compliance set out by the Court of Justice in *Gauweiler*.[88] We can therefore speak of a (perhaps not very sophisticated) constructive attempt of the German court to underline the magnitude of the issue under review in order to demand a higher standard of review of ECB's activities in the monetary field. The German court has used identity review to demonstrate the importance of budgetary autonomy in the Basic Law. As a result, we have witnessed the ECB complying with its request to publish its proportionality analysis and rejected an application for an order of execution relating to the PSPP judgment.[89]

6. Conclusion

The above-described approach of the *Bundesverfassungsgericht* in categorically excluding risk-sharing as a possibility under the German Basic Law, as well as its lack of willingness to balance different values and interests at stake, looms large over the context of the Euro-crisis and the current economic and social consequences of the Covid crisis. However, it is not yet possible to witness a more general trend to use identity review in the monetary field by other member states. Attempts by Hungary and Poland to block the now enacted rule of law conditionality mechanism were not rooted in identity arguments, but rather in an attempt to prevent the expansion of sanctions for breaches of the rule of law.[90]

Presently, the EU's 'Next Generation EU' pandemic programme that forms part of the EU's Own Resources Decision[91] is being challenged before the *Bundesverfassungsgericht* by the founder of the Alternative für Deutschland (AfD) precisely on the basis of constitutional identity.[92] The *Bundesverfassungsgericht* rejected the request for an interim measure to prevent the German

[88] Bobić and Dawson, 'Making sense of the "incomprehensible": The PSPP judgment of the German Federal Constitutional Court', 57(6) *CMLRev* (2020), 1953, 1956–1957.

[89] 2 BvR 1651/15, Order of 29 April 2021.

[90] See, for example, https://www.gov.pl/web/eu/joint-declaration-of-the-prime-minister-of-poland-and-the-prime-minister-of-hungary#:~:text=Back-,Joint%20Declaration%20of%20the%20Prime%20Minister%20of, the%20Prime%20Minister%20of%20Hungary&text=Prime%20Minister%20Mateusz%20Morawiecki%20and, of%20the%20rule%20of%20law

[91] Council Decision (EU, Euratom) 2020/2053 of 14 December 2020 on the system of own resources of the European Union and repealing Decision 2014/335/EU, Euratom OJ L 424, 15.12.2020, pp. 1–10.

[92] More information on the initiative is available at: https://buendnis-buergerwille.de/verfassungsbeschwerde/

ratification of the decision, but stated that in the final proceedings on merits, it is 'at least possible' that constitutional identity is encroached upon.[93] However, the approach of the *Bundesverfassungsgericht* demonstrates that it appreciates the delicate situation the Own Resources Decision is addressing, and in that respect it is possible to expect an interpretation that does not prioritize the autonomy demands over a joint endeavour to address the wide-ranging consequences of the Covid crisis.

In line with the above arguments concerning institutional and substantive balancing in the event of a constitutional conflict, it is expected that the *Bundesverfassungsgericht* will submit a preliminary reference to the Court of Justice and subsequently employ an interpretation that is constructive in relation to the development of the EMU and the use of financial resources. Should we witness an identity review that blocks any further developments in this regard, the limits of constructive conflict and the advantages of judicial interactions in managing autonomy demands will become apparent. This tells us something about the limits that legal and constitutional interpretation can serve in managing the balance between autonomy and integration.

[93] Press Release No. 29/2021 of 21 April 2021, Order of 15 April 2021 in Case 2 BvR 547/21. https://www.bundesverfassungsgericht.de/SharedDocs/Pressemitteilungen/EN/2021/bvg21-029.html

9

Free Movement

A Case Study in State Autonomy and EU Control

Catherine Barnard and Sarah Fraser Butlin

1. Introduction

In the run-up to the UK's Brexit referendum in 2016, a major concern expressed by Brexit supporters was about the extent of free movement rights. There was, in particular, significant disquiet about EU migrants accessing social security benefits. Reports about EU 'benefit tourists' appeared regularly in the tabloid press, along with other, mainly derogatory, messages relating to migration.[1] Immigration therefore took centre stage in the debates running up to the referendum, not least because of the pro-Leave media's 'relentless focus on anti-immigration stories'.[2] Data since the UK's referendum on 23 June 2016 has shown that concerns about the social consequences of EU membership were key to determining how people voted. The British Social Attitudes study No. 34 said that 73 per cent of those who were worried about immigration voted Leave, compared with 36 per cent of those who did not identify this as a concern.[3] The result of the Brexit referendum was the embodiment of complete loss of faith by a certain part of the British public in a key pillar of the single market and thus of the European Union, namely free movement of persons.

This research was funded by ESRC Grant ES/R000824/1.

[1] See also Moore and Ramsay, *UK Media Coverage of the 2016 EU Referendum campaign* (Policy Institute at King's College London, May 2017). https://www.kcl.ac.uk/policy-institute/assets/cmcp/uk-media-coverage-of-the-2016-eu-referendum-campaign.pdf (accessed 9 July 2021). See also Levy, Aslan, and Bironzo, *UK Press Coverage of the EU Referendum* (Reuters Institute for the Study of Journalism, 2016).
https://reutersinstitute.politics.ox.ac.uk/sites/default/files/2017-06/UK%20Press%20Coverage%20of%20the%20EU%20Referendum_0.pdf (accessed 28 June 2021).

[2] Martinson, 'Did the Mail and Sun help swing the UK towards Brexit?', *The Guardian*, 24 June 2016.
https://www.theguardian.com/media/2016/jun/24/mail-sun-uk-brexit-newspapers (accessed 28 June 2021).

[3] Although this is changing. See Curtice et al., British Social Attitudes 37, NatCen, 2019. http://natcen.ac.uk/our-research/research/british-social-attitudes/ (accessed 28 June 2021).

Catherine Barnard and Sarah Fraser Butlin, *Free Movement*. In: *Autonomy without Collapse in a Better European Union*. Edited by Mark Dawson and Markus Jachtenfuchs. Oxford University Press.
 DOI: 10.1093/oso/9780192897541.003.0009

The area of free movement presents an interesting case study of, on the one hand, autonomy by the member states and on the other hand its erosion as the EU tries to exert its influence and control over the operation of a key pillar of the single market project. These tensions and schisms will be explored through two stories: first, the development of free movement of workers under Article 45 TFEU and second, the development of the EU's approach to social welfare benefits. We wish to argue that these two stories show a historic and continued contestation between autonomy asserted by the member states, especially concerning social welfare benefits, and control asserted by the EU. In the case of the UK, that tension became so great that it ultimately resulted in the dramatic departure of the second largest member state from the EU, as the narrative took hold that, as a result of free movement, the UK was unable to 'control its own borders'.

Inevitably, the story is more complicated than this. The narrative is not simply member state vs EU. We see tensions between the member states which, depending on whether they are primarily sending or receiving states, take a different perspective on the autonomy question. We see the Court of Justice as referee between the member states but also a key player in the unfolding narrative, vacillating between furthering EU integration and upholding the fundamental bargains struck in the early years of the Union. And we see the EU legislature—itself of course composed of state actors—trying to navigate a course between national autonomy and the effective operation of the single market. The resulting story is ultimately messy, confused, and at times tempestuous. It does not lend itself to a simple narrative arc of autonomy to central control and back again. This can be seen particularly clearly in the debates around the development of EU-wide social welfare provision, the issue of utmost sensitivity, which is discussed in section 3.

The chapter is structured as follows. Section 2 considers free movement of workers and tells an initial story of a surrender of autonomy by the states, subsequently reinforced by decisions of the Court of Justice and by legislation. Section 3, the main focus of the chapter, concerns the extension of social welfare provision to EU migrants. The section also tells a story of the surrender of autonomy but after a lengthy period of contestation and debate especially over the position of migrant work seekers and their access to benefits, and over migrants' entitlement to housing. It is also largely a story of surrender of autonomy subsequently reinforced by legislation and decisions of the Court of Justice. Section 4 looks at attempts by the member states—including the UK—to reassert that autonomy, largely to no avail. The UK left the EU on 31 January 2020. Section 5 concludes.

2. The Development of Free Movement of Workers

2.1 The Initial Surrendering of Autonomy?

The introduction of free movement of workers in 1957 was a quite remarkable development. Immigration had long been an area of national sovereignty which states had guarded jealously. Yet, as we have argued elsewhere,[4] member states of the EU agreed to the introduction of free movement of workers with relative ease and little discussion about the sovereignty-limiting implications of the decision. Contemporary writers did not make much play about this dramatic shift either, although one or two noted it had occurred. So, for example, Barzanti, writing in 1965, noted the dichotomy between the strict immigration rules operated by the member states and the liberal approach to free movement encapsulated by EU law. He said that:

> the principle of free circulation of workers between Member States of the Community, assured by Article 48 et seq. of the Treaty [now Article 45 TFEU], sharply contrasts with existing legislation in the nations of the [then European] Economic Community. Indeed, in all these States the immigration of foreign workers is strictly regulated, and in no case even approaches the freedom which is the final aim of the Treaty of Rome.[5]

So why did the member states agree to this significant change? Our archival research supports Dahlberg's view that 'The provisions in the Rome Treaty dealing with the free movement of labour resulted not only from the economic logic involved in establishing a common market, but also, and perhaps even more, from the particular constellation of the labour market of the Six in 1958.'[6] Specifically, he noted the need for Italy to export labour, and for Germany to receive labour, and that the economic conditions of the time were favourable towards free movement of labour.[7] But it was also clear that from a relatively early date the member states acknowledged that creating the Common Market was a means to a more political end. For example, in 1963, Kitzinger argued the 'economic task' of setting up the Common Market was 'chiefly valued as a step

[4] Barnard and Fraser Butlin, 'Ceding control and taking it back: the origins of free movement in EU law', *ILJ* (2022). https://doi.org/10.1093/indlaw/dwab032

[5] Barzanti, *The Underdeveloped Areas within the Common Market* (Princeton Press, 1965), p. 147.

[6] Dahlberg, 'The EEC Commission and the politics of the free movement of labour', 6 Journal of Common Market Studies (1967), 310, at 311.

[7] Ibid., at 311 and 331.

towards political integration'.[8] In other words, the then six founding member states (fairly) willingly agreed to curtail their own sovereignty (autonomy) for the greater economic and political good of the Community (Union) as a whole. It was also of particular mutual benefit to the economies of Germany and Italy.

Yet, given the sensitivities surrounding immigration issues it seems surprising that member states did not seek to give themselves some sort of safeguard clause, limiting free movement if the numbers were too great. In fact, in the run up to the Treaty of Rome there had been various discussions about the possibility of introducing an emergency brake to protect national labour markets faced with an excess of migration (an issue which re-emerged during the Brexit negotiations in 2016)[9] or, at least, a gradual implementation of the rules on free movement of workers. So, for example, the resolution adopted by the Foreign Affairs Ministers at the Messina Conference in June 1955 said that the setting up of a common European market had to be established in stages: 'Its introduction will necessitate a study of the following questions .... f) *gradual* introduction of freedom of movement for workers'[10] [emphasis added]. The Inter-Governmental Committee's working paper (No. 7), dated 6 December 1955, also proposed a gradual increase in the number of migrant workers in each State, namely at least 1 per cent of the total number of salaried workers in the member state.[11] This progressive mechanism would have allowed for the harmonization of unemployment insurance systems, which would facilitate free movement. When the Sub-Committee on Social Problems submitted their observations on 22 July 1955, they noted the French delegation's reservation that migration should be limited according to the capacity of the member state to absorb migrant workers.[12]

These attempts to reassert national autonomy never made it into the final version of the Treaty. All that resulted was the power for member states to prevent free movement on the grounds of public policy, public security, and public health, and to limit employment in the public service to nationals only.[13] Most striking is the ambitious approach to free movement laid down in the final text of Article 48 EEC, now Article 45 TFEU, a text whose substance

[8] Kitzinger, *The Politics and Economics of European Integration* (New York: Praeger, 1963), p. 18. He also suggests that the provisions of the Rome Treaty created a 'field in which the citizens of the Six will progressively be treated as if they had not French or Italian, but Community citizenship' (p. 40).

[9] See further Barnard and Fraser Butlin, 'Free movement vs. fair movement: Brexit and managed migration', 55(2) *Common Market Law Review* (2018), 203.

[10] HAEU-CM3-005 (EU archive).

[11] HAEU-CM3/NEGO-040 (EU archive).

[12] 'Le marché commun général sera fondé, en principe, sur la libre circulation des marchandises, des capitaux, des personnes et des services'. HAEU-CM3/NEGO-044 (EU archive).

[13] Articles 45(3) and (4) TFEU.

has remained unaltered since 1957. Article 45(1) TFEU recognizes that 'Freedom of movement for workers shall be secured within the Union'. Article 45(3) TFEU allows workers:

(a) to accept offers of employment actually made;
(b) to move freely within the territory of Member States for this purpose;
(c) to stay in a Member State for the purpose of employment in accordance with the provisions governing the employment of nationals of that State laid down by law, regulation or administrative action; and
(d) to remain in the territory of a Member State after having been employed in that State, subject to conditions which shall be embodied in regulations to be drawn up by the Commission.

At the heart of free movement lies the principle of equal treatment. Article 45(2) TFEU provides: 'Such freedom of movement shall entail the abolition of any discrimination based on nationality between workers of the Member States as regards employment, remuneration and other conditions of work and employment'.

2.2 Did the Member States Lose Their Autonomy?

So, at first sight, the narrative in the field of free movement of workers appears to be a defeat for national autonomy almost from the beginning. But this would be an oversimplification, for three reasons.

First, the narrative overlooks the fact that the principle of equal treatment for migrant workers is provided by EU law but delivered by the host member state. Putting it another way, when migrant workers move, they put themselves under the control of the host state legal system. All EU law requires is that the host state treats migrant workers equally with nationals. So migrant workers will receive equal treatment only in respect of those benefits available to nationals in the host state, not by reference to what the home state would have offered. So, if for example, a German moved from Germany to Romania, equal treatment is provided on the basis of Romanian law and standards, not German ones. As the Court said in *Perfili*,[14] in prohibiting discrimination on the grounds of nationality, Articles 18, 49, and 56 TFEU were not concerned with

[14] Case C-177/94, *Criminal Proceedings against Gianfranco Perfili, civil party: Lloyd's of London*, ECLI:EU:C:1996:24.

disparities in treatment arising from differences between the laws in the member states so long as the laws affected all persons subject to them in accordance with objective criteria and without regard to nationality.[15]

Second, the principle of non-discrimination is not absolute. Directly discriminatory restrictions can be saved by a member state invoking one of the express derogations; indirectly discriminatory measures can be justified by reference to one of the express derogations or by one of the judicially developed public interest requirements (also referred to as objective justification).[16]

Third, EU law applies only where there is an interstate element;[17] in the absence of an interstate element domestic law applies. Despite various attempts to challenge this 'wholly internal' rule, the Court has insisted on its preservation. In the *Walloon* case the Court reasserted the orthodoxy that '[Union] law clearly cannot be applied to such purely internal situations';[18] it added that the citizenship case law does not change this view because 'citizenship of the Union is not intended to extend the material scope of the Treaty to internal situations which have no link with [Union] law.'[19]

Thus, there have always been structural mechanisms in place to protect the (host) member states. However, the erosion of national autonomy plays out through the intervention of the Court of Justice and the EU legislature both in respect of the personal, and the material, scope of free movement rights.

2.3 Control by the EU Institutions

2.3.1 The role of the Court of Justice

In this section we should like to give two examples of how the Court of Justice, through its interpretation of the Treaty, has asserted greater central control over how free movement operates in the EU 27.

First, and most obvious, is the Court's decision to provide an EU definition of 'worker' to ensure a uniform approach to the personal scope of EU employment rights. The 'worker' definition, still used today was developed by the Court in the seminal case of *Lawrie-Blum*.[20] The Court held that a 'worker' is any person who 'performs services for and under the direction of another in

[15] For a more recent example, see *Erzberger* v. *TUI AG* ECLI:EU:C:2017:562.

[16] Case C-237/94, *O'Flynn* v. *Adjudication Officer*, ECLI:EU:C:1996:206.

[17] Case C-212/06, *Government of French Community and Walloon Government* v. *Flemish Government*, ECL:EU:C:2008:178.

[18] Ibid para 38, although cf. para 40. The Court repeated this point in Case C-250/08, *Commission* v. *Belgium (immovable property)*, ECLI:EU:C:2011:793), para 41.

[19] Ibid., para 39. See also Case C-127/08, *Metock*, ECLI:EU:C:2008:449, para 77.

[20] Case C-66/85, *Deborah Lawrie-Blum* v. *Land Baden-Württemberg*, ECLI:EU:C:1986:284.

return for which he receives remuneration.'[21] Three criteria have since emerged as relevant for the assessment—'the performance of effective and genuine economic activities', 'remuneration', and 'subordination. The 'control' exercised by the employer, however, does not have to be direct or absolute—more subtle forms of power relations also count. Hence, presidents of national authorities,[22] directors of companies,[23] judges,[24] and other senior officials have been found to be 'workers' even though they enjoy a large margin of discretion in the performance of their duties. The Court has also found work seekers to be workers.[25] The more the Court has expanded the definition of worker, the larger the number of individuals falling within the personal scope of Article 45 TFEU and the more those individuals enjoy EU rights. However, as section 3.1 below shows, these decisions, especially concerning work seekers, were contentious.

Second, although the Treaty was premised on equal treatment, the Court has gone beyond this, at various times. It has applied its obstacles/restrictions case law[26] to the field of free movement: non-discriminatory national measures which (substantially) impede access to the market breach Article 45 TFEU unless objectively justified. So, for example, in *Bosman*[27] the Court found that the football transfer fee rules, albeit non-discriminatory, 'directly affect[ed] players' access to the employment market in other Member States'[28] and therefore constituted an unjustified 'obstacle to the freedom of movement of workers.'[29] The market access approach is highly effective in striking down barriers to free movement created by the host state. It is essentially deregulatory. Yes, the host state can justify its rules, but the steps taken by the host state must be both proportionate and compatible with fundamental rights. So often, if the host state cannot satisfy that requirement, the national rule as a whole is struck down. This contrasts with the position under the equal treatment model where the unjustified discriminatory element of the rule is removed, but the rule itself remains intact.

[21] Ibid., para 17.
[22] Ibid.
[23] Case C-232/09, *Danosa*, ECLI:EU:C:2010:674.
[24] Case C-393/10, *O'Brien*, [2012] ECLI:EU:C:2012:110.
[25] Case C–292/89, *R. v. IAT, ex p. Antonissen*, ECLI:EU:C:1991:80, para 21.
[26] Barnard, 'Fitting the remaining pieces into the goods and persons jigsaw', 26 *European Law Review* (2001), 35.
[27] Case C–415/93, ECLI:EU:C:1995:463.
[28] Ibid., para 103.
[29] Ibid., para 104.

2.3.2 The role of the legislature

The legislature has, of course, also played an important function in a tightening of EU control over free movement. Regulation 1612/68[30] has been important in this regard; this is considered in the next section. But the Citizens Rights Directive (CRD) 2004/38 has been equally important.[31] There was remarkably little commentary about the substance of the CRD when it was first adopted, which is striking given its importance. The Directive was clearly located in the context of the evolution of the Citizenship of the Union. This is evident from the opening paragraphs of the Directive:

> Citizenship of the Union confers on every citizen of the Union a primary and individual right to move and reside freely within the territory of the Member States, subject to the limitations and conditions laid down in the Treaty and to the measures adopted to give it effect.

And with a nod to *Grzlecyzk*,[32] the third paragraph of the Preamble notes 'Union citizenship should be the fundamental status of nationals of the Member States when they exercise their right of free movement and residence.' Two illustrations will show the extent to which member states' autonomy is undermined.

First, equal treatment by the host state is required from day one, except in respect of social assistance (but only for the first three months) and student grants and loans (for the first five years) (Article 24(2) CRD)). Putting it another way, host member states must always respect the principle of equal treatment except in those two limited areas.

Second, and perhaps more strikingly, member states' ability to not admit/deport EU nationals is significantly curtailed the longer they reside in the host state. So, after three months non-nationals can be deported only on the grounds of public policy and public security (not public health). After five years, individuals can be deported only on 'serious' public policy grounds (and public security) and after ten years, they can be deported only for imperative reasons of public security. In all cases, the proportionality principle applies, as does the Article 28 requirement to take into account the personal

[30] OJ [1968] L257/2.
[31] OJ [2004] L158/77.
[32] Case C-184/99, *Grzelczyk* v. *Centre Public d'Aide Sociale d'Ottignes-Louvain-la-Neuve*, ECLI:EU:C:2001:458.

circumstances of the individual. This restriction has been introduced because, according to the 24th Recital of the CRD:

> the greater the degree of integration of Union citizens and their family members in the host Member State, the greater the degree of protection against expulsion should be. Only in exceptional circumstances, where there are imperative grounds of public security, should an expulsion measure be taken against Union citizens who have resided for many years in the territory of the host Member State, in particular when they were born and have resided there throughout their life.

Yet all of this does represent a significant gloss on the wording of the Treaty and a restriction on member states' ability to 'control their own borders'.

Yet a narrative that simply asserts that the CRD represents a further defeat for state autonomy would also be inaccurate. In particular, Article 7(1) does allow member states to insist that those who are not economically active can stay in the host state beyond three months only if they are students or persons of independent means with sufficient resources and comprehensive sickness insurance; and, as we have seen, Article 24(2) CRD does contain some limits on the equal treatment principle.

2.3.3 Preliminary conclusions

The story told so far has broadly been one of greater control by the EU and loss of member state autonomy. The principle of free movement—the most extensive in the world[33]—was already realized in the Treaty of Rome but reinforced by subsequent EU judicial decisions and legislative measures. But in reality, in the early days of the EU, individuals made little use of it because they were worried about the loss of rights in their own states to social security protection and an inability to gain it in the host member state. So the second part of our story looks at this issue: how this highly sensitive question of social security should be understood and how it fits into the broader narrative of autonomy and control.

[33] A. Pécod (ed), *Migration, Free movement and Regional Integration* (UNESCO Publishing, 2020), https://www.academia.edu/35491413/Migration_Free_Movement_and_Regional_Integration?auto=download&email_work_card=download-paper

3. Social Welfare Provision

3.1 The Initial Surrendering of Autonomy?

Debates around who should be entitled to access social welfare benefits in other EU member states are not new. This has been a controversial and contentious issue since before the Treaty of Rome was signed. Throughout the negotiations leading up to the Treaty of Rome, and then to Regulation 1612/68 (the important legislation on free movement following on from the Treaty of Rome), access to social security benefits and other social provision, was hotly contested. In their final versions, both the Treaty and Regulation 1612/68 made a clear link between being an economically active migrant worker and the right to access the same social advantages as national workers. Workers were also required to have adequate housing before they were entitled to bring their family to join them in the host state. The EU was asserting control.

3.1.1 The initial debates

From the outset, the narratives surrounding extending social provision to migrant EU nationals were mixed. Different member states had different understandings as to what social provision for migrant workers actually meant. Some states had serious ambitions for either the full harmonization of the welfare state or the establishment of a central social security fund to pay certain benefits to migrant workers. Others were more limited in their approach, simply ensuring that families in the home state could still obtain benefits despite the worker being in a host state.

In 1955 at the Messina Conference, the six member states of the European Coal and Steel Community ('ECSC') met to discuss the progress of the ECSC and proposed further European integration, ultimately leading to the creation of the European Economic Community. Prior to this conference, three themes emerged in the debates of why work on social provision was necessary, whatever form that might take.

Firstly, there was a need to address social provision as a means of removing obstacles to free movement of workers. This can be described as the instrumental approach to dealing with social security. This approach can be seen in Article 8 of the Paris Treaty 1948 establishing the Organisation for European Economic Cooperation (OEEC), which eventually became the OECD, in which Contracting Parties agreed to 'take *the necessary measures to facilitate* the movement of workers and to ensure their establishment in conditions satisfactory from the economic and social point of view'. [Emphasis added]. On 21 June 1954 a briefing paper prepared by the Secretariat of the Workforce Committee of the OEEC set out the unanimous agreement of the Committee of Experts that measures should be taken to ensure that families could still access social security benefits, particularly family allowances and sickness benefits, when they remained in the home country and the worker was working abroad. However, the means of achieving this would be left to individual states.[34] The briefing paper noted that there were fifteen bilateral agreements that were already in place between the member states addressing social provision, that the view of the Workforce Committee was that the OEEC should take further measures to facilitate free movement, and that these measures should be focused on filling remaining lacunae and ensuring equality of treatment between migrant and non-migrant workers.

Social provision as a means to facilitating free movement was also the focus of the 1952 Paris Treaty establishing the European Community for Coal and Steel, in which Article 69 provided:

1. The Member States bind themselves to renounce *any restriction* based on nationality against the employment in the coal and steel industries of workers of proven qualifications for such industries who possess the nationality of one of the Member States; this commitment shall be subject to the limitations imposed by the fundamental needs of health and public order.

...

4. They will prohibit any discrimination in remuneration and working conditions between national workers and immigrant workers, without prejudice to special measures concerning frontier workers; in particular, they will work out among themselves any arrangements necessary so that *social security measures do not stand in the way* of the movement of labour.

[Emphasis added]

In November 1953 the High Authority of the ECSC emphasized that member states, by agreeing Article 69(4), had undertaken to implement an agreement 'to ensure that the provisions on social security do not hinder the change of workplace'.[35]

For the ECSC, the removal of obstacles to free movement was tied up with the improvement of social conditions and living standards and creating a

[34] HAEU-CM1.1954-208 (EU archive).
[35] CMI/1954-194 (EU archive).

(higher) level playing field, the second theme that appears in the debates from that period. This is the more aspirational approach to the role of social security. The ECSC's work was focused on whether an equalization fund[36] should be created to provide short-term benefits such as family allowances, sickness benefits, and unemployment benefits, to migrant workers and their family members, remaining in the home country. Thus, in May 1955 the General Assembly noted that 'the realisation of free migration and the free movement of workers will greatly contribute to hastening and facilitating *the progressive harmonisation of living standards and working conditions* and that a wider application of Article 69 [ECSC] will ensure at the same time, the development of continuity of employment.' [Emphasis added].[37] In the same resolution, the General Assembly highlighted the need for 'adequate and safe housing ... in order to achieve the social objectives of the Treaty'.

The third theme that emerged from the contemporaneous debates was that the provision of social security benefits was part of the more substantive aim of political integration. In other words, as the states of Europe started working more closely together, they needed to have rules which would address the social needs of its citizens, including their social security needs. This was a particular feature of the work of the Council of Europe but subsequently became an important narrative of the EU. Thus, at the first session of the Consultative Assembly of the Council of Europe, on 6 September 1949, concerning the role of the Council of Europe in the field of social security, a recommendation was made for member states to take inspiration from 'measures already taken in bilateral or regional treaties, in order to prepare a multilateral agreement that makes their social legislation fully applicable to nationals of other states'.[38]

On 7 November 1949, the Multilateral Convention on Social Security was signed by the five signatory states of the Brussels Treaty, and Belgium proposed that its provisions should be extended to all member states. The Committee of Experts in Social Security concluded that the extension would be unfeasible because of the vast number of bilateral treaties and the difficulties of the diverse systems of social security across the member states.[39] However, they decided that interim agreements should be enacted providing for equal

[36] Original. 'un fonds de péréquation'.
[37] HAEU-CM3-004 (EU archive).
[38] Original: 'des mesures déjà prises par voies d'accords bilatéraux ou régionaux en vue de préparer un accord multilatéral qui rende leur législation sociale entièrement applicable aux ressortissants des autres pays.' See HAEU-CM1.1954-208 at para 3 and Rapport explicative des Accords intérimaires européens concernant les régimes de Sécurité Sociale, Council of Europe (EU archive).
[39] See HAEU-CM1.1954-208 at para 5 (EU archive).

treatment between nationals of Contracting Parties. The First Interim Agreement covered old age, disability, and survivors' schemes, the second concerned social security regimes, except those covered by the First Agreement.[40] Matters of Public Assistance were covered by the European Convention on Social and Medical Assistance, which came into force on the same day. Importantly, the preamble to both interim agreements recalled that the aim of the Council of Europe is 'to achieve a closer union between its members, particularly to facilitate social progress' (the second and third themes identified above) and emphasized the importance of equal treatment of the nationals of signatory states. Nevertheless, even with this aim, there was ongoing debate within the Committee of Experts around the provision of social security to families of migrant workers. Whatever the justification, at heart it was about more EU control.

3.1.2 The evolution of the debates: Attempts to assert state autonomy

So how did this play out in the run up to the conclusion of the Treaty of Rome? At the Messina Conference itself in June 1955, the resolution adopted by the Foreign Affairs ministers proposed two aspects of social life that were to be part of the European integration idea: the gradual establishment of the free movement of the workforce and the progressive integration of social policies[41] (the first and third theme outlined above). Indeed, the draft minutes of the Conference record that Paul-Henri Spaak argued that: 'It is of great importance for the sure success of the European idea that it should not appear that the unification of Europe merely posed economic, financial or political questions, but that it also had social aspects.'[42] However, thereafter the work of the Inter-Governmental Committee and the Sub-Commission on Social Problems moved to focus on social security provision as a means of removing obstacles to free movement of workers, thus prioritizing the instrumental objective of social security law. What is striking in this period is the tension between member states, such as France, asserting autonomy, and other states advocating a greater role for the EU.

On 21 July 1955, the Belgian delegation produced a note regarding social problems, recalling the Messina resolution that proposed the establishment of the free movement of the workforce. They emphasized that countries needed

[40] Interim Agreements (No. 12 and 13): European Interim Agreement on Social Security Schemes Relating to Old Age, Invalidity and Survivors (1953) and European Interim Agreement on Social Security other than Schemes for Old Age, Invalidity and Survivors (1953). European Treaty Series.

[41] HAEU-CM3-005 (EU archive).

[42] Original: 'Es sei seines Erachtens von grosser Bedeutung für den sicheren Erfolg der europäischen Idee, dass es nicht den Anschein habe, die Einigung Europas werfe lediglich wirtschaftliche, finanzielle oder politische Fragen auf, sondern dass sie auch soziale Aspekte habe'. HAEU-CM3-005 (EU archive).

to harmonize their social security systems to ensure that the national regimes did not constitute an obstacle to the geographical mobility of the workforce. They highlighted the importance of resolving the remaining issues such as whether to create an equalization/compensation fund, as discussed by the ECSC, and how to ensure equal treatment of workers in difficult situations, for example, the granting of family benefits to children of migrant workers who remained in the home country.[43] The French delegation responded, favouring a central fund to pay social security benefits to migrant workers and emphasizing that French social security benefits were based on the principle of territoriality and so it was 'impossible' to envisage migrant workers having the benefit of French social security provision.[44] When the Italian delegation suggested that there was a need to work towards harmonizing social security legislation, the Dutch and Belgian delegations indicated that this was a matter for individual member states depending on the demographics in their country. The German delegation suggested that harmonization should be considered as part of economic, financial, and social coordination measures.

On 2 August 1955, the Italian delegation returned to the issue of social security provision, arguing that the realization of a common market had to be based on the harmonization of social security regimes 'in order to arrive gradually at a sufficient degree of equilibrium of social standards and social changes'.[45] However, the conclusions of the Sub-Commission on Social Problems published on 4 August 1955 were that the problems with social security were intimately linked with the problems of free movement of people and the harmonization of regulations protecting workers. They recalled the earlier project by the ECSC to establish a Convention and noted that, were it to apply to all workers, not just coal and steel workers, 'the conclusion and subsequent implementation of this Convention, which provides, inter alia, for the granting of social security benefits to migrant workers and their families irrespective of the place of residence of the persons concerned, would be a very important step in the opening of the common market.'[46]

Going forward, the linkage between social security provision and the free movement of persons was a consistent theme: the Doublet report of 22 August

[43] HAEU-CM3-005 (EU archive), at p. 4.

[44] HAEU-CM3/NEGO-044 (EU archive).

[45] Original: 'afin d'arriver graduellement à un degré suffisant d'équilibre du niveau social et des charges sociales'. HAEU-CM3/NEGO-044 (EU archive).

[46] Original: 'la conclusion puis la mise en vigueur de cette convention qui prévoit notamment l'attribution des prestations de sécurité sociale aux travailleurs migrants et à leurs famille quel que soit le lieu de résidence des intéressés représenteraient une étape concrète fort importante dans la perspective de l'ouverture du marché commun.' MAE 174 f/55yd (EU archive).

1955[47] and the Commission report of 11 October 1955 both addressed this. The Commission report went even further, suggesting that harmonization of social security provision was important 'eventually for reasons of political order'.[48] But the French delegation to the Common Market Group in October 1956 started to raise concerns: it noted that given the relationship between free movement and the problem of harmonization of payroll taxes 'if there are still significant disparities in this area, there will be a fear of too large an influx of labour in countries where welfare benefits are high.'[49] This was an early example of the expression of what today is described as welfare or benefit tourism.[50]

The Treaty drafters could not agree on the role and purpose of social security and so the can was eventually kicked down the road. The EEC Treaty merely contained a provision—Article 51—empowering the Council to adopt the 'necessary measures in the field of social security for the establishment of free movement of *workers*' in relation to social security benefits. [Emphasis added]. It took until 1968 for the first major Regulation, Regulation 1612/68 to be agreed which touched upon this issue, and another three years for Regulation 1408/71 on the application of social security schemes to employed persons, to self-employed person and to members of their families moving in the Community, to be agreed.[51] We shall focus on Regulation 1612/68.

3.1.3 Legislation: Regulation 1612/68

Regulation 1612/68 provided for migrant workers to 'enjoy the same social and tax advantages as national workers' (Article 7(2)). This principle of non-discrimination appears to have been uncontentious within the negotiations of the Regulation. However, it is important to note that the principle of non-discrimination was to apply as between *workers* and there was no reference to it applying to categories beyond those who were economically active. Family members were given the right to join a worker, whether the worker was

[47] HAEU-CM3/NEGO-037 (EU archive).

[48] Much of this was repeated again in their further report dated 17 October 1955: HAEU-CM3/NEGO-040 (EU archive).

[49] Original: 'étant donné que s'il subsiste des disparités importantes dans ce domaine, il y aura de craindre un afflux trop grand de main-d'ouevre dans les pays où les prestations sociales sont élevées'. HAEU CM3/NEGO-229 (EU archive).

[50] See, e.g., AG's Opinion in Case C-138/02 *Collins* EU:C:2003:409, para 75: 'In the present case, however, I take the view that a condition as to residence, which is intended to ascertain the degree of connection with the State and the links which the claimant has with the domestic employment market, may be justified in order to avoid what has come to be known as "benefit tourism", where persons move from State to State with the purpose of taking advantage of non-contributory benefits, and in order to prevent abuses. I do not believe that that condition goes beyond what is necessary to attain the objective pursued since it is applied after examination of claimants' personal circumstances in each case.'

[51] OJ [1971] L149/2.

employed or self-employed, in the host state and even if they were a third-country national they could then seek employment (Article 11). However, there was no right for them to independently access the social advantages equivalent to those of national workers.

Two issues came to the fore in this period—the position of work seekers and the issue of housing, both areas of significant sensitivity for the member states. In respect of work seekers, the question was whether a worker who had become unemployed in a member state should be entitled to assistance and which family members should be allowed to join workers in a member state. The question about family reunification raised a further question: whether workers had to have housing available of a certain standard before family members could join them, and whether they could achieve this level of housing by relying on state housing provision. The latter question became a further aspect of the heated debate about social welfare provision.

In April 1967, the Commission produced its proposal for Regulations and a Directive on the free movement of workers.[52] The proposals included the removal of article 17(3) in Regulation 38/64 (requiring migrant workers to have accommodation equivalent to national workers before being allowed to bring their family) because this provision was discriminatory against migrant workers. In addition, the Commission said that the provision could not be justified because, in reality, families only joined migrant workers in the host state if there was housing available to them that was suitable. This became an area of key concern, particularly for the Dutch delegation. When the Group on Social Questions met on 24 and 29 January 1968 to discuss drafts of the Regulation, the Dutch delegation raised particular concerns about whether a national of a member state who visited another member state to find work should be recognized as a worker who already enjoyed all the rights provided for in the Regulation and in particular the principle of equal treatment with national workers. This was of considerable importance to them because in the Netherlands when a person signed on as a jobseeker, the person was also eligible to certain social security rights, including the ability to join social housing lists. The point at which a jobseeker became entitled to worker rights was unresolved at this point.[53]

On 23 February 1968, the Group on Social Questions met again to discuss the text of the provisions.[54] The issue of 'normal housing' continued to be heavily debated. The German and Belgian delegations proposed the addition as

[52] HAEU CES/1967-2232 (EU archive). COM(67) 134 final.
[53] CM2/1968-1005 (EU archive).
[54] CM2/1968-1005 (EU archive).

recommended by the Economic and Social Committee, requiring workers to have housing 'considered normal' before being permitted to have their family join them. The Commission considered that this was discriminatory. The German and Belgian delegation disagreed and argued that without a requirement for proper housing, families would join the worker and end up living in slums with precarious hygiene and sanitation.

The Dutch delegation agreed and noted that despite efforts to date, an imbalance persisted between supply and demand of housing. They had introduced a system of waiting lists for housing allocation, depending on the length of wait, number of family members, situation of the family etc., with priority given to those in most need and urgency. The waiting lists were open to all who were resident in the Netherlands, not just nationals. The Dutch delegation was concerned that if families of migrant workers were allowed to come to the Netherlands without having normal housing in place, and if they found themselves in a precarious position after arrival, they could use their situation to be given priority for housing and overtake Dutch families who had been living for a long time in unsatisfactory housing.

The French disagreed with these proposals but, by way of compromise, said that public authorities could still object to housing that did not meet basic sanitation requirements, just as they did for nationals. The Luxembourg delegation agreed with this proposal and noted that competence for matters of public order and public health remained with member states. The Italians also agreed with the French proposal. They disagreed with the German and Belgian amendment because they considered that it was discriminatory to add conditions to migrant workers before they could bring their families over.

In March 1968, a summary of the different positions was produced by the Council dealing with both the provision of social benefits and housing issues. In particular, it was suggested that the then Article 6 (which became Article 7) should read a worker 'shall enjoy the same social benefits as national workers when they are dependent on the exercise of an employed activity or on the status as the family'.[55] The French delegation wanted to add '*des travailleurs*' at the end of the provision to make it clear that the Regulation did not concern benefits which were not linked to the status of worker.

Debates regarding the details of the provisions continued throughout April 1968. Of note is the suggestion from the Dutch delegation recorded on 8 April 1968 that Article 6(3) should read:

[55] Original: 'bénéficie des mêmes avantages sociaux que les travailleurs nationaux, lorsqu'ils dépendent de l'exercice d'une activité salariée ou de la situation de famille.' CM2/1968-1002 (EU archive).

> Without prejudice to the provisions of Regulations 3 and 4, an involuntary unemployed worker shall, in relation to measures tending to ensure his reintegration or re-employment, be entitled to the same treatment as those applied to national unemployed persons by the authorities, professional organizations, enterprises and institutions, or with their agreement.[56]

On 29 July 1968, the Council met in Brussels to consider the draft Regulations.[57] There was a lengthy discussion about the severe housing shortage in the Netherlands, with which the Belgian delegation agreed. The Belgians raised concerns about overcrowding and the lack of proper housing at reasonable rents relative to workers' earnings. They raised concerns of exploitation. The Italian delegation emphasized that this was a human and social problem. They were concerned that some countries could use this to protect national interests and that an EU-level solution was required. The President of the European Parliamentary Assembly, M. Schuman, agreed and said that 'the time had come to consider migrants from the Member States of the Community not as a complementary labor force, but as a settled population, and that it would not therefore be proper to introduce into the text of the Regulation a clause prohibiting such an establishment.'[58] He proposed the addition of the final clause of Regulation 10(3) that 'this provision [requiring the worker to have available for his family housing considered as normal for national workers in the region] ... must not give rise to discrimination between national workers and workers from other Member States'. It was in this form that the Regulation was passed and came into force on 15 October 1968 and in this way the tentacles of EU law began to reach deep into national systems.

3.1.4 Preliminary conclusions

The discussion of the origin of the social provisions for migrant workers and their families shows that this issue has been controversial and contentious since the outset of the debates around free movement of people. Although prior to the Treaty of Rome some member states had argued for full harmonization of social security provision as a step towards fuller political union,

[56] Original: 'Sans préjudice des dispositions des règlements 3 et 4, le travailleur en chômage involontaire a droit, lors de l'application des mesures tendant à assurer la réintégration ou le réemploi, au même traitement que celui qui est appliqué aux chômeurs nationaux par les autorités, les organisations professionnelles, les entreprises et les institutions, ou avec leur accord.' HAEU CM2/1968-1006 (EU archive).

[57] CM2/1968-1011. 1297 f/68 (PV/CONS 21) (EU archive).

[58] Original: 'le temps est venu de considérer les migrants en provenance des Etats membres de la Communauté non pas comme une main-d'oeuvre d'appoint, mais comme une population d'établissement, et qu'il ne conviendrait pas par conséquent d'introduire dans le texte du règlement une clause interdisant cet établissement.' CM2/1968-1011. 1297 f/68 (PV/CONS 21) (EU archive).

this was strongly contested by other member states determined to assert control. An examination of the historical debates shows the compromises that were reached to seek to resolve these widely disparate positions taken by the member states.

The debates following the Treaty of Rome tied the provision of social security benefits to the status of being economically active: only workers and self-employed individuals were entitled to access social security benefits. Family members were entitled to join a worker and reside within another member state in suitable housing. By Article 11 they were also entitled to take up employment. However, it was only by virtue of being a worker, or having been a worker, in the member state that an individual was entitled to social and tax advantages. The idea that someone who was not a worker would be able to avail themselves of social security benefits was not even suggested or debated. This was not raised as an idea by even the members states, like Italy, which were pushing for the broadest possible concept of free movement. Moreover, the ability of workers to have access to state housing, and thereby bring their family to the host state, was also contentious and resulted in tightly negotiated provisions that had been debated over a lengthy period ultimately favouring EU control.

3.2 Disintegration of Free Movement?

3.2.1 The role of legislature: Part two

Clearly the position has moved on since 1968. Rights for the semi-economically active (students, the retired and persons of independent means (PIMs)) were given via the Residence Rights Directives in the early 1990s which were then repealed and replaced by the Citizens' Rights Directive 2004/38 (CRD). The Directive provides that after three months, students and PIMs enjoy the right to reside in another member state provided that they have comprehensive sickness insurance (CSI) and sufficient resources. Article 24(1) CRD, provides:

> all Union citizens residing on the basis of this Directive in the territory of the host Member State shall enjoy equal treatment with the nationals of that Member State within the scope of the Treaty. The benefit of this right shall be extended to family members who are not nationals of a Member State and who have the right of residence or permanent residence.

Article 24(1) is subject to exceptions (social assistance, student grants and loans) and justifications (express deroations and objective justification), as noted above in section 2.2.

3.2.2 The role of the Court of Justice

The notion of EU citizenship was introduced by the Treaty of Maastricht, with accompanying rights (now Arts. 18–21 TFEU): the right to move to, and reside in, another member state for those holding the nationality of a member state and the right to equal treatment subject to the limitations laid down by EU law. The right to equal treatment under Article 18 TFEU was because 'Union citizenship is destined to be the fundamental status of nationals of Member States, enabling those who find themselves in the same situation to enjoy the same treatment in law irrespective of their nationality, subject to such exceptions as are expressly provided for.'[59] Starting with *Martinez Sala*, the Court adopted a creative reading of Article 21 and Article 18 to ensure that migrant, but impecunious, citizens could have access to benefits in the host state. Having relied on the principle of equal treatment to obtain benefits, this gave migrant citizens (who were not necessarily economically active) sufficient resources to stay in the host state.[60] It was this very broad reading which caused concerns in a number of member states, including the UK.

However, perhaps in recognition that the judges read newspapers too,[61] the Court of Justice did something of a U-turn in its interpretation of the CRD in *Dano*[62] and other post-2014 cases. It appears that the change in approach was specifically because of concerns across the EU about benefit tourism, exemplified by the ministerial letter sent to the President of the European Council by the UK, Germany, Austria, and the Netherlands in April 2013 seeking urgent discussion about 'arrangements at national or EU level that allow those who have only recently arrived in a Member State and have never been employed or paid taxes there to claim the same social security benefits as that Member State's own citizens.'[63]

[59] Case C-184/99, *Rudy Grzelczyk* v. *Centre public d'aide sociale d'Ottignies-Louvain-la-Neuve*, EU:C:2001:458.

[60] Case C-85/96, *María Martínez Sala* v. *Freistaat Bayern*, EU:C:1998:217.

[61] M. Blauberg et. al., 'ECJ Judges read the morning papers. Explaining the turnaround of European citizenship jurisprudence', 25 *Journal of European Public Policy* (2018), 1422. See also S. Schmidt et al, 'Free movement and equal treatment in an unequal union', 25 *Journal of European Public Policy* (2018), 1391.

[62] Case C-333/13, *Elisabeta Dano and Florin Dano* v. *Jobcenter Leipzig* ('*Dano*'), ECLI:EU:C:2014:2358.

[63] Letter to President of the European Council. http://docs.dpaq.de/3604-130415_letter_to_presidency_final_1_2.pdf (accessed 9 July 2021).

In *Dano*, the Romanian migrant applicant lived in Germany and had never worked as she was raising a young child. She was refused particular special non-contributory cash benefits by the German authorities, and this was upheld by the Court of Justice on the ground that she did not satisfy the requirements laid down by Article 7(1)(b) CRD that non-economically active EU citizens had to have sufficient resources. The Court specifically held that 'Article 7(1)(b) of Directive 2004/38 seeks to prevent economically inactive Union citizens from using the host member state's welfare system to fund their means of subsistence.'[64] In other words, benefit tourism will not be encouraged under EU law. In *Commission* v. *UK*, the Court confirmed that there was nothing to prevent, in principle, the grant of social benefits to Union citizens who were not economically active being made subject to the substantive condition that those citizens meet the necessary requirements for possessing a right to reside lawfully in the host member state. It also said that while a residence requirement was indirectly discriminatory, the need to protect the finances of the host member state justified in principle the possibility of checking whether residence was lawful when a social benefit was granted, in particular to people from other member states who are not economically active.[65] In this way, the Court reasserted some state control. In *CG*[66] the Court confirmed its ruling in *Dano* but added a significant caveat. It said that where

> a Union citizen resides legally, on the basis of national law, in the territory of a member state other than that of which he or she is a national, the national authorities empowered to grant social assistance are required to check that a refusal to grant such benefits based on that legislation does not expose that citizen, and the children for which he or she is responsible, to an actual and current risk of violation of their fundamental rights, as enshrined in Articles 1, 7 and 24 of the Charter.

4. Reassertion of Autonomy

There are clear parallels between the debates during Brexit and the positions of different delegations to the negotiations over the Treaty of Rome. Concerns about the level of EU8 and EU2 migration during Brexit were similar to the serious concerns raised by the Belgian and Dutch delegations about the

[64] Ibid., para 76.
[65] Case C-308/14, *Commission* v. *UK*, ECLI:EU:C:2016:436.
[66] Case C-709/20 *CG* v. *The Department for Communities in Norther Ireland* EU:C:2021:602, para 93.

ability of host member states to deal with an influx of migrants in the 1950s. During the Brexit campaign, there was extensive public concern too about the impact of significant EU migration on the health service (NHS), housing, and school places, mirroring the debates about housing provision in the Netherlands seventy years ago. Concerns about the impact of migration on benefits and housing were noted by David Cameron in a speech on immigration in May 2015:

> The British people want these things sorted. Over the past 5 years, we've been working towards that ... Paying the rent and dole of jobless migrants—we stopped it ... I said on the steps of Downing Street we would be a 'one nation' party. That means governing for every single person in Britain: ... for the young couple praying that someone won't jump ahead of them on the housing list.[67]

Though there is no evidence of migrant workers getting priority on local housing lists,[68] this was a key narrative within the Brexit debates.

Concerns about benefit tourism are not a uniquely 'British' issue. The UK was one of four signatories to the 2013 ministerial letter referred to above, indicating a desire by states to reassert their autonomy. 'Benefit tourism' has been a particular concern in Germany, with German judicial decisions drawing criticism from the Commission.[69] The German government has been seeking to change EU provisions to allow them to adjust child benefits to living costs in the recipients' home country.[70] Fears of 'welfare magnetism' have also been prominent in Denmark, with its generous welfare state.[71] In Denmark in 2016, the government announced that it was working on a policy to make it more difficult for EU citizens to receive social benefits by requiring them to earn the right to them by working for a period of time.[72] This followed controversial

[67] https://www.gov.uk/government/speeches/pm-speech-on-immigration (accessed 9 July 2021).

[68] EEA migrants: access to social housing (England) report (House of Commons Library, March 2016). https://researchbriefings.parliament.uk/ResearchBriefing/Summary/SN04737#fullreport (accessed 9 July 2021).

[69] In particular, the decisions of the Bundessozialgericht of 03.12.15 B4AS 44/15 R and the Sozialgericht Berlin of 11.12.15, S 149 AS 7191/13.

[70] The Local, 'Germany paying €350 million in child benefits to children abroad', *The Local*, 21 March 2018. https://www.thelocal.de/20180321/germany-paying-350-million-in-child-benefits-to-children-abroad (accessed 9 July 2021).

[71] Martinsen and Rotger, 'Evidence from Denmark: How EU immigration can benefit the welfare state', LSE blogs, August 2017. https://blogs.lse.ac.uk/europpblog/2017/08/16/evidence-from-denmark-how-eu-immigration-can-benefit-the-welfare-state/ (accessed 9 July 2021).

[72] Martinsen and Werner, 'No welfare magnets—free movement and cross-border welfare in Germany and Denmark compared', 26(5) *Journal of European Public Policy* (2018), 637–655.

decisions by the CJEU, in particular the ruling in *LN*,[73] that an EU migrant, if classed as a worker, was entitled to the Danish study grant even if they had entered Denmark with the express intention of studying there.[74]Austria announced that it would be cutting child benefit for residents whose children lived in other member states where the cost of living was lower.[75] Finland has faced enforcement proceedings because of applying a waiting period for the aggregation of periods of unemployment insurance.[76] Thus, it is clear that migration, free movement of people, and access to benefits has become controversial within the wealthier states of the EU.

Perhaps the most obvious signs of a resurgence in the desire for the member states to reassert their autonomy came with the British negotiations for a revised arrangement with the EU, the so-called 'New Settlement' deal, over these sensitive questions, in February 2016. Of particular note for the purposes of this chapter were the proposed arrangements:

(1) to allow states to justify discrimination by reference to a broader range of objective justifications including encouraging recruitment, reducing unemployment, protecting vulnerable workers, and averting the risk of seriously undermining the sustainability of social security systems. In the case of benefits 'conditions may be imposed in relation to certain benefits to ensure that there is a real and effective degree of connection between the person concerned and the labour market of the host Member State'.
(2) to confirm the *Dano* principle (the right of economically non active individuals to reside in the host Member State depends under EU law on them having sufficient resources for themselves and their family members not to become a burden on the social assistance system of the host Member State, and on them having comprehensive sickness insurance. Member States have the possibility of refusing to grant social benefits to individuals who exercise their right to freedom of movement solely in order to obtain Member States' social assistance although they do not have sufficient resources to claim a right of residence)

[73] Case C-46/12, *LN* v. *Styrelsen for Videregaaende Uddannelser og Uddannelsesstotte*, ECLI:EU:C:2013:97.

[74] See also Leonhardt Hjorth, 'EU ruling: Danish SU student grants for all EU citizens', University of Copenhage, 11 April 2013. https://uniavisen.dk/en/eu-ruling-danish-su-student-grants-for-all-eu-citizens/ (accessed 9 July 2021).

[75] Reuters Staff, 'Austria's new government plans to cut child benefits abroad', *Reuters*, 4 January 2018. https://www.reuters.com/article/us-austria-politics/austrias-new-government-plans-to-cut-child-benefits-abroad-idUSKBN1ET1RB (accessed 9 July 2021). In Case C-328/20 *Commission v Austria* the Austrian rule was challenged. The AG found in contrary to EU law as did the Court of Justice.

[76] European Commission press release. http://europa.eu/rapid/press-release_IP-13-1107_en.htm (accessed 9 July 2021).

(3) to relax the criteria when the state can deport an individual (individuals whose personal conduct is likely to represent a genuine and serious threat to public policy or security)

(4) a legislative proposal to enable host Member States to have an option, in the case of migrants who export child benefits to another Member State to index such benefits to the conditions of the Member State where the child resides.

(5) an emergency brake not on the number of migrants but on their access to benefits (on a proposal from the Commission after having examined the notification and the reasons stated therein, the Council could authorize the Member State concerned to restrict access to non-contributory in-work benefits to the extent necessary. The Council would authorize that Member State to limit the access of newly arriving EU workers to non-contributory in-work benefits for a total period of up to four years from the commencement of employment. The limitation would be graduated, starting with an initial exclusion but gradually increasing access to such benefits to take account of the growing connection of the worker with the labour market of the host Member State. The authorization would have a limited duration and apply to EU workers newly arriving during a period of 7 years.)

These proposals, while not exactly allowing member states, particularly the UK, to take back control, at least allowed a degree of reassertion of autonomy.

But it was too little, too late. 52 per cent of UK voters voted to leave the EU and, as a result, these proposals never came into effect. This reassertion of autonomy—through Brexit—has led to a significant convulsion in the EU and a major upheaval in the UK, where immigration policy has been radically overhauled. As the Home Secretary proudly announced on 9 November 2020: 'After many years of campaigning, I am delighted the Immigration Bill which will end free movement on 31st December has today passed through Parliament. We are delivering on the will of the British people.'

5. Conclusions

So what do these two stories - the development of free movement of workers under Article 45 TFEU and the development of the EU's approach to social welfare benefits - tell us about member states' autonomy in this field? It is clear that the states surrendered more than they probably thought and expected back in the early days of the EU. As the Court and, to an extent, the legislature have pushed to secure the effective operation of the single market, the consequences for member state autonomy only slowly became clear. This was particularly the case with the United Kingdom.

The 2016 New Settlement deal would have tipped the balance back somewhat towards autonomy. The benefits of the New Settlement deal were multiple, but two points are of particular relevance to the discussion in this chapter. First, the express reconnection between economic activity and free movement by confirming the *Dano* principle. Second, and relatedly, the flexibility that member states would have been granted in justifying differential treatment of migrant workers, and ultimately their ability to apply an emergency brake in relation to access to benefits. These points would have represented a compromise between the disparate positions of the different member states, much as was achieved originally in relation to social security provision, allowing a return of control by individual states.

Of course, with that increased autonomy there would have been a risk of a loss of cohesion, and perhaps therefore of integration. Flexibility could easily become disparity in the application of the principles to be applied under the New Settlement deal. Different states might take different views of when discrimination was justifiable, as they could in relation to the application of the emergency brake. The New Settlement deal might have become the beginning of a multi-tiered Union with different rules applying in each state, effecting the disintegration of the Union.

In practice, this seems unlikely. The original settlement of social security provisions was a pragmatic compromise between the different and diverse positions taken by states. Space was left for individual state autonomy. In many ways, it can be argued that the balance between autonomy and compromise was what was so successful. The New Settlement deal might have been an equally successful compromise in the new and different circumstances of much greater economic migration across the Union.

However, that is now lost and tainted by its association with the UK. The pandemic has changed things again, as EU migrants have often returned to their own countries where the cost of living may be cheaper when no work was available in the UK. While this may take away some of the urgency of the issue, there may come a time when the EU member states regret not implementing the New Settlement Agreement to take back some of the levers of control. Were there to be a return to significant economic migration across the Union by EU citizens, fresh consideration will be needed of how to balance autonomy and EU control. A compromise will need to be sought, and perhaps the New Settlement deal, allowing some flexibility to member states to regain some autonomy over such matters as access to social security or its connection with economic activity, will return to the fore.

Index

Tables are indicated by an italic *t* following the page number; 'n.' after a page number indicates the footnote number.